WHY HITLER?

WHY HITLER?

The Genesis of
the Nazi Reich

SAMUEL W. MITCHAM, JR.

Westport, Connecticut
London

Library of Congress Cataloging-in-Publication Data

Mitcham, Samuel W.
    Why Hitler? : the genesis of the Nazi Reich / Samuel W. Mitcham,
Jr.
       p.   cm.
    Includes bibliographical references (p.   ) and index.
    ISBN 0–275–95485–4 (alk. paper)
    1. Germany—Politics and government—1918–1933. 2. Germany—
Politics and government—1933–1945. 3. Germany—Economic
conditions—1918–1945. 4. Hitler, Adolf, 1889–1945. 5. National
socialism. I. Title.
DD238.M58   1996
943.085—dc20   96–16246

British Library Cataloguing in Publication Data is available.

Library of Congress Catalog Card Number: 96–16246
ISBN: 0–275–95485–4

First published in 1996

Praeger Publishers, 88 Post Road West, Westport, CT 06881
An imprint of Greenwood Publishing Group, Inc.

Printed in the United States of America

The paper used in this book complies with the
Permanent Paper Standard issued by the National
Information Standards Organization (Z39.48–1984).

10 9 8 7 6 5 4 3 2 1

This book is dedicated to my daughter,
Lacy Meredith Mitcham

Contents

Tables

Introduction

During my travels and after my speeches, the most common question I am asked is why the Germans—a civilized and educated people—came to choose Adolf Hitler as their chancellor, unleashing upon the world one of the most barbaric and inhuman regimes in history. The purpose of this book is to answer that question.

Taken as a whole, it is a complex story. Hitler owed his rise to both external and internal factors. First of all, he was a great politician. This comment may horrify some Americans, many of whom mentally conceptualize the terms "greatness" and "goodness" as if they are somehow related. This is not necessarily true and certainly is not true in the case of Hitler. There have been (and are) great criminals and great villains. Hitler was unquestionably both, especially in terms of the enormity of his crimes. In fact, his memory is so repugnant to us that many are reluctant to ascribe to him any traits that might be construed as positive for fear of somehow being conceived as pro-Hitler or pro-Nazi. The truth, however, is that just as the devil has the power to assume pleasing forms so do some of his human allies, and Hitler certainly exhibited a touch of political genius in making himself appear pleasing to the average German voter. This was made all the easier by the relative mediocrity of his opponents, which brings up the second major point: the external factors.

Despite his undeniable political skill, Hitler would never have come to power in times that were in any way normal. Reasonably happy and prosperous people, regardless of nationality, do not elect extremists like

Hitler to high office in normal times. But for Germany in the 1920s and early 1930s, times were anything but normal; they were desperate. Collectively, the Germans were like a drowning man, and a drowning man will take anybody's rope. Hitler offered them hope, and they grabbed his rope by the millions.

I once knew a German who was the type of man one would not mind having as a neighbor—just a good, solid, helpful, pleasant sort of fellow who was getting up in years and who was more overweight than I was—another mark in his favor. Certainly, he was not the type of monster who committed murder on such a massive scale in the 1940s. I was appalled when he told me, in a confidential manner, that he had voted for Hitler. After I expressed my shock, he became very thoughtful. He reminisced about being a young man lying in bed next to his wife at night, but neither of them could sleep since their children in the next room were crying because they had not had enough to eat. Then his eyes focused directly on mine. "Yes," he declared forcefully, "You're damn right I voted for Hitler. He offered us hope!"

This brings up the question, "Could it happen again?" Absolutely. It already has. In Cambodia alone, two to three million people were exterminated out of a population of eight million by the Khmer Rouge, and the world press hardly noticed. But one of the most sobering experiences I ever had was a visit to Russia after the collapse of the Soviet empire. I found the conditions almost identical to those that existed in the Weimar Republic as it tumbled toward its end. The purpose of this book, therefore, is not only to inform and entertain: it is also meant as a warning because it *could* happen again!

ACKNOWLEDGMENTS

I would like to acknowledge everyone who assisted me in the production of this book, including Waldo Dalstead, Gene Mueller, and Colonel John Angolia, who furnished insights and much needed information. I would also like to thank the staffs of the U.S. National Archives and the U.S. Army's Institute of Military History, U.S. Army War College, Carlisle Barracks, PA. Sincere gratitude is also extended to Ms. Melinda Matthews, director of the interlibrary loan department at Northeast Louisiana University, Monroe, LA, for her invaluable assistance in tracking down research material. Sandel Library is indeed fortunate to have this incredibly efficient and knowledgeable professional. Finally, the greatest thanks go to my wife and my hero, Donna Mitcham, who helped in ways too numerous to mention.

1 The Fall of the Second Reich

The Second World War had its roots in the first, which began in 1914. By early 1918 Germany had overrun all or most of Belgium, Poland, Lithuania, Latvia, Estonia, and Romania. Russia had sued for peace; Italy was on the verge of defeat after General Otto von Below's victory at Caporetto (where 275,000 Italians were captured and another 100,000 deserted); and Imperial Germany's two most revered military leaders, Field Marshal Paul von Hindenburg and General Erich Ludendorff, were massing a million men for a final blow, aimed at knocking France—Germany's archenemy and strongest remaining opponent in numerical terms—out of the war.

Unfortunately for Imperial Germany, these facts concealed the true gravity of the situation. Germany was, in fact, on her last legs militarily. She had been diplomatically outmaneuvered almost constantly since young Kaiser Wilhelm II removed the brilliant Otto von Bismarck as chancellor of the empire on March 19, 1890. As a result of Wilhelm's ineptitude, the Second Reich went to war in 1914 with only the weakest allies: the Ottoman Empire (later Turkey), the Austro-Hungarian Empire, and eventually Bulgaria. On the other hand, by 1917 all of the world's major powers were arrayed against her. By 1918 the ships of the German High Seas Fleet had either been sunk or bottled up; her U-boat offensive had been defeated by the British convoy system; her allies were on the verge of collapse; and hunger, starvation, and war weariness had gripped the German people, who were unable to import food due to the British blockade. Already there were signs of civil unrest in the fatherland. Also, as a result of Germany's decision to adopt a policy of unrestricted submarine warfare, the United States had declared war on Germany on April 6, 1917. Germany, then, had only two possible ways out of her deteriorating and increasingly grim strategic position in early 1918: either quickly seek and negotiate the best peace treaty she could get or launch a major offensive and defeat France and Great Britain, before the fresh American troops arrived in Europe in strength. Characteristically General Erich Ludendorff, whom the Germans called the "National Commander" and who had been the virtual military dictator of the Reich since 1916, chose the latter course. He recalled some of his best formations from Russia, Italy, and the Balkans and assembled more than 3,500,000 men for the decisive campaign.

The big blow (dubbed Operation "Michael") came at 4:40 A.M. on March 21. Sixty-two German divisions advanced out of the fog and struck the British right wing along a 43-mile front. By the end of the month, when the offensive bogged down near Amiens, Ludendorff had advanced 40 miles in 8 days, capturing 70,000 prisoners and 500 guns, and inflicting 200,000 other casualties on the Allies. However, he had failed to achieve any strategic results, and losses in his elite shock divisions had been heavy.

Operation "Michael" was just the first of five major offensives, which together constituted the so-called "Great Offensive" or "Ludendorff Offensive." On April 9 the Germans struck again near the Lys River with 35 divisions. Initially they gained ground rapidly and even broke into open territory, but the British rallied quickly and stalled the advance. By the time Ludendorff called off this series of attacks on April 29, he had lost 350,000 men, as opposed to only 305,000 for the Allies. A significant feature of this offensive was the fact that the German troops frequently slowed their drive to forage for food.

After a month-long respite, Ludendorff lashed out again on May 27, determined to push the British Army against the sea and separate them from the French. The great Quartermaster General was now showing distinct signs of mental strain, which today might be called combat fatigue. His tremendous responsibilities were weighing heavily on him; also, his stepson had been killed in action in the first days of the Great Offensive, and his wife's reaction was one of inconsolable grief, which would contribute to their divorce.[1] Despite his terrible personal and professional burdens, however, General Ludendorff took French Marshal Ferdinand Foch, the Allied commander-in-chief since March, by surprise. Striking with 17 divisions, the Germans overran Chemin des Dames Ridge, crossed the Aisne and the Vesle Rivers, and gained up to 20 miles on the first day. By the end of the month they had reached the Marne at Chateau-Thierry, less than 50 miles from Paris. Although the Allied High Command was on the verge of panic, Ludendorff had already overextended himself and was halted by three fresh American divisions at Chateau-Thierry and Belleau Wood during the first week in June. Each side lost about 128,000 men in the Aisne Offensive, but the Germans had no way of replacing their casualties. By now, a quarter of a million American troops were arriving in France every month, and some German divisions—for the first time in the war—were showing a marked reluctance to attack.

By July 4 there were a million American servicemen in France, and each of their 19 divisions was about twice the size of a German, French, or British division. The thin German numerical superiority of the spring was now gone, but Ludendorff nevertheless decided to launch two more offensives. In the first, General Oskar von Hutier's 18th Army would thrust toward Paris, forcing Foch to commit his reserves to defend the French capital. Then Ludendorff would launch his major blow—against the British in Flanders. This last offensive would be decisive, one way or the other.

Hutier pushed forward on June 9 but gained less than 10 miles. The time and place of his attack had been betrayed to the Allies by a German prisoner—another sign of a deteriorating army. Prior to 1918, German prisoners almost never cooperated with their captors; now, however, it was becoming a fairly common event. As a result, by June 11 Hutier was under counterattack by five French and two U.S. divisions and was forced over to the defensive. The fourth German offensive was a clear failure: The great majority of Foch's reserves remained uncommitted. Ludendorff nevertheless persisted with his original plan and struck on July 15 with 3 armies, totalling 52 divisions. He compounded his mistake by calling this the *Friedensturm*—the Peace Offensive, implying to the German soldier that it would decide the outcome of the war. When it failed, the man in the ranks would not be psychologically prepared to deal with the despair that followed.

Ludendorff's final roll of the dice was met by 57 Allied divisions (9 of them American). Tipped off as to the timing of the attack, the French opened the battle with a huge artillery bombardment, catching the German assault regiments in their assembly areas and slaughtering them. East of Rheims the decisive German offensive was a total disaster—so much so that Ludendorff ordered his 1st and 3rd armies to go over to the defensive on July 16. To the west, however, General Max von Boehn gallantly pushed his 7th Army forward, breaking through and crossing the Marne west of Rheims. It was a forlorn hope, however. On July 18 the 7th was counterattacked by two French armies, supported by several American divisions and 350 tanks. By evening six German divisions were fighting for their lives and were in danger of being cut off south of the Marne. Boehn exhibited considerable tactical skill in extricating his army, but his success did little to mitigate the extent of the German disaster. The Ludendorff Offensives were over. They had cost the Imperial Army more than a million casualties, and the best German divisions had been destroyed or bled white. Imperial Germany now had no choice except to make peace with the Allies.

The slowness with which the Second Reich began peace negotiations is symptomatic of the leadership bankruptcy that led to its demise. The German Army was physically and spiritually exhausted after four years of trench warfare. In addition, an epidemic of the deadly Spanish influenza had broken out in June. Over the next 10 months it would claim the lives of 20,000,000 people—more even than the Black Death of the Middle Ages. The men of the German Army, already worn out and suffering from long-standing malnourishment, were especially easy victims for the disease, and they died by the thousands. Morale slumped even further as retreat followed retreat and they were pursued by fresh Allied divisions, supported by thousands of tanks—a newly introduced innovation against which the Germans as yet had little defense. On August 8, for example, hundreds of British, Canadian, and French tanks swamped General Georg von der Marwitz's 2nd Army in the Amiens Salient. At a cost of fewer than 9,000 men, they inflicted more than 27,000 casualties on the Kaiser's legions and broke through into open country for the first time in 4 years. Worse still, the first cases of large-scale German surrenders occurred: 15,000 men lay down their arms, and 400 guns were taken intact. Ludendorff called it the "black day" of the German Army in this war. "We have nearly reached the limit of our power to resist," Hindenburg said. "The war must be ended."[2] When Ludendorff agreed, Kaiser Wilhelm II instructed his foreign ministry to begin peace negotiations, but with the idea of retaining as much of the conquered territory as possible. With such a condition, there was little real chance for successful negotiations.

Meanwhile, Ludendorff fell back across the Vesle and Aisne to the main Hindenburg Line, abandoning all the territory he had seized since March. He still had 197 divisions, but only half were still battleworthy. Marshal Foch followed him with 220 divisions. Even though its long-range prospects appeared more hopeless each day, the German Army was still capable of tenacious resistance. In September it rallied, checking the Allies at Ypres on the left flank, while the Americans bogged down in heavy fighting in the Argonne Forest on the right. In the center, three French armies continued to gain ground, but only very slowly. On the Western Front, the danger seemed to have passed, at least for the moment. Trouble, however, broke out elsewhere. To bolster his sagging defenses in the West, Ludendorff had to strip his southern and eastern flanks of most of their German formations. As a result, a Franco-Serbian army under General Franchet d'Esperey was able to rout Germany's Bulgarian allies, who fled almost without firing a shot. By the third week in September the Bulgarian Army had dissolved itself, their king had abdicated, most of the Balkans had been lost, and Germany's link to Istanbul had been effectively severed. Meanwhile, the armies of the Ottoman Empire also collapsed. British General Edmund Allenby decisively defeated the Turks at Megiddo, overran Jordan, and pursued the Turkish remnants all the way to Damascus. Another British army under General William Marshall overran Iraq, pushing up the Tigris all the way to the oil fields at Mosul. Turkey sued for peace and was granted an armistice on October 30. In northern Italy the Austro-Hungarian forces, stripped of the German divisions that put backbone into their defenses, also began to disintegrate, and mass surrenders took place; 300,000 men capitulated in the Vittoro Veneto area alone. Simultaneously a new Republic of Hungary was formed, and it promptly recalled all Hungarian units from the front. Elsewhere the Austro-Hungarian Empire, which Stokesbury rightly called a "dynastic anachronism," was unable to keep its minorities in line any longer. The Poles in the Austrian Army were deserting, as were the Czechs, Yugoslavs, Romanians, and others. The Czechoslovaks formally declared their independence on October 21, followed by the Yugoslavs eight days later. The Austro-Hungarian Empire, which in reality no longer existed, formally signed an armistice with the Allies on November 3.[3]

Signs of disintegration were apparent in Germany as well. Unrest had, in fact, broken out in April 1917. On April 15 the government announced a further reduction in the bread ration. The next day, led by Independent Socialists and Communists, 200,000 workers went on strike in Berlin. Two days later the more moderate Majority Socialists (also called the Social Democrats) issued a manifesto publicly welcoming the triumph of the revolutionaries in Russia. Only the firm opposition of the Kaiser and his reactionary Conservative supporters prevented their delegates in the *Reichstag* (the national parliament) from establishing a ministerial government (that is, one responsible to the Reichstag, rather than to the emperor alone). The debate was nevertheless a clear sign that the Reichstag—not previously noted for its independence—was ready to play a more dynamic role in the political life of the country.

Shaken by the attitude of the moderate parties and the obvious depth of their support with the general public, the unpopular Chancellor Theobald von Bethmann-Hollweg belatedly jumped on the bandwagon of constitutional reform. Bethmann, who had no real support from either side, was promptly attacked by the parties of the left (for not supporting reform earlier and more strongly) and by the parties of the right (for supporting reform at all). It was Ludendorff, however, who drove him from office. Always the ardent expansionist and reactionary nationalist, he told the Kaiser that he and Hindenburg would resign from the Supreme Command if Bethmann remained. Because the public believed that these two were the only men who could lead Germany to victory, Wilhelm II had little choice but to withdraw his confidence from Bethmann-Hollweg, who resigned on July 13, 1917. He was replaced by the Prussian commissioner of food, Dr. Georg Michaelis, an obscure bureaucrat whose only qualification for the post was that he was an acceptable front man for the arrogant and uncompromising Ludendorff. The appointment was made without consulting the leadership of any of the civilian political parties, which was too much—even for the Reichstag. Five days after Michaelis assumed office, the Catholic Center Party, led by Matthias Erzberger, succeeded in passing an ambiguous peace resolution by a vote of 212 to 126. It called for peace without annexation of territory. The Kaiser, of course, chose to interpret the resolution as nonbinding. After that the Reichstag relapsed into insignificance, but the seeds of a parliamentary republic had been sown.

So were the seeds of discontent. In the autumn a mutiny broke out in the great naval base at Kiel. It was severely put down, and its leaders were executed or given long prison terms, but the incident led to the fall of the Michaelis government on October 26, 1917. The next government was formed by Count Georg von Hertling, a conservative former chief of the Catholic Center Party and a veteran parliamentarian. A friend of Ludendorff but not of constitutional reform, he was greeted with little enthusiasm by the left, but at least he was more acceptable than Michaelis had been. As a sop to the moderate left, a leading member of the Progressive Party was named vice chancellor.

Count von Hertling was unable to stop the decay at home, and the unsympathetic attitude of the military to the woes of the civil population did nothing to help; in fact, the military leadership unwittingly undermined its own cause, for it looked upon the civilian sector as a source of tax money and cannon fodder—and little else. Partially as a result of this attitude, when the Bolsheviks came to power in Russia in November, their movement in Germany gained new enthusiasm and support among the hungry, disillusioned, and disgruntled working classes. When the Soviets asked for a negotiated peace with the Reich in late 1917, they were greeted with terms that were totally at variance with the lip service the Kaiser's government had been paying to the idea of a just and democratic peace. The Germans demanded Poland, Lithuania, and Courland (eastern Latvia)—areas that in no way could be considered German. Russia would also have to evacuate Finland and the Ukraine and cede some of her southern provinces to the Turks. So severe were the proposed terms that the Soviets actually returned to the war, albeit only briefly. The smashed Russian armies were simply no longer capable of fighting the Germans, so the Red government agreed to the terms. By the Treaty of Brest-Litovsk, which was finally signed on February 28, 1918, Russia lost 34 percent of her people, 32 percent of her agricultural land, 54 percent of her industry, and 89 percent of her coal mines.[4] This treaty, and the uncompromising attitude of the German delegation that negotiated it, disillusioned those who took the Peace Resolution of July 1917 seriously, undermined what confidence the German people had in the justness of the Kaiser's cause, and dampened even further the eroding enthusiasm the people felt for the war. Their faith was further undercut by United States President Woodrow Wilson's speech to Congress on January 8, 1918, in which he outlined the "Fourteen Points" on which he felt peace should be based. Wilson's fair-sounding and idealistic points stood in marked contrast to the harsh terms of Brest-Litovsk. The American called for freedom of the seas, the removal of trade barriers, armament reductions, impartial settlement of colonial claims, the withdrawal of foreign troops from Russia and Belgium, the creation of an independent Poland, and the establishment of a League of Nations to protect the independence and territorial integrity of all nations and to settle international disputes without war. The Fourteen Points clearly implied lenient terms for Germany should she ask for an armistice; she would only be asked to give up Alsace-Lorraine. "Wilson's advocacy of a just peace on this and subsequent occasions had a tremendous effect on German public opinion," William Halperin wrote later. "His remarks multiplied their yearning for peace, and Wilsonian idealism . . . became the Allies' most potent psychological weapon."[5]

Later that same month, strikes broke out again in Berlin, but this time half a million workers were involved. The strikes called for demilitarization, political amnesty, an immediate end to the war, and a negotiated peace based on the Bolshevik plan of no indemnities and no annexations. The government reacted quickly and with great severity. Denouncing strikes in wartime as treason, it declared strict martial law and conducted mass arrests. Many of the strikers were taken from jail and conscripted directly into the army—a mistake that boomeranged on the authorities, because the new draftees began spreading Communist and defeatist propaganda within the armed forces. Soon Ludendorff found it necessary to secretly order each army commander to keep two battalions ready for use against the civilian population at all times.[6]

The Great Offensive temporarily stabilized the domestic political situation, but as soon as it became obvious that it had failed, events raced beyond the ability of the German leadership to control them. Nothing, in fact, exhibits the isolation and ineptitude of the Kaiser's government more than the leisurely approach it took toward the armistice negotiations. It was not until October 4, 1918, that Hertling was replaced as chancellor by Prince Max of Baden, a man widely known for his liberal viewpoints. Prince Max formed a broad-based, peace-oriented coalition government. He also assumed the foreign minister's portfolio for himself and immediately appealed to Wilson for an armistice based on the Fourteen Points. The Germans acted too late, however, because now that the American Doughboys had suffered a quarter of a million casualties, Wilson was not as inclined to deal as leniently with the Central Powers as he was 10 months before. The U.S. president therefore hedged, issued demands, stated preconditions, requested clarifications of the German positions, and in general conducted a complicated delaying action in the finest traditions of international diplomacy. Among other things, he categorically refused to deal with the "military masters" of Germany. Meanwhile, for Kaiser Wilhelm II, time ran out.

THE REVOLUTION AND THE ARMISTICE

Erich Ludendorff, who was by now clearly unstable, reacted to Wilson's tactics by changing his mind and demanding that the war be continued and turned into a last-ditch struggle if need be. The Kaiser, for once, reacted angrily to his "National Commander" and gave him a fierce dressing down. Shocked and very hurt, Ludendorff resigned on October 26 and, because the Allies wanted to put him on trial as a war criminal, went into exile in Sweden. Hindenburg submitted his resignation at the same time as his deputy, but the Kaiser begged him to stay on and eventually persuaded him to do so.

Like the Kaiser, Hindenburg, and Prince Max, Vice Admiral Franz von Hipper, the commander of the High Seas Fleet, also saw disaster on the horizon in the hopeless military situation and in the ugly riots that were now sweeping Germany. Determined to carry out one last act of defiance, he ordered the fleet to break out for one last, desperate battle against the Royal Navy, which had bottled up Germany's big ships since the Battle of Jutland two years before. This order triggered the disaster that led to the fall of the monarchy, for the best officers and men of the High Seas Fleet had long since been transferred to the submarine service, or to the torpedo boats, or to the elite naval infantry divisions fighting on the Western Front. All that remained were mediocre crewmen, often led by overage officers of indifferent quality, who were demoralized by two years of festering inactivity. Infected by Red propaganda, disillusioned with the Kaiser and the Supreme Command, affected by the unbroken string of defeats and retreats on the Western Front, and aware that armistice negotiations were underway, they only wanted peace so that they could go home. Certainly they did not want to be part of some heroic but useless last-minute act of self-sacrifice.

Unrest broke out in the fleet on October 27, when the orders came to sail. Rumors were rift—and many of them were true—although no official word was forthcoming. Hipper issued his instructions to his squadron leaders on the evening of October 29. They were to sail the following day, he ordered. That night word of this decision, made independently of the government, swept through the fleet like wildfire, and mutiny followed right behind. Riots swept the *Thueringen, Helgoland, Markgraf,* and other main surface ships. The men simply refused to put to sea. They would defend their ports and coasts, they told their officers, but they refused to be needlessly sacrificed. Confronted by such determined opposition from his own men, Admiral Hipper cancelled his orders that night. After daybreak, however, he reconsidered and changed his mind. He decided that, for the sake of the navy's honor, he had to do something to help the army in Flanders; therefore, he would send out his U-boats and torpedo boats (which had thoroughly reliable crews) to attack the British vessels off the Belgian coast. Due to the mutinies, he would not commit the surface vessels to battle; however, he did intend that the surface ships escort the submarines and torpedo boats to the deep water mine belt and await their return there. When he revealed his new plan to the squadron commanders, some of them expressed doubts that it could be carried out. Admiral von Hipper, however, was determined to act and could not be deterred.

When the order to weigh anchor came, many of the seamen of the First Squadron mutinied. The *Thueringen* was disabled by its own crew, and riots immobilized the *Helgoland.* Hipper thereupon cancelled his orders a second time but simultaneously declared that the mutiny would be put down—by force, if necessary. Reliable marine platoons, several torpedo boats, and a submarine converged on the *Thueringen* and *Helgoland.* Just as they were about to open fire, the mutineers lost their nerve and surrendered. About 400 men were taken off the *Thueringen, Helgoland, Markgraf,* and *Grosser Kurfuerst* and thrown into the brig in Wilhelmshaven, and the mutiny seemed to be over. It flared up again that night, however, when disorder broke out aboard the vessels of the Fourth Squadron, including the *Friedrich der Gross, Koenig, Albert,* and *Kaisern,* but the officers agreed to give the mutineers amnesty if, in exchange, they would go back to work. Hipper hesitated for some time and then decided to disperse the fleet, sending the First Squadron to the Elbe and the Third to Kiel. The Fourth remained at Wilhelmshaven. This decision was a serious mistake on his part, because it further spread the mutiny and, at the same time, put the ships beyond centralized control.

When his ships dropped anchor at Holtenau, near Kiel, Admiral

Kraft, the commander of the First Squadron, signaled the alarm. When his crews went to their battle stations, 47 of them were arrested and another 200 were transferred to a penal battalion on shore. Kraft then insisted upon taking his ships into Kiel, despite the objections of Admiral Wilhelm Souchon, the commander of the Baltic Naval Station. Souchon realized that Kiel was rife with unrest and that he would be unable to control the rebellious sailors once they reached shore, but he could not get the stubborn and repressive Kraft to listen to him. On the afternoon of November 2 several hundred sailors, marines, and dock workers, urged on by local Independent Socialists, held a major rally at Kiel and demanded the release of the mutineers. The next day they rallied again, but this time there were several thousand servicemen, union members, and workers who were determined to free the rebels. Marching to the tune of the "Internationale," the drunken and disorderly crowd headed for the naval prison on the Feldstrasse, gaining in numbers with each bar they passed. They were blocked just short of the prison by a patrol of 48 mates and officer-candidates, commanded by a Lieutenant Steinhaeuser. When the mob refused to disperse, Steinhaeuser ordered a volley fired into the air. When the mob continued to press forward menacingly, the sailors fired into it, killing 8 and wounding 39. Lieutenant Steinhaeuser was also seriously wounded when a bullet struck him in the head. Seeing the mob flee, Admiral Souchon thought that he had regained control of the situation and cancelled his earlier request for army reinforcements from the nearby garrison at Altona.

Souchon's optimism was disastrously premature, for the mob had not dispersed—it had merely retreated in considerable haste. When it returned, larger than ever, Souchon's troops, including the entire 1st Torpedo Division, most of the Dock Division, and even the usually reliable Submarine Division, went over to it *en masse*. Souchon now had little choice but to negotiate with the sailors' and workers' councils that represented the insurrectionists, and the imprisoned mutineers were soon released. The mutiny was not over, however; it was blossoming into a full-scale revolution.

The next day, Monday, November 4, the sailors' and workers' councils declared a general strike in Kiel, and red flags were hoisted on most of the ships in the harbor. By the following day the entire city was in the hands of the rebels. Hipper was powerless to intervene because most of his men had gone over to the revolutionaries. On November 5 the Third Squadron revolted, took over Travemuende, and marched on Luebeck. There the entire garrison went over to the revolution without firing a shot.[7] From Kiel, Travemuende, and Luebeck, the rebellion spread with incredible swiftness across northern Germany, engulfing Wilhelmshaven, Cuxhaven, Bremen, and Hamburg, the second city of the Reich, where 40,000 demonstrators were rioting in the streets on November 6, disarming officers, and ripping off their epaulettes. The government ordered the Hanover garrison to attack the rebels, but it joined them instead. On the evening of November 6 Prince Max made the difficult decision to tell the Kaiser that he must abdicate, but Wilhelm was too stubborn to consider such a course of action. The next day Hanover, Brunswick, and even Cologne went over to the revolution. Then Munich exploded. At 3 P.M. on November 7 more than 100,000 workers waving red flags marched on the palace of the Royal House of Wittelsbach. When he learned that all of the troops in the city had either deserted or gone over to the rebels, and that all of his palace guards had fled, Ludwig III, the benevolent, grandfatherly 73-year-old Bavarian king, tucked a box of cigars under his arm and headed for the Royal garage, along with his four daughters, one of whom had a more practical turn of mind than the monarch: She took jewels. (Queen Maria Theresa was seriously ill and could not travel. She was left to the clemency of the rebels.) At the garage, Ludwig discovered that the Royal chauffeur had also deserted, with the Royal gas supply. Fortunately, a nearby private garage furnished him with cars and drivers so that he could flee his capital. After leaving Munich, Ludwig's car ran off the road and got stuck in a potato field. An exhausted Ludwig did not reach his mountain retreat at Wildenwarth until 4 A.M. the next morning. He eventually made his way into exile in Hungary, where he died in the fall of 1921. He never saw Munich again.

The Bavarian capital was taken over by the Independent Socialists, Reds, and workers' and soldiers' councils, which were led by Kurt Eisner, who was named minister-president. Eisner was a Berlin drama critic who, at the age of 40, had deserted his wife and five children and fled to Bavaria, where he moved in with a woman journalist and habitually haunted the artists' cafés of the Schwabing district. Here he became active in socialist politics and eventually became the founder of the Munich branch of the Independent Socialists. Eisner acquired a reputation as an antiwar martyr by spending the first eight months of 1918 in prison for organizing a peace strike. Charles B. Flood described him as a "birdlike little man" with a "long wispy grey beard . . ., [a] big black hat, thick steel-rimmed glasses, and seedy suits."[8] He certainly did not look the part of a great political leader—and indeed would prove that he was not. In fact, he had no idea how to run a province of 7,000,000 people.

Meanwhile, all of Germany was shocked by the passing of Ludwig. The House of Wittelsbach, Germany's oldest dynasty, had endured for a thousand years. Now it fell without a shot being fired in its defense. The ignominious fall of the Bavarian monarchy had a snowballing effect for the revolution and a domino effect on the royalty. By the evening of

November 8, all 22 of Germany's lesser kings, princes, grand dukes, and ruling dukes had been deposed, and Soviet republics had been proclaimed in Cologne, Munich, Leipzig, Stuttgart, and Frankfurt-am-Main. Of the old monarchy, only Kaiser Wilhelm II remained, temporarily secure with the army headquarters in Spa. But he no longer had the slightest control over events. That same day a German armistice commission, led by Matthias Erzberger, now state secretary for foreign affairs, arrived at Allied headquarters at Compiegne. Here a frigid Marshal Foch handed the Allies' harsh conditions over to the delegation. They were designed to make it impossible for Germany to resume the war after the armistice expired (that is, to force Germany to accept the terms of the subsequent peace treaty, whatever they might be). In exchange for an armistice, the Germans were required to evacuate all territory west of the Rhine within 30 days and to hand over 3 bridgeheads east of the river: the Mainz area to the French, the Colbenz sector to the Americans, and the Cologne area to the British. The entire east bank of the Rhine was to be demilitarized for a distance of 10 kilometers, except for those zones occupied by the Allies. German troops were to withdraw at once from Turkey, Romania, Austro-Hungary, and eventually from Russia, and all of her Eastern territorial claims were to be renounced. In the West she must surrender 30,000 machine guns, 5,000 trucks, 5,000 railroad locomotives, and 150,000 railroad cars, as well as 5,000 heavy guns and 1,700 aircraft. In addition, 10 battleships, 6 battle cruisers, 8 light cruisers, and 50 destroyers were to be interned in British or neutral ports, and all U-boats were to be surrendered. All Allied prisoners of war were to be released at once, but no provision was to be made concerning the release of German POWs until later. Worst of all, the Allied blockade was to remain in effect until the signing of the final peace treaty—an event that would no doubt be months away. The German delegation was given 72 hours in which to reply. In view of the gravity of the situation and the chaos in Germany, Erzberger asked for a one-day extension of the time limit. The uncompromising Foch refused to grant even this.

Meanwhile, inevitably and somewhat belatedly, the revolution reached Berlin. Prior to midnight on November 8 Prince Max wired Spa that the rebellion could no longer be put down unless the Kaiser's abdication was announced in the morning newspapers. The emperor, however, had already gone to bed, with orders not to be disturbed. Consequently it was Hindenburg and Ludendorff's successor, Quartermaster-General Wilhelm Groener, who were forced to tell Wilhelm that he had to abdicate. It took them several hours to convince him of this fact, for he simply refused to face reality. In the end, he signed the act of abdication. As usual, however, he had waited too long. On the morning of November 9 Emil Eichhorn, a member of the extreme left wing of the Independent Socialists who worked in the telegraph department of the Soviet embassy, led an armed mob into the headquarters of the Berlin police and installed himself as chief. As Eichhorn and his militants liberated some 650 prisoners and inducted them into the new, radical police force, the regular police stacked their arms and went home. Following this collapse of law and order, left-wing mobs seized newspaper offices, the city hall, the main telegraph office, and other strategic points. By 11 A.M., when Prince Max learned of the emperor's decision to step down, the Social Democrats had already left the government, and mobs of workers and deserters were marching into the center of Berlin (and the government quarter) unopposed. It was now too late for Prince Max to save the institution of the monarchy. A few minutes after noon a delegation of Social Democrats arrived and informed Max that they were taking over the government. Prince Max of Baden had no choice but to turn the chancellery over to the head of the Social Democratic Party, Friedrich Ebert, a former saddle maker and a *Gasthaus* owner from Heidelburg. The last Imperial chancellor then faded from the stage of history, and on November 9, 1918, the first German Republic (soon to be known as the Weimar Republic) was established.

Elsewhere the Kaiser and the monarchy also faded into history. Early on the morning of November 10 Wilhelm II boarded his gold and cream colored private train at the Spa station and crossed into Holland. As a final indignity, the Supreme War Lord of Germany had to give up his sword to a Dutch customs official. Thus ended the rule of the House of Hohenzollern, after 507 years and 19 generations.

In the meantime it was left to Germany's first parliamentary government to bare the onus of signing the harsh terms of the armistice. Erzberger pled with the Allies for softer terms, pitifully pointing out that the blockade was inhumane and, if it were not lifted, thousands of innocent women and children would die. "Is this fair?" he asked the British delegate, First Sea Lord Sir R. Wemyss.

"Fair?" Wemyss shot back. "Remember that you have sunk our ships without making any distinction of sex." The Allies did, however, promise to undertake to provide Germany with food during the armistice period.[9]

In three hours of early morning negotiations this promise was the only concession the small, roundish state secretary could wrest from the victors. Even his request to retain some of the 30,000 machine guns, which were needed to suppress the domestic Communist insurrections, was rejected. Finally, at 5 A.M. on November 11, 1918, the German plenipotentiaries signed the armistice. The fighting stopped at 11 A.M. that same day. The First World War was over, but the Allies had already taken a wrong turn down the road that led to the second. They would unwittingly pursue this same course at top speed over the next several years.

The Allies had already made a number of mistakes vis-à-vis Germany—mistakes that Adolf Hitler and the Nazis would take full advantage of in the years ahead. First of all they unwittingly allowed German militarism to obtain a new lease on life. By refusing to deal with the "military masters" of Germany, Wilson had spared Germany's military leaders from participating in the all-important signing of the armistice—the symbolic act of surrender. Had Hindenburg signed, the myth held by many Germans that their armies were invincible would have been exploded, and the legend that the frontline troops had been "stabbed in the back" by traitors at home would not have been able to germinate. Later it would be recalled countless times that not one foot of German territory was occupied by foreign armies at the time of the armistice; on the contrary, German forces still held most of Belgium, much of France, and large expanses of territory in the East. Hindenburg himself became a leading proponent of the "stab in the back" legend *(Dolchstosslegend)*. As early as 1919 he, Ludendorff, and others were asserting that the army had never been defeated in the field but rather had been betrayed by the subversive elements at home, including pacifists, socialists, Communists, liberals, and Jews. By allowing the German military to escape responsibility for its part in the collapse of the Second Reich, the Allies indirectly encouraged the rebirth of German militarism and helped pave the way for the rise of the militaristic Third Reich.

Secondly the Allies forced the newly born civilian parliamentary government to bear the odium of the surrender. Thus even at the time of its birth, the German people's faith in the Republic was undermined by the Allies—the very people who should have been doing all they could to ensure that Germany's fledgling democracy was successful, because it was in their national interests to do so.

Thirdly the harsh armistice terms bore little resemblance to Wilson's Fourteen Points. Many Germans felt that they were being hoodwinked by the Allies—although many others still had faith in the Wilsonian principles and were sure that the terms of the final peace treaty would be just. Still, the seeds of mistrust had been planted.

As if these blunders were not enough, the Allies maintained their economic blockade but did not really keep their promise to feed Germany. True, some provisions were sent, but not enough to keep tens of thousands of people from starving to death. The food situation was actually worse after the armistice than before it, and the first winter of peace was worse than any winter of the war. Before the cease-fire, Germany could at least draw some food from the occupied territories. Now these were denied to it. Even where small surpluses of food became available, it often could not be shipped to where it was needed, because the Allies had taken so many of Germany's locomotives and much of her rolling stock in exchange for the armistice. For a time even the Baltic Sea was closed to German fishermen by order of the victors. The results of all of this were tragic. In some districts, 20 percent of the babies were born dead due to malnourishment in the mothers, and another 40 percent of the newborns did not live a month. When the death of these innocents (predicted by Erzberger) is taken into account, there is small wonder that hatred for the Allies festered in the hearts of many of the Germans. But the Allies had even more unpleasant surprises in store for them, as we shall see.

2   The Freikorps and the War after the War

Germany in November 1918 was not only suffering from blows delivered by external forces: It was suffering from internal fragmentation as well. The sudden collapse of the Second Reich took Germans of all political persuasions completely by surprise. The chancellorship had been thrust into the hands of Friedrich Ebert, but real power did not come with the title. In fact, no one was in power in Germany at that time. The collapse of the House of Hohenzollern had created a geopolitical power vacuum into which several factions wished to expand. The Ebert government was, at best, a weak and disunited minority, in grave danger of being overthrown by the Bolsheviks or their allies, the Independent Socialists. Ebert, who had lost two sons during the war and said he "hated revolution like sin," realized the true nature of the situation. On the night of November 9, after only a few hours in office, he was pacing up and down in his chancellery office, his shirt drenched in sweat, nearly in a state of nervous exhaustion. The crowds on the Wilhelmstrasse below did not reassure him. They were singing the "Internationale" (the Bolshevik theme song) and carrying signs that read "Down with the Traitors to the Revolution" and "Down with Ebert-Scheidemann." An occasional shot rang out in the distance. Suddenly one of the three telephones on his desk rang, and Ebert answered it hurriedly, for this was Number 988: the direct line to OHL *(Oberste Heeresleitung)*, the Headquarters of the Supreme Command, located at Spa.

"Yes, who is there?" Ebert asked.

"Groener speaking," came the reply.

Ebert was relieved. He liked the smooth Wuerttemberger staff officer from the Swabian district of southern Germany, who was so unlike the dictatorial Ludendorff and many of the other arrogant and overbearing Prussians. The two had worked together on the program to increase munitions production during the war and had gotten along fine.

After a brief but nervous exchange of courtesies, Ebert asked that OHL supervise the withdrawal of the field armies from France, Belgium, and the East. This Groener agreed to do. Then Ebert came to the point and asked what the army expected from the government in exchange for its support.

"The Field Marshal [Hindenburg] expects that the government will support the Officers' Corps, maintain discipline, and preserve the punishment regulations of the Army," Groener replied. He went on to demand that the government provide the army with complete and satisfactory provisions and maintenance.

"What else?" the chancellor asked.

"The Officers' Corps expects that the government will fight against Bolshevism and places itself at the disposal of the government for such a purpose."

A relieved Ebert promptly agreed and asked Groener to convey the thanks of the government to the field marshal.[1]

By this brief conversation, Ebert had allied the government to the army and had made the civilian government both the protector and the dependent of the High Command of the Army. It was, however, an army with its own ideas—one that would function with a high degree of independence from (and contempt for) the republic that it had pledged to defend. However, the General Staff of the Army, which was composed mainly of reactionary, aristocratic officers who hated democracy and who longed for the return of the Kaiser, considered the republic a viable alternative to a Soviet Germany—in which they would have no place. And, if their support for the Weimar Republic was halfhearted at best, their desire to suppress the Bolsheviks, Communists, and extreme left-wing factions in the fatherland was very, very real; in fact, they would do so with the greatest enthusiasm.

First, however, they had to get the army out of France and Belgium. This the General Staff accomplished within 30 days and with the greatest discipline and marvelous efficiency. (The move from the East was less successful.) This success, however, caused the High Command to overestimate its power over its own troops. They failed to grasp the fact that most of the soldiers in the ranks were no longer obeying commands because such instructions reflected the will of some Prussian general or the officers of the General Staff; they were obeying orders because that was the safest and quickest way to get back home. Once they arrived back in Germany, the bulk of the divisions simply melted away like snow in the sun; many of the men did not even bother to report to their demobilization stations. Most of those who remained in the ranks of the so-called reliable divisions were, in fact, no longer reliable.

The first attempt of the army to use one of its divisions against the left-wing mobs was a complete fiasco. The scene was Berlin in December 1918. The streets of the capital were in complete anarchy. Police President Eichhorn, as he himself admitted, was unable to form a reliable or disciplined force. His police, now about 2,000 strong, were mostly criminals, anarchists, leftists, and hoodlums—men who were not the least bit interested in establishing and maintaining law and order. They spent most of their time drinking, looting, stealing, engaging in extortion, and committing random acts of rape and murder. They were not bothered when the People's Naval Division *(Volksmarine Division)*, a force of about 3,000 deserters from the navy and army, seized the castle *(Schloss)* and stables *(Marstall)* of the former Kaiser at the end of November.

The People's Naval Division was led by Lieutenant Dorrenbach, a mentally deranged officer who had been one of the instigators of the Kiel mutiny. Using the palace (and its well-stocked wine cellar) as its headquarters, the naval division went on a spree of looting and pillaging, which Dorrenbach did nothing to discourage. Soon the Schloss was attracting the worst elements of the Berlin underworld. By early December, Dorrenbach was actually blackmailing the government. He promised that he and his men would leave the palace and stables if Ebert would pay them 125,000 marks. Ebert paid, but Dorrenbach's men did not leave; rather, they used their money to buy liquor and prostitutes and began a drunken orgy that lasted for days. As Christmas Eve approached, however, the deserters began to run low on money and booze. Dorrenbach therefore demanded more money. Sick of and frightened by the lawless and outrageous behavior of the Volksmarines, Ebert and the five People's Commissioners who made up his government (which at that time was called the Council of People's Representatives) decreed that the sailors must leave the Schloss and Marstall and reduce the size of their division to 600 men by New Year's Day. The Council authorized Otto Wels, the Majority Socialist Commandant of Berlin, to pay them 80,000 marks "back pay" to leave the castle and stables. The crisis came when Dorrenbach demanded the money in advance, but Wels, not trusting him, refused to pay until the Schloss was actually vacated. Dorrenbach thereupon went berserk. On the afternoon of December 23 he declared the entire government under arrest; surrounded the chancellery; occupied the main telephone exchange; seized the city commandant, the commandant's headquarters, and the 80,000 marks; and hauled Wels and his two principal assistants back to the castle, where Wels was beaten to a bloody pulp. Dorrenbach and his colleagues, however, did not know that Telephone 988 was a direct line to Spa and thus bypassed the main switchboard, which the rebels controlled.

The Council of People's Representatives was now divided as to what to do. The three Independent Socialists opposed using the army against the mob under any circumstances. Ebert, supported by the two other Social Democrats on the Council, favored military action. He picked up 988 and called for help.

Groener was out when Ebert's call arrived, so he spoke with his assistant, Major Kurt von Schleicher, who held influence far beyond his rank. "You have always told me that you would help," cried the worried Ebert. "Please act now!"

Major von Schleicher was only too happy to help. He at once ordered Lieutenant General Arnold Lequis's Guards Rifle Cavalry Division to attack the buildings and free the hostages. The 300 men of Lequis's special street-fighting detachment surrounded the Imperial grounds that evening.

Realizing that they had gone too far, the rebels impeached Lieutenant Dorrenbach and elected a Lieutenant Fischer to replace him. They refused to surrender or release their hostages, however, so the stage was set for a battle the following day.

"The Battle of the Schloss" began at 7:40 A.M. on Christmas Eve, 1918. General Lequis had 800 men and a battery and a half of field artillery. He faced about 1,200 sailors in the castle and stables.

Lequis opened the fighting with a point-blank bombardment on the palace. Then the Prussian Guards quickly stormed the castle, killing seven sailors and losing two of their own in the process. At 9:30 A.M. the sailors raised the white flag and asked for a 20-minute truce, to which Lequis agreed. This turned out to be a disastrous mistake, because, at about 9:45 A.M., Emil Barth (the Independent Socialist leader) and several Spartacist (Communist) leaders arrived with a large mob, including many women and children, which proceeded to surround the cavalrymen. Many of the civilians interposed themselves directly in the line of fire, between the sailors and the Guards.

The confused and horrified regular soldiers would not fire on the crowd, which jeered them and called for them to throw down their weapons and join them. Many of the Guards did just that, while others simply allowed themselves to be disarmed. Meanwhile, some of the sailors took advantage of the situation by grabbing women and children and using them as human shields. Meanwhile, an order arrived from the Council of People's Representatives, ordering the Guards to cease fire. All of this was too much for the cavalrymen: They threw down their weapons and ran away. The "undefeated Army" had been vanquished by a rabble of civilians, workers, and deserters. Thus began what the Germans came to call *"der Krieg nach dem Krieg"*—the war after the war. The Battle of the Schloss was the nadir of the old army. Yet General Groener, for one, was rather pleased with the result. The three Independent Socialist members of the Council of People's Representatives resigned in protest of Ebert's using the army against the mob, causing a rupture between the two major Socialist factions that never healed. Ebert and the Majority Socialists (also known as the Social Democrats) were thrown into a situation in which they were publicly dependent upon the army. Finally, as General Groener gloated, "Ebert has been made to cross his Rubicon. Now he can no longer oppose a cleaning up of Berlin by force of arms."[2]

Groener could afford to be smug, in spite of the embarrassment at the Schloss, for his assistant, Major Kurt von Schleicher, had come up with a brilliant alternative to using the army against the mob. Young Schleicher, who was getting along very well with Paul von Hindenburg, suggested to the field marshal that the government be encouraged to organize volunteer units recruited from the old army and commanded by former Imperial officers, for use against the Reds. It was a beautiful idea, from the perspective of the army. If the experiment succeeded, the army leadership would have accomplished its objectives without having become directly involved—and thus would have avoided the stigma of having to fire on German crowds. However, because most of the volunteer bands would be commanded by officers of the former Kaiser, the army generals would be in effective control. On the other hand, if the experiment misfired, the government—not the army—would bear responsibility for the failure. As an additional bonus, the government would have to pay and supply the new formations. Meanwhile, the army could regroup and reform itself into an effective military weapon once again. These new organizations were called the *Freikorps* (free corps). They were also the forerunners of the Storm Troopers and the SS of Hitler's Nazi Party.

The men of the Freikorps were called "Freebooters" and were almost all products of either the prewar Youth Movement or the trenches of World War I. The Youth Movement, according to Robert G. L. Waite, was characterized by action without conscious purpose; high (if naive) idealism and optimism; gentle good will; acceptance of the Fuehrer Principle (that is, orders from the leader—whoever he was—were to be followed without question); and a willingness to follow a charismatic leader.[3] The World War I veterans, on the other hand, were men who could or would not return to civilian life after the war. Hermann Goering referred to them as "fighters who could not be de-brutalized." "War could not release them from its grasp," Ernst von Salomon said of them.[4] They were more than a match for the undisciplined radicals, extreme Leftists, and Reds that they would have to face.

The Freikorps recruits were also none too happy with the reception they had received when they got home from the front. One World War I veteran recalled an all-too-typical experience. When the troops returned to the fatherland, he wrote,

> a disgusting sight met their eyes. Beardless boys, dissolute deserters and whores tore off the shoulder bands of our front-line fighters and spat upon their field-gray uniforms. At the same time they muttered something about liberty, equality, and fraternity. . . . People who never saw a battlefield, who had never heard the whine of a bullet, openly insulted men who through four and a half years had defied the world in arms, who had risked their lives in innumerable battles, with the sole desire to guard the country against this horror. For the first time I began to feel a burning hatred for this human scum that trod everything pure and clean underfoot. Young as I was, I determined I should never have anything to do with those people.[5]

This young man later joined the Freikorps, the Black Reichswehr, and finally the Nazi Party. Unfortunately, his story was all too typical of what happened to the returning soldiers. Captain Erwin Rommel, who was later to win fame as the "Desert Fox," was shouted at and insulted several times because he continued to wear his many decorations. Lieutenant Ernst Udet, a former member of Baron Manfred von Richthofen's fighter wing and the leading German ace to survive the war, was attacked by a deserter with a red arm band, who tried to rip his *Pour le Merite* (that is, the "Blue Max," Germany's highest decoration) from his throat. (Fortunately for the much smaller Udet, the Bolshevik had a huge red beard; Udet grabbed it with both hands and held on tightly, until a sympathetic streetcar conductor banged the Red upside the head.) Even General Groener and Major von Schleicher were assaulted on a public train while travelling from Spa to Berlin to meet with the chancellor. Literally thousands of other soldiers had similar experiences. Bitter memories of this nature served to alienate many of the returning warriors from the Republic and later were major contributing factors in their support of the Nazi Party, but this is getting ahead of our story.

The first Freikorps formed was also the best. General Ludwig Maercker, the former commander of the 214th Infantry Division, began recruiting his Freikorps in a Franciscan convent near Salzkotten, Westphalia, in mid-December 1918. Maercker demanded and received strict discipline, moderation, and military bearing beyond reproach. By the end of the month he already had 4,000 men. About that time he moved his command (which he dubbed the "Maercker Volunteer Rifles") to Zossen, a little garrison town about 35 miles south of Berlin. On the morning of January 4, 1919, the Maercker Freikorps was inspected by the chancellor, General Groener, and Gustav Noske, the new strongman in the Ebert government. When the Independent Socialists resigned in protest during the Schloss affair, Ebert (at Groener's suggestion) appointed Noske minister of national defense. Variously known as "the Brandenburg woodcutter" and the "Bloodhound of the Revolution," Noske had created order out of chaos in Kiel and now promised to do the same in Berlin. He was well equipped to do it, too. Massive of body and sporting a walrus mustache, he exuded a tough solidness that was not belied by his actions. His firm and direct approach and clear, easy-to-understand instructions stood in marked contrast to the timid vacillation that characterized the rest of the Ebert administration. He had, for example, already sacked General Lequis for his failure at the Schloss and replaced him with General Baron Walter von Luettwitz, the former commander of the III Corps of the Imperial Army and a Prussian aristocrat to the tip of his toes. Noske was also planning to oust Eichhorn as police president of Berlin, even though he knew such a move might spark a Communist *coup* attempt against the government, and he had won Ebert over to his position. All the two politicians needed now was a military force capable of suppressing such a rebellion. On the morning of January 4 they found it. As they stood on the edge of the parade field at Zossen, Ebert's eyes were moist as he heard the boom of a Prussian military band, followed by thousands of good-looking troopers marching in perfect formation. "These are not amateur soldiers like Eichhorn's Republican Security Force," he said to Noske. "These are the real thing. They are every bit as smart as the Kaiser's army."[6]

Gustav Noske agreed. "No need to worry any more, Fritz," he said to the chancellor as they drove away. "Everything will be all right now."[7]

Noske was so impressed by the Maercker Volunteer Rifles that he gave official sanction to the Freikorps movement, which was already sweeping the country. When he arrived back in Berlin, he persuaded Paul Hirsch, the premier and minister of interior of the province of Prussia, to sack Eichhorn at once. It is perhaps ironic that the supposed champions of German democracy felt compelled to put their faith and the fate of their government into the hands of these reactionary mercenary soldiers, but that is exactly what happened in early January 1919. By the peak of its power in 1920 the Freikorps would have a strength of about 400,000 men.

Meanwhile, back in Berlin, the strength of the Communist (or "Spartacist") forces had grown to alarming proportions. The Communist Party, which formally broke with the Independent Socialists on December 30, was led by Karl Liebknecht, the chief of the National Association of Deserters *(Reichsbund der Deserteure),* and Rosa Luxemburg, a tiny young woman (barely five feet tall) noted for her girlish charm, her brilliant pen, and her quick and biting tongue, which made her a terror and a threat to the Ebert regime and coleader of the Spartacists in an era when women were seldom directly involved in politics. Despite her youth, she had spent considerable time in both German and Russian prisons and had just been released from a Breslau prison, where she was serving time for antigovernment activity, but this had not cooled her idealism and revolutionary ardor. Clearly the more intelligent of the two, Luxemburg urged caution when Hirsch relieved Eichhorn of his post. But Karl Liebknecht, who was determined to disrupt the national election that Ebert had called for January 19, could not be restrained. A vehement and effective orator, he possessed Luxemburg's gift for speaking but was without her gift for thinking, and he swept the Revolutionary Committee and the party along with him. "The hour of action has struck!" he roared as the Spartacists declared the Ebert government deposed and a general strike in effect. In the first week in June the Independent Socialists joined the Spartacists in staging the largest public demonstrations yet seen in Berlin. Entire sections of the city were seized by the rebels, and anarchy reigned in the streets of the capital. It seemed to many that the day of the Soviet Republic had arrived in Germany.

In fact, they had played into the hands of the army. From his headquarters at Dahlen, Noske organized the Freikorps that would be used to clean out Berlin. General von Luettwitz organized several Freikorps under his personal command. Collectively known as Freikorps von Luettwitz, they included the Potsdam Freikorps (1,200 veterans of the 1st Foot Guards and Imperial Potsdam Regiments of the old army under Major von Stephani); the remnants of the Guards Rifle Cavalry Division; and the Reinhard Freikorps under Colonel Wilhelm Reinhard, the future SS-Oberfuehrer[8] of Berlin. Reinhard's command included the reliable elements of his former regiment, the 4th Guards, plus the 1,500 men of Freikorps Suppe, which came mainly from the old 2nd Guards Regiment. To these Noske added the Maercker Volunteer Rifles, General von Roeder's *Landeschuetzen* (local defense troops, in this case made up largely of provincial police and also known as von Roeder's Scouts), the Iron Brigade from Kiel (1,600 men), the Kuntzel Freikorps, and several smaller units. By January 10 Luettwitz had more than 22,000 men under his command.

While the government massed this impressive array of forces, the Leftists in Berlin met. And met. And formed committees. And met. And formed subcommittees. And talked. And met. And met again. They could not make up their minds to do anything. By doing nothing, they let the initiative slip into the hands of the government, which, thanks to Gustav Noske and the officers of the old Imperial General Staff, was not handicapped by a similar paralysis of leadership.

The Freikorps struck on the morning of January 10, spearheaded by the Reinhard Brigade, which took the Spandau district after a sharp battle. Meanwhile, Major von Stephani's Potsdam Freikorps bogged down in the Belle-Alliance-Platz in heavy fighting. The next day they advanced again, supported by flamethrowers, machine guns, trench mortars, and field artillery. Overwhelmed, many of the Spartacists surrendered, after which several were directly shot by the men of the Freikorps—an incident that was repeated all too frequently during Germany's civil war. Meanwhile, Maercker's Rifles, the Iron Brigade, and von Roeder's Scouts converged on Berlin from the south and west. The people of Berlin—longing for peace and some semblance of order—had changed sides by now. Sick of anarchy and lawlessness, they greeted the disciplined field-gray battalions with cheers of joy.

The battle ended on January 13, when the Revolutionary Committee called on the rebels to stop resisting and go back to work. Actually how many people were killed in the fighting is not known, but the number exceeded 1,000; few of them were Freebooters. Karl Liebknecht and Rosa Luxemburg fled to the Wilmersdorf district of the city, where they were captured by an armed citizens' patrol. They were then taken to the elegant Eden Hotel in Berlin's west end, where the Guards Rifle Cavalry Division had established its headquarters. Here they fell into the hands of Captain Waldemar Pabst, the Ia (chief of operations) of the division.

Waldemar Pabst was an extremely reactionary officer who saw no need to subject the state to a long and expensive trial. He ordered that the prisoners be taken to Moabit prison for interrogation, but in separate cars. Liebknecht was led outside first, where a hussar named Otto Runge smashed his head with a rifle butt. Semiconscious and bleeding profusely, Liebknecht was driven to a lonely spot on the Charlottenburg Highway. Here the soldiers pretended that the car had broken down. Liebknecht was dragged out of the vehicle and asked if he could walk. When he did, Captain Horst von Pflugk-Hartung shot him twice in the back and once in the back of the head. The official announcement stated that he had been "shot while attempting to escape."[9]

Rosa Luxemburg was next. She had already been severely beaten when she was escorted out of the Hotel Eden for her rendezvous with Private Runge. His blow was so hard that it was heard inside the hotel. More dead than alive, she was dragged into a car and taken to the Landwehr Canal. En route, Lieutenant Kurt Vogel amused himself by firing his revolver into her head until he ran out of ammunition. Her body was then wired to stones and tossed into the canal, where it finally floated to the surface—bloated and unrecognizable—four months later. The entire incident reminds one of the "one-way rides" soon to be made infamous by American gangsters. Vogel kept a tiny shoe as a memento of the event.

The Liebknecht-Luxemburg murders set a pattern for political violence in Germany that continued until Hitler finally fell in 1945. In a sense, the pattern of murder and massacre that began in Berlin in 1919 continued, with occasional periods of dormancy, until millions had been put to death in gas chambers across Europe. Germany during this era was indeed a country undergoing a nervous breakdown. In this period of revolution and social and moral collapse, violence and murder had indeed become acceptable political weapons. They would remain so for the next 26 years.

It is perhaps appropriate to note that Lieutenant Vogel and Private Runge were eventually sentenced to two years in prison for their parts in the murders. Only Runge, the lowest-ranking of those involved, actually served time behind bars, and he was pardoned after a few months. Vogel escaped to Holland and was eventually amnestied. Waldemar Pabst was never convicted and never served a day in prison. As late as 1962 (at the age of 82) he still freely acknowledged his involvement in the affair, although he denied actually giving the order to kill the pair. Pabst never had the slightest regret about his part in the incident. He finally died, a retired major, in West Germany in 1970—in bed.

THE WEIMAR REPUBLIC: ROTTEN FOUNDATIONS

The Battle of Berlin did not end the German civil war, but it certainly determined which side was going to win it. Meanwhile, Fritz Ebert moved the government from Berlin to the city of Weimar, 150 miles to the southwest. Long a cultural center, many people still believe the myth that the regime moved to Weimar because it was the home of Goethe (Germany's Shakespeare) and Schiller and because Franz Liszt conducted the symphony there. Actually the reason for the move was purely military: Noske could not guarantee the safety of the National Assembly in Berlin, but the isolated and much smaller Weimar would be easy to defend. Accordingly, General Maercker occupied the place with 7,000 of his reliable volunteers between January 30 and February 3. Meanwhile, the first democratic general election in the history of Germany was held on January 19.[10] More than 30,000,000 people went to the polls (out of 35,000,000 eligible voters), and the result was a solid victory for Ebert. His Social Democratic Party garnered 11,500,000 votes (37.9 percent of the total) and captured 163 of the Reichstag's 421 seats. The moderate Catholic Center Party received 19.7 percent of the ballots and took 89 seats, followed by the liberal Democrat Party (18.6 percent of the votes and 74 seats). All totalled, these three pro-democracy parties (collectively referred to as the "Weimar Coalition") received 76.2 percent of the votes and garnered 331 of the 423 seats in the First Reichstag. The reactionary Nationalists, who accused Ebert of betraying the Kaiser, got only 42 seats, and the Independent Socialists could capture only 22. The Communists, who still harbored the illusion that they could seize power in the streets, boycotted the election and got nothing. This election proved to be the first and only time in the history of the Weimar Republic that the pro-democracy parties received more than half of the ballots.

Ebert opened the Reichstag with an address on February 6 and formed the "Weimar Coalition" of Social Democrats, Centrists, and Democrats. He was overwhelmingly elected the first president of the Weimar Republic and on February 11 named Philipp Scheidemann chancellor. The assembly then went to work on the new constitution, the initial version of which was drafted by Hugo Preuss, a liberal Jew who was a professor of law at the University of Berlin. Over the next several weeks, because they had little experience in democracy, the German legislators produced a dangerously flawed document that based the government on a system of proportional representation. For national voting purposes, Germany was divided into 35 electoral districts, but the outcomes of Reichstag elections in individual districts had little to do with the final composition of the national parliament. In Reichstag elections, a party was allotted one seat for each 60,000 votes it received. If it had 30,000 votes or more left over after the seats had been awarded, it was allocated another seat. This system resulted in considerable fluctuations in the number of Reichstag delegates (from 459 in 1920 to a high of 608 in 1932); it also ensured the proliferation of small, splinter parties. At various times over the next 13 years no fewer than 40 parties were represented in the Reichstag. Under this setup, it was virtually impossible for any party to gain a majority, which doomed the Weimar Republic to a series of short-lived coalition governments and eventually brought the very process of government to a standstill. (Table 2-1 shows the chancellors of the various cabinets that governed the Weimar Republic.) Also, the provincial state governments were granted limited autonomy, which would soon allow the Nazis to flourish in Bavaria, beyond the reach of the central government in Berlin. Finally, Article 48 of the constitution allowed the president to rule by decree—without the Reichstag—in time of emergency. Although it was used properly to solve Germany's financial crisis in 1923, this article would eventually help propel Adolf Hitler into the chancellery in 1933. However, as Otto Friedrich points out, the main problem at Weimar did not rest with the constitution but with the society it was supposed to govern.

It was a society fiercely divided against itself . . . [not only] between extremes of radical and conservative ideology but between classes, regions and religions. It was a society shattered by both psychological and economic consequences of military defeat, and still facing the crises of reparations, inflation, foreign invasion, and intellectual demoralization.[11]

In short, the Weimar Republic was not the kind of government to weather a crisis. "Any system can stand in fair weather," British historian A. J. P. Taylor wrote later. "It is tested when the storm begins to

Table 2-1
Reich Chancellors during the Weimar Era, 1918–1933

Chancellor (Party)	Date Left Office
Friedrich Ebert (S. D.)	Feb 11, 1919
Philipp Scheidemann (S.D.)	Jun 21, 1919
Gustav Bauer (S.D.)	Mar 27, 1920
Hermann Mueller (S.D.)	Jun 21, 1920
Konstantin Fehrenbach (Center)	May 10, 1921
Dr. Joseph Wirth (Center)	Oct 26, 1921
Wirth (Center)	Nov 22, 1922 (2nd cabinet)
Dr. Wilhelm Cuno (None)	Aug 13, 1923
Dr. Gustav Stresemann (People's)	Oct 6, 1923
Stresemann (People's)	Nov 30, 1923 (2nd cabinet)
Dr. Wilhelm Marx (Center)	Jun 3, 1924
Marx (Center)	Jan 15, 1925 (2nd cabinet)
Dr. Hans Luther (None)	Jan 20, 1926
Luther (None)	May 17, 1926 (2nd cabinet)
Marx (Center)	Jan 29, 1927 (3rd cabinet)
Marx (Center)	Jun 29, 1928 (4th cabinet)
Mueller (S.D.)	Mar 30, 1930 (2nd cabinet)
Heinrich Bruening (Center)	May 30, 1932
Franz von Papen (Center)	Nov 17, 1932
Kurt von Schleicher (None)	Jan 30, 1933
Adolf Hitler (Nazi)	*

S.D. = Social Democrats (Majority Socialists)
* = established the Nazi dictatorship, March 23, 1933

blow. This test the German republic could not pass: with few supporters and no roots, it fell at the first roar of thunder." [12]

While the Reichstag debated endlessly over minor modifications in the constitution, the army and its Freikorps were winning the civil war against the forces of the Left. After Berlin the pattern was more or less the same: The Communists and their Leftist allies would seize power in a city that had no Freikorps presence; frequently a Soviet Republic would be proclaimed and a "Red Terror" would ensue against the more-moderate citizens; then the Freikorps would arrive, crush the Reds, and institute a "White Terror" of its own. Finally, after the old, Republican government was reinstated, the Freikorps would march off to its next battle in another city, leaving the locals behind to bury the bodies it had left in the streets.

Bremen was the first test case. It was seized by the Reds in January 1919. Noske ignored threats of a general strike by soldiers' and workers' councils throughout the country and dispatched the Kiel Iron Brigade, Gerstenberg's Freikorps, and elements of Maercker's Rifles and von Roeder's Scouts to restore order. By February 5 the People's Commissars were dead or in hiding, and the bourgeois government had been rees-tablished. Bremen was followed in rapid succession by outbreaks in Bre-merhaven, Cuxhaven, and Wilhelmshaven, all of which were subdued in turn. No sooner was the north pacified than a general strike broke out in the west. Lichterschlag's Freikorps occupied Muelheim in Westphalia, while Maercker subdued Halle in particularly bloody fighting. He then moved on to Magdeburg, which was followed rapidly by battles for other cities, often with the support of other volunteer bands. The Frei-korps was victorious in every case.

Because his Freikorps was needed to put down insurrections at every point on the compass on short notice, General Maercker did not have the manpower to garrison the cities he conquered; therefore, he hit upon the idea of establishing smaller units of local citizens (called *Einwohner-wehren*, or civil guards), supervised by a small cadre of Volunteer Rifles, to maintain order and keep the Spartacists from rebelling again. Eventu-ally these civil guards grew into the *Orgesch* (Organization Escherich), a reserve militia for the German Army, under the command of Major Dr. Forstrat Escherich. [13]

Berlin erupted again on March 3, when the Spartacists proclaimed another general strike. The government responded by making Noske the virtual dictator of Germany. With his usual decisiveness, Noske de-clared martial law. This time the People's Naval Division, which had maintained a discreet neutrality in the January uprising, joined the battle on the side of the Reds. The fighting began on the night of March 3 and was particularly bitter, with more than the usual number of atrocities. Artillery and mortars were used by both sides, and even bombers and fighter aircraft were involved. On March 5 future SS-Oberfuehrer Reinhard's Freikorps stormed the Alexander Platz and the Berlin subway, and the following day the police headquarters, which had been converted into a virtual fortress by the Communists, was taken after a bombardment by mortars, bombers, heavy machine guns, and howitzers. That evening the Spartacists withdrew into the Lichtenberg suburbs, pursued by the better armed and much better led Freikorps. The unequal street fighting continued on March 7, but the next day the strike committee withdrew the general strike proclamation and made peace overtures to the government. Unfortunately for them, the men of the Freikorps found that several of their comrades had been lynched after being taken prisoner or had had their throats cut. The Freebooters responded savagely by beating their own prisoners in the faces with whips, or simply lining them up against the nearest wall.

On Sunday, March 9, wild rumors of Communist massacres swept the capital. Noske ordered that any man bearing arms against the government be shot on the spot. Meanwhile, a full-scale offensive was launched against Lichtenberg. Reinhard's brigade attacked from the north and east, von Huelsen's Freikorps and von Roeder's Scouts struck from the west, and the soon-to-be infamous Ehrhardt Naval Brigade advanced from the south. Supported by tanks, flamethrowers, artillery, and heavy machine guns, the Freikorps clearly had the insurgents in a death grip. The following day, March 10, Noske ordered the People's Naval Division to dissolve. They were instructed to report to the division's main office at 32 Franzoesischestrasse between 9 A.M. and 1 P.M. the following day, to receive their mustering out pay and demobilization certificates. Incredibly enough, many of the Volksmarines actually complied with the order, instead of going into hiding or trying to slip out of town. The "paymaster" at Franzoesischestrasse was Lieutenant Marloh, one of Reinhard's more ruthless officers. Marloh arrested hundreds of the sailors and deserters and had 29 of them shot at random. He intended to kill 300, but the executions were stopped on the orders of an unidentified officer. Marloh was later arrested for murder, tried, acquitted, and given a judgeship in the Freikorps' legal section by Wilhelm Reinhard. Eventually he followed his colonel into the Nazi Party.

The killing in Berlin continued for days after the resistance collapsed. Between 1,200 and 1,500 people were killed, and martial law remained in effect in Berlin for the next eight months. Meanwhile, three other cities were subdued by the Freikorps: Dresden on April 14, Brunswick on April 18, and Leipzig on May 10. However, the worst fighting, outside of Berlin, took place in Munich.

THE BAVARIAN REVOLUTION

Bavaria has been likened to America's Deep South in that it had (and has) its own way of life, which was distinctly different from that of the *"Saupreuss"* (Prussian swine), as they called the northerners. It will be recalled that the government of Bavaria had been taken over by Kurt Eisner, a Jewish theater critic and a member of the "cafe intelligentsia." Eisner was one of those well-meaning but fuzzy-headed Leftists who was so idealistic that he was totally incapable of coming to grips with the reality of governing. The people of Bavaria were not very receptive to Utopian ideas and, shrinking from the high-handed and arbitrary actions that had characterized past governments, Eisner preferred all-night discussions with social philosophers to making decisions. As a result, nothing was accomplished. After 100 days in office, the idealistic Eisner sought a mandate from the people. He expected to receive about 95 percent of the vote; however, on election day—January 12, 1919—only 3 percent of the ballots were cast for Eisner and his Independent Socialist Party. His supporters won only 3 seats in the *Landtag* (provincial legislature or diet), as opposed to 66 for the conservative Bavarian People's Party. Nevertheless, even though he had been afraid to use power, Eisner did not want to let it go. He therefore delayed convening the Landtag until he was absolutely forced to, causing a great deal of unrest on all sides of the political spectrum. Some, completely misjudging Eisner, thought he must have been planning to nullify the results of the election and remain in office illegally; the anti-Semitic Thule Society went so far as to secretly circulate a handbill that contained a veiled threat against his life if he did not step down. Finally, yielding to the pressure accumulating on all sides, Eisner agreed to convene the Landtag in Munich on February 21. That morning he walked to the provincial parliament building, where he probably intended to resign as premier of Bavaria.

Waiting for him was a handsome, 22-year-old lieutenant named Count Anton von Arco-Valley. A charming Austrian, Arco-Valley had served in the 1st Bavarian Heavy Cavalry Regiment on the Russian Front, where he had been highly decorated and badly wounded. Still weak from his wounds when the war ended, he had been totally humiliated when a Leftist mob attacked him on the street and ripped the cockage from his hat. A firm believer in the "stab in the back" legend, he had undergone further humiliation when the right-wing Thule Society rejected him for membership because his mother was half Jewish. Now, Arco-Valley resolved, he would show them all. As Eisner neared the Diet building, the count jumped out of a doorway and fired his revolver twice. One bullet struck Eisner in the back, the other in the brain. He was dead before he hit the sidewalk.

Arco-Valley himself was quickly shot five times by Eisner's bodyguard, and then trampled and stomped by a Spartacist mob. He was
then left for dead on the sidewalk. But Count Anton von Arco-Valley
did not die. Eventually someone discovered that he was still alive. He
was taken to a hospital and later was tried, convicted, and sentenced to
five years in prison. He was briefly a prisonmate of Adolf Hitler but
refused to have anything to do with the Nazi leader. In 1933 he was
arrested for plotting against the Fuehrer. Remarkably he survived the
war, only to be run over by an American jeep just after the German
surrender.

Despite the turmoil caused by Eisner's assassination, the Landtag met
at 11 A.M. One of Eisner's most influential opponents, Minister of the
Interior Erhard Auer, the leader of the Social Democrats, rose to deliver
a eulogy to the late premier and to warn against the danger of anarchy.
Unfortunately, in this emotionally overheated political atmosphere, the
totally false rumor had already spread that Auer had masterminded the
assassination. As he spoke, one of Eisner's most fervent supporters, a
saloon waiter named Alois Linder, entered the Diet with a rifle. He shot
Auer twice, severely wounding him, and killed a Major von Jahreiss,
who attempted to capture him when he fled. Then several of Eisner's
armed supporters in the spectator's gallery opened up on the floor. One
delegate was killed, and the others ran away, dove for cover, or jumped
out of the windows. At least two cabinet ministers suffered nervous
breakdowns that day, and government in Bavaria ceased to exist.

The murder of the idealistic premier made him a martyr and produced a groundswell of Leftist support much greater than any Eisner
had been able to generate when he was alive. "He was instantly elevated to the status of a proletarian saint," Hanser wrote later.[14] Huge
demonstrations took place in his honor, and the University of Munich
was closed because some of the students hailed Arco-Valley as a hero.
Priests were forced at gunpoint to toll the bells for days on end and
dozens of aristocrats were held hostage, in anticipation of a right-wing
coup. Thousands mourned Eisner, and large portraits of him were gar-
landed with flowers and set up on the streets of the city. In response,
the Thule Society rubbed burlap sacks in the sweat of bitches in heat
and rubbed them on or dropped them near the pictures. The Leftists
were shocked and outraged when sexually excited male dogs—attracted
by the scent—attacked the pictures and defiled them.

Government did not resume in Bavaria until March 7, when an anti-
militarist former schoolteacher named Adolf Hoffman, the new leader
of the Majority Socialists, was able to put together a shaky coalition
government. He wanted to restore order and preserve democracy, but
he was not given a chance to do so, because on March 20 a 33-year-old
Transylvanian Jew named Bela Kun created a Soviet republic and in-

stalled his dictatorship of the proletariat in Hungary. The Kun regime was to be an economic disaster and was characterized by terror and murder. It would only last 130 days and would set the stage for conservative rule in Hungary for a generation; nevertheless, at the time of its inception, it had an electrifying effect on Communist parties throughout Europe. The revolutionary dreamers in Munich met in the Queen's bedroom in the Wittelsbach Palace on the night of April 6/7 and proclaimed Bavaria a Soviet republic with a 26-year-old poet and playwright named Ernst Toller as chief of state. Toller issued a proclamation establishing a dictatorship of the proletariat and called on the Bavarian Red Army to ruthlessly suppress any counterrevolutionary activity.

There was no Red Army in Bavaria, and Toller and his "Coffee House Anarchists" could easily have been suppressed by the Munich Sanitation Department. The proclamation itself, however, was enough to send Hoffman fleeing northward, where he reestablished his capital in Bamberg, in the Bavarian province of Upper Franconia. Six weeks before, Bavaria had had no government; now it had two of them.

Events in Munich now assumed comic proportions. "It was as if Greenwich Village had moved into city hall *en masse*," one author wrote.[15] Toller named a former mental patient named Dr. Franz Lipp commissar of foreign affairs. Lipp promptly sent notes to Lenin and the pope, officially protesting the fact that Hoffman had taken the keys to his lavatory with him when he fled to Bamberg. Lipp also called upon His Holiness to bless their arms (a strange thing for a supposedly Godless communist to do) and demanded that Switzerland and the neighboring province of Wuerttemberg supply him with 60 locomotives. When they failed to comply, he declared war on both of them. Meanwhile, a part-time railroad track maintenance worker was named commissar for transportation, a burglar with a conviction for moral turpitude was appointed police president of Munich, a former waiter became commissar for military affairs, and a Jew was named commissar for education—in strongly Catholic Bavaria, where nuns still ran the schools. Shortly thereafter, the commissar for public housing decreed that henceforth no house could contain more than three rooms, and living rooms must always be placed above the kitchen and bedroom.

The Toller regime lasted only six days. After an abortive *coup* attempt by troops of the Munich garrison still loyal to Hoffman, the hard-line Communists seized power in Munich, and leadership was invested in a pair of Russians: Towia Axelrod (Lenin's former press chief) and Max Levien, who became the new head of state. They instituted a reign of terror and held mad sex orgies that shocked even the sophisticated Munichers. At the same time Rudolf Eglhofer, the 23-year-old chief of the army, was busy enrolling mercenaries in what was one of the best-paid armies in history. The privates were paid 25 marks per day (in advance), with bonuses of up to 15,000 marks, free housing for them and their families, free liquor, and free prostitutes.

Meanwhile, in Bamberg, Hoffman and his war minister, Ernst Schneppenhorst, tried frantically to build an army of "anti-militaristic Republicans." Noske offered to lend them Freikorps von Epp, led by former Imperial Major General Ritter Franz von Epp, but Hoffman replied that he did not need "foreign" help.[16]

The clash between the two Bavarian governments occurred at Dachau, a village about 10 miles north of Munich, on April 18, when the 8,000 antimilitary soldiers of Hoffman and Schneppenhorst met 30,000 of Eglhofer's well-paid mercenaries, led by none other than Ernst Toller, who had gone from poet to premier to field general in less than two weeks. He was also victorious, for the republican forces either fled or went over to the Reds at the first shot, leading one author to comment that "Anti-militarist soldiers are and remain a contradiction *per se.*"[17] What happened after Dachau is not at all amusing, however; now Hoffman had no choice but to turn to Noske, who was none too happy with him. The national defense minister still offered him the use of the Freikorps but only with a number of conditions attached, the most important of which was that Lieutenant General Burghard von Oven, the former commander of the Kaiser's 24th Infantry Division and overall Freikorps commander in the area, would not take any orders from Hoffman or his government until after Munich was under control.

Unlike Toller, Eglhofer et al., von Oven was a Prussian general who knew his business. By April 27 his Freikorps, which included at least 20,000 men, had formed a ring around Munich, and the next day began to contract it. On April 30 they took Dachau, despite the fact that the Spartacist forces had resorted to the use of poisonous gas and dumdum bullets. Then word reached the Freebooters of a Red atrocity committed in Munich earlier that day. Rudolf Eglhofer had been told that there was absolutely no hope of defending Munich. Terrified, he ordered the execution of the hostages he had seized and held prisoner in the Luitpold-gymnasium (high school). When Ernst Toller heard the news, he rushed to Luitpold to save them, but he arrived too late: Several of the most prominent citizens of Munich had been executed, including 32-year-old Countess Hella von Westarp, the beautiful secretary of the Thule Society. A prince, a distinguished Jewish professor, a painter, a baron, an industrial artist, and two captured cavalrymen were among the dead. Some of the bodies were so badly mutilated that they could not be identified. These were just the kind of people the German Freebooters had been taught to admire and respect since childhood. A cold fury gripped the men of the Freikorps, who were now out for revenge.

On May Day, traditionally the day of the worker and Communism's most sacred holiday, the men of Freikorps Oven, Ehrhardt, and Epp surged forward and broke through the Munich defenses on all sides. The city was in their hands by the following day, but von Oven would not declare it secure until May 6. In the meantime at least 1,000 and perhaps 1,200 Reds were executed. Many of the firing squads deliberately aimed low, so their victims were gut-shot. Then the squads walked away, while the Spartacists screamed in agony, begging for a mercy bullet that did not come. Some of them took a long time to die. Others, like Rudolf Eglhofer, were not shot. He was captured as he attempted to flee the city, and when his identity was discovered, he was beaten to the ground and kicked to death by his guards. The two Russians, Axelrod and Levien, managed to escape to Austria. Ernst Toller was hidden by a woman friend until a reward of 10,000 marks was offered for him; then she turned him over to the police. Luckier than most, he was eventually sentenced to five years in prison for high treason.

It is interesting to note the names of some of the men who were members of the Freikorps that stormed Munich, for this list shows the close relationship between the Freikorps and the Nazi Party. Their future positions in the Nazi Party and/or government are also given. They included Lieutenant Rudolf Hess, deputy Fuehrer and chief of the Nazi Party; Karl Fritsch, minister-president of Saxony; Robert Bergmann, colonel of SS; Hans Frank, Reichs Commissioner for justice; Dietrich von Jagow, commander of Hitler's first SA (storm trooper or Brownshirt) company and later Obergruppenfuehrer (full general) of SA and Reichs Commissioner for Wuerttemberg; Karl Kaufmann, Gauleiter (Nazi governor) of Hamburg; Manfred von Killinger, SA Obergruppenfuehrer, minister-president of Saxony, and Nazi minister to Slovakia (1940) and Romania (1941); Johann Ulrich Klintsch, accomplice in the murder of Erzberger (1921) and later a Brownshirt recruiter and organizer; Ritter von Krausser, general of SA; Johann von Malsen-Ponickau, SS-Brigadefuehrer, police president of Nuremberg-Fuerth, and a member of the personal staff of SS chief Heinrich Himmler; Hans Schemm, Gauleiter of Upper Franconia and director of the National Socialist Teachers' Association; Karl Schlumprecht, Gauleiter and mayor of Bayreuth; Wilhelm Stuckart, mayor of Stettin and director of the Prussian ministry of culture; Adolf Huehnlein, SA general and commander of the National Socialist Motor Corps (NSKK); Wilhelm Weiss, SA Gruppenfuehrer (lieutenant general); Friedrich Wilhelm Brueckner, Hitler's personal adjutant; and Karl Wolff, Himmler's adjutant and later SS commander in Italy. One non-Nazi Freebooter who later achieved fame was Lieutenant Baron Hasso von Manteuffel, who later commanded the 5th Panzer Army in the Battle of the Bulge.[18]

3 The Treaty of Versailles

While the Freikorps was fighting and winning the war after the war, the Allies were busy trying to ensure that Germany would never be able to fight another world war. As is typical for politicians, however, they accomplished exactly the opposite of what they set out to do.

In April 1919 the German government issued its directives to its delegates attending the peace conference, which had at last been scheduled to convene in Paris the following month. The instructions emphasized the fact that the German government regarded Wilson's Fourteen Points as binding on both sides, and they would have to be the basis of any settlement. Among other things, the Germans wanted a free plebiscite in Alsace-Lorraine, Posen, and northern Schleswig; the evacuation of German territory under Allied occupation when the treaty was concluded; the formation of a League of Nations to settle international disputes by arbitration; a prompt lifting of the blockade; and the return of the German merchant marine and of all German colonies lost during the war. They agreed to pay reparations for civilian losses and civilian property damage. They unequivocally denied that Germany alone was responsible for the war and rejected the cession of Upper Silesia or of a Polish Corridor through Prussia to the sea.

The chief of the German delegation was Count Ulrich von Brockdorff-Rantzau, a man of genuine liberal views who had served for years as an Imperial ambassador, most recently at Copenhagen. Not affiliated with any political party, he had accepted the post of foreign minister in December 1918 with the stipulation that the Allies' peace conditions could be rejected if they would not allow the German people the chance to lead half-way decent lives.

The German representatives arrived in Paris on April 29, 1919, and their reception was anything but friendly. They were kept practically under house arrest until May 7, when the Allies were at last ready to meet with them. The terms of the peace treaty were handed to the German delegation at Trianon, not far from the Palace of Versailles, where Bismarck had proclaimed the creation of the second German Empire *(Reich)* on January 18, 1871. Georges Clemenceau, the French premier, rose and briefly addressed the Germans, while copies of the 70,000-word document (which he called the "Second Treaty of Versailles") were passed out. Then Foreign Minister von Brockdorff was given a few minutes to respond. He remained seated because he had severe stage fright (he said later) and did not trust his knees; the Allies, however, took it as a gesture of arrogance and were livid. Brockdorff-Rantzau spoke bitterly about "the hundreds of thousands of non-combatants starved by the blockade since November 11" and deplored how they had deliberately been killed after the Allies had won their victory. This speech was not what the Allied leaders wanted to hear. Clemenceau's face turned red with rage and Lloyd George, the British prime minister, broke a letter opener on the desk in front of him. After Brockdorff concluded his remarks, he was tersely informed that the Germans had 15 days to read the treaty and to prepare any objections, questions, or counterproposals they had in writing, but only in French or English. Oral discussions and verbal communications were forbidden, as was any response in German.[1]

These high-handed tactics were a serious blunder. Excluding the Germans from the peace process until the treaty was drafted and then refusing to verbally discuss it with them lent considerable credibility to the charge that it was a dictated peace. Even Woodrow Wilson, who had been voted down by his former allies, said that, if he were a German, he would not sign it. When he saw the treaty, Marshal Foch, who certainly had no love for the Germans, exclaimed: "This is not a peace treaty. It is a 20 years' truce." It was also a punitive peace, for the terms of the treaty were harsh, to say the least. Alsace and Lorraine were to be ceded to France without a plebiscite. The German territory west of the Rhine presently under Allied occupation—including the cities of Cologne, Koblenz, and Mainz—was to be occupied by Allied troops for at least 15 years, although they might evacuate it piecemeal if Germany fulfilled all of her treaty obligations. The right bank of the Rhine was to be permanently demilitarized for a distance of 50 kilometers. The Saar basin—a clearly German area that possessed some of the richest coal deposits in Europe—was to be administered by a League of Nations commission for 15 years, during which the French would be in charge of the mines; thereafter it might be returned to Germany by a plebiscite. If the Saar voted to return to the Reich, Germany would have to purchase the mines. The districts of Moresnet, Eupen, and Malmedy were to be turned over to Belgium; Schleswig would choose by plebiscite whether it wanted to be German or Danish. (Ultimately it was split, with northern Schleswig voting to join Denmark.)

In the east, Germany was to hand over the rich (and largely German) industrial area of Upper Silesia to France's ally, Poland, along with most of Posen and West Prussia. The so-called Polish Corridor would cut across Germany to the Baltic, giving Poland access to the sea and completely severing East Prussia from the rest of the Reich. The city of Danzig was to be set up as a Free City under the administration of the League of Nations, despite the fact that its population was 95 percent German—a clear violation of the Wilsonian principle of self-determination. The Poles would have extensive economic and trade rights in the Free City. In addition, Germany would have to give up the East Prussian city of Memel (which eventually became part of Lithuania). In all, Germany would lose one-eighth of its national territory. None of her colonies would be returned. The treaty also forbade an *Anschluss* (union) between Germany and Austria, as did the Treaty of Saint Germain (the peace treaty between the Allies and Austria).

In addition, the Treaty of Versailles sought to reduce Germany to a state of military impotence. Germany would have to reduce its army—still 500,000 strong, excluding the Freikorps—to 100,000 men, of which only 4,000 could be officers. Officers would have to sign up for terms of 25 years and the enlistment for other ranks would be 12 years—provisions designed to prevent Germany from establishing a significant military reserve. The types of weapons the army could have were severely curtailed, and all excess war materials were to be surrendered to the Allies. The treaty went so far as to specify how many rounds of ammunition the army could have in reserve, and even German hunting clubs were to be regulated, to eliminate them as a potential source of paramilitary training. The great General Staff would be dissolved, and the elite cadet school at Gross-Lichterfeld was to be closed, along with most other training establishments. Of the four great weapons innovations of World War I (tanks, poisonous gas, the airplane, and the submarine), Germany was to be denied all four. The German Navy was to be reduced to what Halperin called "innocuous proportions": 6 small battleships, 6 light cruisers, 12 destroyers, 12 torpedo boats, and a few coastal guns. An Inter-Allied Control Commission was to be set up to ensure German compliance with the military clauses of the treaty. It would have the right to go anywhere on German soil to conduct inspections on demand, at German expense.[2]

The commercial articles of the treaty were as unfair as the others. In these clauses, the Allies granted themselves most-favored-nation status in the German market, but without reciprocation. All commercial agreements that allowed Germany to trade with other countries on advantageous terms were abrogated, thus effectively barring German products from Allied markets. These clauses would deny Germany— already saddled with a huge war debt—the ability to accumulate foreign capital and cut her off from one of her few potential sources of revenue. As if this were not enough, almost all of her foreign financial holdings were to be confiscated and her merchant fleet reduced to less than one-tenth its prewar size. In addition, German shipyards would have to construct 200,000 tons of new shipping per year and hand it over to the Allies, free of charge.

Germany also had to agree to pay whatever reparations the Allies demanded, even though the exact amount to be paid had yet to be determined. Germany, in effect, would have to sign a blank check worth billions.

Finally came the so-called "shame paragraphs." Germany would have to assume sole responsibility for starting the war—something she clearly did not do; in fact, Germany was the last of the major European powers to mobilize in 1914. Also, Germany would have to agree to hand over to the Allies anyone they decided to try as a "war criminal" and would have to assist the Allies in compiling evidence against these people. Finally, Germany would not be granted admission into the League of Nations.

Up until this point, most Germans had deluded themselves into believing that they would receive a just peace; the Allies had, after all, led them to believe the treaty would be based on Wilson's Fourteen Points. Now their final illusions were shattered. "The unbelievable has happened," Reichstag President Konstantin Fehrenbach exclaimed. "Our enemies have presented us with a treaty which surpasses the worst fears of our greatest pessimists."[3] President Ebert denounced the treaty as "unbearable,"[4] and Chancellor Scheidemann instructed Brockdorff to inform the Allies that the terms were unfulfillable and would ruin Germany. Simultaneously, he issued a proclamation denouncing the treaty and forcefully pointed out that it was not in accordance with the promises made prior to the armistice. "May the hand wither that signs such a treaty!" he cried. For the first time in years, Germans of every class and every political persuasion were united on one issue: They had been deceived by men who had never had the slightest intention of honoring their pledges. Throughout the war, the Allied leaders had declared that they were waging war against the House of Hohenzollern, not against the German people; now the German civilians unanimously felt that they had been lied to. Countless mass meetings were held, and protests were widespread. All forms of public entertainment were suspended for a week, and a period of official mourning ensued.

The German public reaction to the treaty caused the Allies to hesitate and even to offer a few concessions. The deadline for German acceptance was extended to June 23; though the Saar was under Allied occupation, its local governments could now be administered by Germans, but the French still got the mines; and the area subject to plebiscite in Schleswig was reduced somewhat. Most significantly, the Allies agreed that the fate of Upper Silesia would be determined by a plebiscite, rather than by outright concession to the Poles. Nevertheless, the protests continued throughout Germany. However, protesting an unjust treaty was one thing; refusing to sign it was something else altogether, for the alternative to signing was going back to war, and this Germany could not do. Most of the German Army had already gone home, but the Allies—especially the French—had the means to resume the conflict very quickly and were clearly prepared to do so. Also, in accordance with the terms of the armistice, the army had evacuated its foreign-held territory and had given the Allies major bridgeheads across the Rhine. If the war resumed, it would be fought on German territory. Nevertheless, at Versailles, Foreign Minister von Brockdorff berated the treaty and urged its rejection. He then informed the Allies that he was returning to Weimar. As he left, he and the German delegation were stoned by an angry French mob.

When Count von Brockdorff arrived at the German capital on the morning of June 18, he found the cabinet and every political party sharply divided. Some, like Chancellor Scheidemann, adamantly opposed signing. Others, while expressing dismay at the treaty, were even more dismayed about the prospect of resuming the war. This could mean the rise of separatism, especially in Bavaria (Germany had only united 48 years previously, after all); renewed Bolshevik uprisings; and the eventual disintegration of the Republic which would, in the end, be forced to sign anyway. Gustav Noske, who was very worried about more Red uprisings, was in favor of signing, but it was Matthias Erzberger who took the lead in urging ratification. After considerable debate, Noske signaled the High Command (now headquartered in Kolberg) and asked what the prospects of armed resistance were. Hindenburg replied that the army could resist successfully in the east, but not in the west, where French and American armies were poised to invade. He called upon the administration to reject the treaty anyway; as a soldier, he said, he preferred honorable annihilation to a dishonorable peace. After receiving this message, the Social Democrats joined the Centrists in supporting ratification.

The result was yet another governmental crisis. Chancellor Scheidemann could not support his party's position and resigned, leaving Germany without a government—three days before the Allied deadline (and with it the armistice) expired. Ebert had a difficult time finding someone to form a new government. He turned to Otto Landsberg, but he refused to have anything to do with the treaty, even though his stand meant giving up the chancellorship. Finally, with the expiration of the deadline only 24 hours away, Ebert was rescued by a Centrist-Social Democratic coalition under Gustav Bauer, the former minister of labor. Ulrich von Brockdorff-Rantzau resigned in protest and was replaced as foreign minister by Hermann Mueller.[5] Field Marshal von Hindenburg and his deputy, General Groener, the chief of the General Staff and the Quartermaster-General of the army, respectively, announced their retirements. Matthias Erzberger, the man who had originally signed the armistice and who led the proponents of the treaty, was named minister of finance in the new cabinet.

On June 22, 1919, the German Reichstag ratified the Treaty of Versailles by a vote of 237 to 138. Many Social Democrats, most notably Scheidemann and Landsberg, were absent. The German resolution contained two exceptions: the shame paragraphs (which stated that German aggression was solely responsible for the war) and the war criminals paragraphs. The Allies refused to accept even this. Finally, only 19 minutes before the Allied ultimatum ran out, the German delegation capitulated and informed the French that the Reich accepted the treaty under duress. It was signed in the Hall of Mirrors in the Palace of Versailles on the afternoon of June 28, 1919—the very room in which the German Empire had been declared in 1871. Hermann Mueller and Dr. Hans Bell, the Centrist minister of transportation, signed for the Weimar Republic.

The Treaty of Versailles dealt the Weimar Republic a blow from which it never fully recovered. "Instead of using their powers as victors to help democracy in Germany," one historian wrote,

> the Allies made its position infinitely more difficult. They refused to recognize the fact that the November revolution had transformed the Reich into a state in which the people were sovereign. They treated as of no account the impressive victory which moderate republicanism had won in the elections of January, 1919. They persisted in regarding the Germany of Ebert and Scheidemann as in no essential regard different from the Junker-dominated Germany of 1914. What they failed to see was that the consolidation of democracy in Germany was the first prerequisite of European and world peace. In their anxiety to weaken and fetter Germany, they overlooked the all-important fact that nowhere were there stauncher believers in Wilsonian idealism than the men and women who composed the parties of the Weimar coalition.[6]

Professor Abel of Columbia University would have agreed with the above statement. He wrote:

> In retrospect it is clear that the affair of the Versailles Treaty was the primary factor in the debacle of democracy in Germany. It discredited the leaders who for months maintained that only a new, democratic Germany could count upon a just peace from the Western democracies. This became the mainspring of all subsequent attacks on the republican regime.[7]

Another historian went even further and called World War II "the war over the settlement of Versailles,"[8] and Eliot Barculo Wheaton wrote:

> quite aside from the question of practicability, the crushing nature of the Versailles terms was unwise, for it gave German extremists the most combustible material wherewith to inflame nationalist passions and perpetuate a sense of cruel injury.[9]

At least two Allied leaders at the time would have agreed with Wheaton. Winston Churchill denounced the economic clauses as "malignant and silly,"[10] and Woodrow Wilson said of the treaty: "If I were a German, I think I should not sign it."

Niccolo Machiavelli advised the prince to never inflict small hurts. This is exactly what the Allies did with the armistice and the Treaty of Versailles. The German people were humiliated, and their faith in democracy—which was fragile to begin with—was almost totally destroyed. However, they were not annihilated. Their industrial plants remained largely intact, their skilled workers and inventors remained valuable assets, their young men remained warlike and military-oriented, their talent in technological and military matters remained unimpaired, and their extreme nationalism—which they were in the process of abandoning in late 1918—had been thoroughly and fatefully restored. The Allies should have either totally destroyed and dismembered Germany or else have made a sincere effort to make a fair and just peace with her and bring her into the family of nations as a full partner. By doing neither, they set the stage for Adolf Hitler and the Second World War. In my view, it is not going too far to state that the Nazi dictator should have worn a stamp on the seat of his pants with three words on it: "Made at Versailles."

4   Enter Adolf Hitler

Many historians, who would accept nothing else from Hitler's book, *Mein Kampf*, as the gospel truth, have accepted all of what he wrote about his early life as unquestioned fact. This might seem strange or remarkable to the reader until he or she considers that Hitler's account of those days was about all the historian had to work with between 1933 and 1965. Prior to that date, much of the information was inaccurate, legend, or just plain lies. From 1945 until 1965 much of the documentary evidence was locked up in a U.S. government facility and unavailable to the researcher. Since then much has been brought to light, especially by the German historian Werner Maser, author of *Die Fruehgeschichte der NSDAP, Hitlers Weg bis 1924* (1965); *Hitlers Mein Kampf* (1966); and *Adolf Hitler: Legende, Mythos, Wirklichkeit* (1971). However, so many books on Adolf Hitler and the Nazi era were written in that 20-year period (and some of them are still in print) that the myths deliberately started by the German Fuehrer are still believed and repeated today. The fact that many historians still use the earlier biographies has not helped in exposing the myths.

Adolf Hitler's father was born Alois Schicklgruber, the illegitimate son of Maria Anna Schicklgruber (1795–1847), who was the daughter of a fairly prosperous farmer from the village of Strones in lower Austria. Maria kept the name of her lover secret for years; in fact, his identity was never revealed with absolute certainty, but he was probably Johann

Nepomuk Huettler, the brother of Johann Georg Hiedler, whom she married in 1842. She passed away in 1847, five years after marrying her lover's brother. Alois, her only child, did not officially become legitimate until 1876, when he was 39. At that time the word "illegitimate" was scratched out of the place for the father's name on the baptismal register, and the name Johann Nepomuk Huettler was entered, despite the fact that he had been dead since 1857 and (as far as is known) had never acknowledged that the child was his. Alois then adopted the name "Hitler," a simplified form of his father's name.[1] The motivations behind this rather bizarre and irregular procedure are not known today, but it probably had something to do with the Huettler family inheritance. In any case Alois's son, the future dictator, later joked that he was very glad that his father went through the ceremony. After all, who could imagine 100,000 uniformed Nazis, all screaming "Heil Schicklgruber!" in unison?

In 1946, while on Death Row at Nuremberg, Hans Frank, the Nazi Governor-General of Poland and a recent convert to Catholicism, stated that Maria Anna Schicklgruber worked in Graz as a cook for a Jewish family named Frankenberger and that one of the Frankenberger sons was responsible for Maria's pregnancy. Adolf Hitler was, therefore, one-quarter Jewish, according to that story.

Although Frank's statement has astonished many (especially those who wanted to believe it), it does not bear close scrutiny. First of all, Maria Anna Schicklgruber never lived in Graz. She also never worked for the Frankenbergers of Graz, who apparently did not exist; in fact, all Jews were expelled from Graz (and the entire province of Styria) by Emperor Maximilian I in 1497 and were not allowed to resettle in the region until the 1860s. A few Jews were allowed to visit the region on business after 1781, but none was named Frankenberger. There is absolutely no evidence to indicate that Adolf Hitler had any Jewish antecedents whatsoever.

Why, then, would Hans Frank tell such a momentous lie on the eve of his execution? We can only speculate, of course, but two possible reasons immediately suggest themselves:

1. Frank wanted to disembarrass the Catholic faith for the Catholic mass-murderer, Adolf Hitler.
2. He wanted to embarrass and inflict a sense of guilt on those of the Jewish faith.

Except to a very few he did not succeed, however; like Hans Frank, Adolf Hitler had a great deal of Jewish blood on his hands, but there is not a single piece of concrete evidence to indicate that he had any in his veins.

Alois did not seem to worry much about his illegitimacy as a young man, because about 40 percent of the children born in rural Austria at that time were illegitimate. In fact, he contributed to that statistic himself, having at least two children out of wedlock (a son and a daughter). Throughout his life Alois enjoyed drinking, smoking, and carousing. He also knew when and how to apply himself, however. As a 13-year-old orphan he was a bootmaker's apprentice in Vienna but, by virtue of hard work and self-education, gained admittance into the Austrian civil service, where he enjoyed a successful career, as well as a reputation for being a freethinker and a hard man for whom to work. Through civil service promotions, the acquisition of dowries, and the buying and selling of a series of small properties, he became quite well-off by the standards of the region. In his book *Mein Kampf*, Adolf Hitler made a number of exaggerated or untrue statements, deliberately misleading his reader into believing that his father was poor. This is not true. His father's retirement pension was 2,600 kronen a year—enough for Alois and his family to live quite comfortably.

At home Alois was not an easy man with whom to live. Fortunately for his family, he spent most of his time working or engaged in his favorite hobby, beekeeping. Alois thoroughly enjoyed his bachelorhood until he was 36; then he married a woman named Anna Glassl, who was about 15 years his senior. He probably married her for her money. In any case he was soon having affairs with Franziska "Fanny" Matzelberger (age 19), a waitress at a nearby inn, and his own second cousin, 16-year-old Klara Poelzl, whom he brought into his household as a domestic servant. Why he wanted one of his mistresses living under the same roof as his wife is a mystery.

Anna finally got enough of Alois Hitler and officially separated from him in 1880. He then dropped Klara and moved in with Franziska, who bore him a son (also named Alois) in 1882. The following year, when Anna died of cancer, Alois senior (age 46) married his 22-year-old mistress and legitimized his son. Fanny gave birth again later that year. This time she had a daughter named Angela who, in time, would become the mother of Geli Raubal, the niece of Adolf Hitler and the one great love in the future dictator's life.

Like her predecessor, Fanny also left the brutal, bullying, and habitually unfaithful Alois Hitler. Shortly afterwards she was stricken with tuberculosis and died in 1884, at the age of 23. By this time Klara Poelzl had returned to Braunau, a town on the German-Austrian border where Alois worked as a customs official, and moved in with him as a "housekeeper." She was already pregnant when Franziska died, but their marriage had to be delayed because they were related, and a special dispensation had to be secured from Rome. This was granted (no doubt because Klara was pregnant) and the couple married on January 7, 1885, just in time to legitimize their first son, Gustav, who was born in May. The following year a daughter, Ida, was born, and a second son, Otto, followed in 1887.

Klara Poelzl Hitler was a quiet, simple, good-hearted country girl who was totally subdued and intimidated by her overbearing and domineering husband. Her lot could not have been an easy one, especially with a womanizing spouse, who would occasionally abandon his family for a month or more during the summer, ostensibly to look after his beehives. Then tragedy struck, and Klara lost all three of her children within a single year. Otto died within a few days of his birth; Gustav died of diphtheria on December 8, 1887; and Ida succumbed to the same disease 25 days later. Klara continued to be the model stepmother for Alois, Jr., and Angela, but she was nevertheless overjoyed when Adolf, the future ruler of Germany, was born at Braunau-on-Inn on April 20, 1889.

Klara lavished an immense amount of love and devotion on her young son, who could twist his mother around his little finger and knew it. His father was another matter. Alois retired from the customs service at the age of 58, when Adolf was six. Over the next several years the restless retiree moved from one village to another but remained in the vicinity of Linz. He drank more and more, became more and more short-tempered and irritable, and more and more abusive toward his children. The beatings became so bad and so frequent that Alois, Jr., ran away from home at the age of 14 and never returned. He became a waiter—a career that was interrupted by at least three prison sentences: two for theft and one for bigamy. He then immigrated to England, where he established yet another family and then deserted them. In 1940 he was an aging, portly bar owner in Berlin, living in constant fear that his powerful half-brother (who never liked him) would revoke his liquor license.[2] At last report (1954), he was in his 70s, living in Hamburg.[3]

Meanwhile, in 1895, young Adolf entered the single-class primary school at Fischlam, where he was an excellent student, although sometimes a difficult one to handle. He received Class 1 marks (the equivalent of an "A") in all subjects and the following year entered the second class of the ancient Benedictine monastery school in nearby Lambach, where he remained until the spring of 1898. Again he rated Class 1 in all courses. Here, as he recalls in *Mein Kampf*, he was impressed by the dignity of the Abbot and by the "solemn splendor" of the magnificent church festivals. He became a regular churchgoer and a choirboy, and, for a time, even wanted to become a priest himself.[4] It is interesting to note that the Abbot of the school, a man named Hagen, had a swastika as a part of his coat of arms, which appeared on the pulpit.

Up until about the turn of the century, life was totally carefree for

Adolf Hitler. True, he had few friends, largely because he changed schools five times by the age of 15 due to the job transfers and wanderings of his father. Nevertheless, with his doting mother and frequently absent father, young Adolf's situation was remarkably easy, until he reached the age of 9 or 10. Then the combination of Alois's retirement and worsening drinking problem, coupled with Alois junior's departure, changed all of that. Now Adolf, the oldest son at home,[5] received the brunt of his father's despotic attention, which often entailed a severe pounding. There is no doubt that Adolf Hitler was an abused child. His disputes with his father centered on the issue of Adolf's career. Alois insisted that his son follow him into the civil service, but such a career was anathema to young Adolf, who wanted to become an artist. In the face of his son's opposition, the intolerant Alois invariably lashed out at the child, fiercely beating the screaming boy while his mother cringed in silent horror, too terrorized to intervene. The beatings, however, accomplished nothing except to intensify Adolf's natural willfulness and stubbornness.

Hitler completed his primary education at the village of Leonding (three miles from Linz) in September 1900, and it was decided that he would go to high school. Alois sent him to the *Realschule* at Linz (the equivalent of a technical school of today), instead of to the humanistic *Gymnasium*, which would have given Hitler a liberal arts education. This entailed considerable financial sacrifice on Alois's part, so he was naturally very disappointed when Adolf's grades began to slip. In *Mein Kampf*, Hitler stated that he deliberately neglected his studies in the hopes that his father would see how little progress he was making and would give up, letting him pursue his own career choice. This statement may or may not be true; he may have been trying to pass off his lack of academic success as an intentional failure on his part. When Professor Eduard Huemer, who taught him French and German at Linz, testified concerning his character at his 1924 treason trial, he said:

> Hitler was certainly gifted, although only for particular subjects, but he lacked self-control and, to say the least, he was considered argumentative, autocratic, self-opinionated and bad-tempered, and unable to submit to school discipline. Nor was he industrious; otherwise he would have achieved much better results, gifted as he was.[6]

Nevertheless, 40 years later, his scholastic reverses still rankled Hitler. "When I recall my teachers at school," he said in 1942, he realized that most of them "were somewhat mentally deranged, and quite a few ended their days as honest-to-God lunatics!" On one occasion he stated that his foreign language teacher was "a congenital idiot,"[7] and on another he described his teachers as "absolute tyrants."[8] In fact, Hitler had thinly veiled contempt for higher education for most of his life.

There was, however, one professor whom Adolf Hitler loved: Dr. Ludwig Poetsch, who taught him history at the Linz *Realschule*. Of him, Hitler wrote:

> This old gentleman, whose manner was as kind as it was firm, not only knew how to keep us spellbound, but actually carried us away with the splendor of his eloquence. I am still slightly moved when I remember the gray-haired man whose fiery descriptions made us forget the present and who evoked plain historical facts out of the fog of centuries and turned them into living reality. Often we would sit there enraptured in enthusiasm and there were even times when we were on the verge of tears.[9]

Poetsch certainly exerted a profound and fateful influence upon his young pupil, and he was both an anti-Semitic and a fanatical Pan-German nationalist (that is, a believer that the Germanic people of Europe should be united under one Reich). Indeed, Hitler recorded later that it was during his time in Poetsch's class that he decided to become a young revolutionary.

In 1938, more than 30 years later, Chancellor Adolf Hitler was touring Austria, which he had just annexed into the Third Reich. He decided to look up his old professor, then living in retirement at Klagenfurt. He was delighted to learn that the old man was a Nazi and an underground member of the SS, which had been outlawed in Austria prior to Hitler's takeover. They talked alone for an hour, and, when Hitler emerged, he was almost in tears. "You cannot imagine how much I owe to that old man," he told his entourage later.[10]

Adolf Hitler had excelled in the primary schools at Fischlam, Lambach, and Leonding. At the end of his first year at Linz, he was not promoted to the next form due to deficiencies in mathematics and natural science. One can imagine his father's reaction. He was promoted the following year, but he became even more rebellious and contemptuous of authority, and his grades were always either very good or very poor, depending on whether or not he was interested in a particular subject. "His achievements," Maser writes, "were determined solely by his inclinations, his interests and passing enthusiasms."[11] Certainly, at this point in his life, Adolf Hitler was an unhappy and uninspired underachiever. His problems with his father continued until 10 A.M. on January 3, 1903, when Alois suffered a lung hemorrhage and died in a local tavern a few minutes later. Some sources state that he was stricken while out on a morning walk and was carried into the tavern, where he died; others aver that he was drinking beer when the hemorrhage occurred. In any event, 13-year-old Adolf wept when he saw the body of his father, but he refrained from speaking highly of him in the years ahead.

Following the death of her husband, Klara Hitler moved into an apartment in Urfahr, a suburb of Linz, and continued to raise Adolf and his sister Paula (born in 1896), the two children still at home. Contrary to the myth that Adolf fostered later, the family was not left in poverty by Alois's death. His pension was more than the salary received by the headmaster of a *Volksschule*, for example. Frau Hitler received a cash award equal to three months of her husband's pay, a widow's pension of some 1,300 kronen per year for the rest of her life, plus a fair amount of property. In addition, each of her children would be eligible to draw 250 kronen per year as an orphan's benefit until age 24. Klara settled down with her family and tried to carry out the wishes of her late husband (that is, to guide Adolf into the civil service); as a result, for the first time, a degree of friction developed between mother and son. Unfortunately for Frau Hitler, all she could do was implore, and this cut no ice with Adolf, who had inherited his father's stubborn and willful disposition. His grades continued to suffer, he failed French, and he was thus not eligible for promotion to the fourth form. He appealed to his French instructor to allow him to retake the exam, and Professor Huemer—seeing an opportunity to rid himself of his difficult and headstrong student—consented, but only on the condition that Hitler transfer to another school. Hitler agreed, passed the exam, and entered the fourth form at Steyr Secondary School in September 1904. Now, however, he rented a room in town to spare himself the four-mile walk home each day.

Hitler hated Steyr even more than he had disliked Linz. At the end of the first term he did something he had never done before: He got uproariously drunk and passed out by the side of a road, where a dairymaid found him the following morning. Then the shocked student discovered that his grade report was missing. He had no choice but to ask the school for a duplicate, only to find that the headmaster had the original—which had been torn into four pieces. In his drunken stooper, Hitler had mistaken it for toilet paper! What the headmaster said next is unprintable, but he gave the dismayed student a dressing down and a thorough cursing. Adolf Hitler swore that he would never get drunk again in his whole life, and he never did.

Why Hitler was so concerned about his lost report card is somewhat of a mystery to this author, because he was rated Class 5 ("non-satisfactory" or "failing") in stenography, handwriting, and mathematics, and was Class 4 (almost failing) in diligence, religion, geography and history, chemistry, and geometry. He rated Class 3 in moral conduct and physics, Class 2 in freehand drawing, and Class 1 only in gymnastics.[12] Also, he was absent 30 days without excuse. By the end of the second term, however, he had pulled all of his grades up to the "adequate" level or higher, although he did have to take the descriptive geometry examination twice.[13] Despite his mother's displeasure with his academic performance, young Hitler was quite content with these grades.

The friction between Hitler and his mother over his schoolwork ended in the summer of 1905, when Adolf contracted a serious lung ailment and was unable to reenter the Linz *Realschule* that fall. Upset and alarmed over his health, Klara Hitler let him drop out of high school with the equivalent of a 9th grade education and consented to let him attend the Vienna Academy of Fine Arts. With the cause for friction gone, their relationship became even closer and warmer than it had ever been and would continue to deepen until her death. Now that he had obtained his goal, however, Hitler was in no hurry to apply to the Academy. He ate well, rested, rapidly regained his health, and then led a life of idle laziness from 1905 until the end of 1907. He spent his time reading, drawing, and exploring the countryside. Later he recalled that these were "the happiest days of my life and seem to me almost a dream."[14]

Hitler spent much of this period with the one friend of his youth: August "Gustl" Kubizek. Gustl was a very passive young man, whereas Adolf, he recalled, "was exceedingly violent and high-strung. Quite trivial things, such as a few thoughtless words, could produce in him outbursts of temper . . . quite out of proportion to the significance of the matter."[15] They were both, however, lovers of art and music, and Gustl adjusted to Hitler's domineering ways by knuckling under, so they got along fine.

In the spring of 1906 Hitler's mother allowed him to visit Vienna, where he spent a month roaming the romantic old city, an international center of music, art, and architecture in these, the twilight years of the Austro-Hungarian Empire. He was enthralled with what he saw and returned to Linz even more determined to devote his life to art and architecture. It was not until September of the following year, however, that he returned to the Imperial capital to take his entrance examination at the Academy of Fine Arts's General School of Painting.

Hitler was superbly confident that he would pass this extremely difficult two-day "drawing composition" exam with flying colors. In addition to submitting the best work he had produced in high school, Hitler (under the eyes of an examining board) had to draw half of the following on the first day alone: "the expulsion from paradise"; "the hunt"; "spring"; "farm worker"; "death"; "rain"; "return of the prodigal son"; "flight"; "summer"; "lumberjacks"; "mourning"; "fire"; "Cain kills

Abel"; "homecoming"; "autumn"; "craters"; "joy"; "moonlight"; "Adam and Eve find Abel's body"; "farewell"; "winter"; "shepherds"; "the dance"; and "storm." He had only six hours to complete this task, and the subjects for the second day were just as comprehensive. Hitler passed this test but was not admitted to the Academy because the sample drawings he submitted contained too few heads. In all, 85 of the 113 art candidates failed, including Robin Christian Andersen, who was later to have a distinguished career in art and hold important positions in the very academy that rejected him in 1907.[16]

For Hitler, this failure was as devastating as it was unexpected. Nor was it any consolation that the rector of the Academy recommended he apply for their School of Architecture, because admission there depended upon having a Certificate of Matriculation from the *Realschule*—something that he did not possess. He was still lamenting this fact when he wrote *Mein Kampf* 16 years later.

To make matters worse, Klara Hitler was seriously ill. On January 14, 1907, she called on Dr. Edward Bloch, a Jewish physician, who discovered that she had cancer. Dr. Karl Urban removed one of her breasts four days later, and she began a temporary recovery. However, when Adolf returned to Urfahr in October 1907, he found that her health was again deteriorating. The operation had been performed too late. The cancer had returned, and the treatment was both expensive and primitive: Large daily doses of iodoform were placed on the open wound. The iodoform, which had a nauseating, clinging odor, burned its way through the living tissue toward the cancer, causing agonizing pain. Throughout Klara's last illness, Adolf Hitler devoted himself exclusively to his mother and was tortured by her pain. Gustl Kubizek remembered the remarkable change in Hitler. "Not a cross word, not an impatient remark, no violent insistence on having his own way. . . . He forgot himself entirely . . . and lived only for his mother."[17] Nothing could help her now, however. In the early morning hours of December 21, in the glow of a lighted Christmas tree, she quietly passed away. Dr. Bloch came by the following morning to sign the death certificate and found Hitler still at his mother's side. "In all my career," Bloch recalled later, "I never saw anyone so prostrate with grief as Adolf Hitler."[18] He kept a photograph of his mother near his bed for the rest of his life, and it was in his room the day he committed suicide. And he never had another Christmas tree as long as he lived.

Klara was buried in Leonding, next to Alois, on December 23. Hitler broke down and wept beside her grave. The next day the family paid a visit to Dr. Bloch to settle the medical bill. It is not true, as some authors have reported, that Hitler persecuted the Jews because a Jewish physician had failed to save his mother and then (in Hitler's opinion) tried to cheat them with his bill. The final charge was 359 kronen, of which 59 had already been paid—an extremely reasonable total for 77 home and office visits and 47 treatments. In fact, Klara's funeral cost 11 kronen more than her doctor's bill.[19] This fact was appreciated by the entire Hitler family, who paid the bill with profuse thanks. Later, after the Nazis took power and seized Austria, the order came to expel all Jews from Linz, the Fuehrer's hometown. One exception was made: Dr. Bloch and his family. By order of Adolf Hitler, they could choose to emigrate or could live unmolested in Linz for the rest of their lives. Dr. Bloch chose to move to the United States. Not only were he and his family allowed to leave without harassment, they were allowed to sell their property and take all of their money and possessions with them. This was an almost unique occurrence in the history of Nazi Germany. "Favors were granted to me which I feel were accorded no other Jew in all of Germany or Austria," Bloch wrote later.[20] Whatever Hitler's reasons were for persecuting those of the Hebrew faith, Dr. Edward Bloch's treatment of his mother was not among them.

Writing in *Mein Kampf*, Hitler stated that the years 1908 to 1914 were ones of hardship and misery for him. The family's meager resources, he implied, had been wiped out by his mother's last illness.

> I was forced to earn a living, first as a day laborer, then as a smaller painter; a truly meager living which never sufficed to appease even my daily hunger. Hunger was then my faithful bodyguard.[21]

He was grossly exaggerating when he wrote that. His share of his father's estate produced an income of 58 kronen per month, plus he received an orphan's pension of 25 kronen per month until he was 24—a total income of 83 kronen per month. At that time a court lawyer with one year's practice received 70 kronen a month, a teacher with less than five years' service received 66, and a junior postal employee received 60.[22] He was thus fairly well-off, even if one excludes an undisclosed (but probably modest) inheritance he received from an aunt in 1907. Certainly he had a large enough income to live comfortably, if not exactly luxuriously. Frequently he did, in fact, go hungry, but that was because he preferred to spend his money on theater tickets rather than on food. "The reason which compelled Hitler to lodge in a doss [flop] house at the end of 1909 was certainly not material want," Werner Maser wrote, "although all his pre-1965 biographers are unanimous that it was."[23] In fact, Hitler took temporary refuge in the flop house, a place inhabited by bums, vagrants, and out-of-work laborers, in order to conceal himself from the Austrian authorities, but this is getting ahead of our story.

After helping to settle his mother's affairs, Adolf Hitler deliberately estranged himself from his relatives and departed for Vienna as soon as he could. One reason for his haste was that he was sick of the pressure his family was putting on him to learn a profession and get a job. He was especially resentful of the persistence of his brother-in-law, Leo Raubal, a tax official who had married his half-sister, Angela, and who now wanted Adolf to follow him into the civil service. In any case, from February to September 1908, Hitler lived at Number 29 Stumpergasse with his roommate and only friend, Gustl Kubizek, who was now a student at the Academy of Music. Adolf, now 19, spent his time doing something he had heretofore religiously avoided: He worked extremely hard, preparing to sit for the next entrance examination at the Academy of Fine Arts, which was to be held in the fall of 1908. He even took painting lessons from the Viennese sculptor Panholzer, who was also an art master at a secondary school and an experienced teacher. However, emotional strain and the events of the previous year had left their mark, and he went to pieces during the drawing composition test. He thus failed the first part of the entrance exam (the part he had passed in 1907) and was not allowed to show the sample drawings he had so painstakingly composed during his year of studying under Panholzer.

Hitler was, of course, furious at this second rejection. To Kubizek, he denounced the art faculty as "a lot of old-fashioned fossilized civil servants, bureaucrats, devoid of understanding, stupid lumps of officials. The whole Academy ought to be blown up!" he roared. "His face was livid," Kubizek recalled, "the mouth quite small, the lips almost white. But the eyes glittered. There was something sinister about them. As if all the hate of which he was capable lay in those glowing eyes!"[24] Nevertheless, Adolf Hitler did not allow his failures or his temper to stop him from experiencing the musical joys of Vienna. He and Gustl went to the opera several times a week. Hitler never tired of hearing Wagner (he and Gustl attended the performance of *Lohengrin* alone 10 times), but he also enjoyed symphonic music, especially Bruckner, Beethoven, Schubert, Mendelssohn, and Schumann.

In the autumn of 1908 Kubizek went away for a brief period of compulsory military service. When he returned in November, he found that his friend had moved out and left no forwarding address. Apparently Hitler, embarrassed by his failure to gain admission to the Academy, could no longer face his friend who knew so much about his hopes, ambitions, and aspirations. Gustl would not see Adolf Hitler again for 30 years.

Another reason Hitler left Number 29 Stumpergasse was that he was evading the police. He had deliberately failed to register for military service in the fall of 1908 and was thus in violation of the Austrian Defense Law. For this reason he changed his address frequently over the next year: He lived at 22 Felberstrasse (November 18, 1908, to August 20, 1909), 58 Sechshauser Strasse (August 20 to September 16, 1909), and in the Simon-Denk-Gasse (September 16 to November 1909). Then, after a brief stay in the Meidling doss house, he moved into a large, cheap hotel in the Meldemannstrasse area. This residence was similar to a men's hostel, and Hitler remained here until May 24, 1913, when he finally fled to Germany in order to escape military service.

Hitler's reasons for avoiding the Austrian draft were straightforward enough: He had no wish to serve in the Hapsburg monarchy and the Austro-Hungarian Empire, which he regarded as un-German. He also began to nurture a hatred for Vienna, which had too many ethnic groups to suit him, including Czechs, Italians, Poles, Hungarians, various Slavic groups, and Jews. It was definitely not a German city. Hitler grew to hate the Jews most of all. He states in *Mein Kampf* that he first became anti-Semitic while living in Vienna. This is not true: He was first infected with the anti-Semitic virus before he left Linz and was thoroughly familiar with the Jew-baiting publications of the period long before he arrived in the Austrian capital. He was, for example, a regular reader of the anti-Semitic newspaper *Linzer Fliegende Blaetter* in his early days and was probably first influenced in this direction by his father, Alois, who made it quite clear that he had no use for Jews. In fact, it was Alois—a freethinker—who weened his son away from the Catholic Church and who had a far greater impact on the shaping of his son's character, opinions, and actions than Adolf would ever care to admit. Of course his history professor, Dr. Poetsch, also exerted a strong Pan-German, anti-Semitic influence on young Hitler, as we have seen. It is nevertheless undoubtedly true that Hitler's anti-Semitic views were reinforced and deepened while he was in Vienna. Young Hitler was a voracious and undisciplined reader who deliberately selected books or pamphlets that confirmed his own preconceived ideas.

While living in Vienna (and later in Munich), Hitler earned money drawing and painting innumerable small pictures, sometimes at the rate of six or seven per week. Most of these were watercolors, and many of them were quite good. His subjects were invariably the architecturally significant buildings of Vienna, and he sold them to art dealers (most of whom were Jews) and to private collectors. Some of the paintings and India-ink or pencil drawings that survived included "Parliament," "Old Vienna," "The Michaelerplatz und Dreilauferhaus," "The Old Burgtheater," "The Auersperg Palace," "The Minorities Church," and "Prager." For a time he had an agent of sorts named Reinhold Hanisch, who would sell his paintings for him and then split the proceeds. For a time they both prospered. After eight months, however, Hanisch became dissatisfied with the artist, because his work became more and more careless and he worked less and less. Hitler, it will be recalled, was painting to supplement an already ample income, but Hanisch really needed the money. Also, Hitler now wanted to be an architect, not a painter, and he would stay up all night studying or reading architectural material or some political tract instead of painting. The Hitler-Hanisch partnership ended in August 1910, when Hanisch suddenly disappeared (with a couple of the artist's paintings) and Hitler filed charges against him for fraud. Hanisch was arrested, convicted, and spent eight days in prison. He took revenge later by spreading false stories about Hitler to unsuspecting journalists after Hitler became a public figure. Unfortunately, many of these tales have been accepted as unquestioned truth by certain historians, and Hanisch was never one to let the facts stand in the way of a good story. Telling lies and inventing yarns about Adolf Hitler's background was a dangerous business during the Nazi era, however, and Hanisch was arrested by the Gestapo as soon as Germany annexed Austria in 1938, and no one ever saw him again. He was variously reported as having died of pneumonia and having hanged himself, but it is almost certain that he met with foul play while in SS hands in 1938.

Despite the loss of his partner, Hitler continued to prosper financially. Some of his paintings were apparently quite good. Dr. Bloch, for example, did not keep the watercolors Hitler gave him all those years simply because he was the grief-stricken teenage son of an ex-patient. Hitler also received a considerable but undisclosed amount of Johanna Poelzl's (his aunt's) estate when she died in March 1911. He was so well-off, in fact, that two months later he signed over his orphan's pension to his younger sister, Paula—the only member of his family with whom he remained close. Of course, one must keep in mind that Hitler lived a rather Spartan life-style, did not want much, and his material standards were never high.

Although he had no real financial problems, trouble was brewing in another quarter, because Hitler failed to answer his preliminary call-up to the Austrian Army in the spring of 1910 and did not appear at his mustering in during the spring of 1912. When the Austrian officials began looking for him, he packed all of his belongings into a single bag, fled to Germany, and settled in Munich in May 1913. Here he found a city much more to his liking, and the Bavarian capital became his home for the next 20 years. Initially he rented a room at Number 34 Schleissheimer Strasse from a tailor named Josef Popp for 20 marks a month.

As in Vienna, he earned his living painting the famous buildings of Munich: the Old Rathaus, the Hofbraeuhaus, the National Theater, the Feldherrnhalle, and others. He was so successful that his income was about 100 marks a month—a healthy sum before 1914.[25]

As in Vienna, Hitler worked when the mood struck him and continued to spend much of his time reading, frequently all night long. To Hitler, reading was not something to be done for pleasure, for education, or to acquire a depth of knowledge, but to "provide the tools and building materials which the individual needs for his life's work."[26] He read to reinforce his own prejudices and *Weltanschauung*—a German word that was extremely important in the Nazi era but that has no exact English counterpart. Roughly it means "world view" or "one's view of the world." Reading, to Hitler, was something he did to reinforce his own ideas and prejudices, to support his own arguments, and to defeat those of his adversaries. He read everywhere and continued to do so all of his life, even when at his battle post in World War I. His range of interest was astonishing, but the authors who had the most important influences on his intellectual development were the geopolitical thinkers Friedrich Ratzel, Alfred Mackinder, and later Karl Haushofer; Karl May, a German who wrote adventure novels about the American West, even though he never crossed the Atlantic; Thomas Robert Malthus, who theorized that widespread starvation was inevitable; Charles Darwin; Friedrich Wilhelm Nietzsche, who believed that decadent Western civilization must be swept away and the world ruled by a new type of heroic superman; and Houston Steward Chamberlain, a transplanted Englishman who married Wagner's daughter and became the greatest Pan-German of his day. And there were others. "The truth is," Maser wrote, "that he had simply amassed an astoundingly wide range of knowledge of disconnected facts and it was impossible to say who were his 'master minds.' . . . any attempt to present some particular writer, thinker or scholar as 'the master' and Hitler as his 'pupil' inevitably leads to distortion of the facts."[27] Philosophically, Adolf Hitler was essentially a Social Darwinist, heavily influenced by Pan-Germanism, and would remain so for the rest of his life. He believed that the "survival of the fittest" theory could and should be applied to man. In this struggle, the fittest race (called the "Aryans") would survive; those of inferior racial groups (Jews, Slavs, Gypsies, Blacks, etc.) would perish or become slaves of the "master race." He also believed that fighting for dominance was the basic motivating factor in the history of man, and this natural law could not be changed—indeed, should not be changed. This "might equals right" mentality characterized Hitler's attitudes and actions throughout his career.

Precisely because of his racial views, Hitler did not want to serve in the Austrian Army, which was too thoroughly infested with Jews, Hungarians, and Czechs and other Slavic groups to suit his tastes. For a time, however, it looked as if he would have no choice. In late 1913 the Austrian police contacted their Bavarian counterparts, who ordered Hitler to report to Linz for his military physical on January 20, 1914. He wrote the authorities an abject letter and received a delay but was at last forced to report at Salzburg on February 5. He failed the physical examination and returned to Munich "unfit for military service."

On August 1, 1914—less than six months after he failed his physical in Salzburg—World War I broke out. Adolf Hitler, who had been a fugitive from the Austrian draft for more than four years and who was now exempt from military service, rushed to join the Bavarian Army. Because he was still a citizen of Austria, he had to file a personal petition with King Ludwig III to receive permission to enlist. This he did the day the war began. His request was granted the following day, and he promptly joined the 16th Reserve Infantry Regiment, commanded by Colonel Wilhelm von List. Later this unit would become known as the List Regiment. Hitler reported to the 2nd Company, 6th Replacement Battalion at Munich on August 16 and began his military service. Due to the exigencies of war his training was all too brief, and he was transferred to the 1st Company and sent to France. On October 29 the regiment was thrown into the 1st Battle of Ypres, where it suffered heavy casualties. Indeed this battle, which lasted until November 24, produced enough casualties to fill 40 cemeteries. Hitler's company commander, all of his lieutenants, all but one of the company's sergeants, and most of the corporals were killed or seriously wounded. Meanwhile, Hitler impressed his superiors with his initiative and dash in the hand-to-hand fighting against the British. On October 30 they transferred him to the regimental staff as a dispatch runner. Colonel von List was killed the following day, and his deputy was badly wounded a few hours later. Under heavy fire Private Hitler dragged this man—a lieutenant colonel—out of no-man's land. After he had been attended to by a medic, Hitler and Private Ernst Schmidt carried the colonel to a dressing station. The following day, November 1, Hitler was promoted to *Gefreiter* (lance corporal).

By all accounts, Adolf Hitler was a good soldier and a brave one. Colonel von Lueneschloss recalled "Hitler never let us down and was particularly suited to the kind of task that could not be entrusted to other runners." Major General Friedrich Petz said that Hitler's "pluck was exceptional, as was the reckless courage with which he tackled dangerous situations." Colonel Spatny referred to him as a "shining example" and recalled in 1922 that his "admirable unpretentiousness earned him the respect of superiors and equals alike." Lieutenant Colonel Baron

Anton von Tubeuf remembered that no circumstances would prevent him "from volunteering for the most difficult, arduous and dangerous tasks" and Lieutenant Colonel Baron von Godin referred to his "coolness and dash" and his "exemplary" behavior when he recommended him for the Iron Cross, 1st Class.[28] Lieutenant Colonel Philipp Engelhardt remembered him as "exceptionally brave, effective, and conscientious," and his last regimental commander, Lieutenant Colonel Maximilian Baligand, called him a "courageous and outstanding soldier and comrade."[29] All of these testimonials came long before anyone could foresee that he might become the chancellor of Germany.

Of the eight dispatch runners on the staff of the List Regiment at Ypres, three were killed, and one was seriously wounded. Hitler and a group of soldiers were selected for the Iron Cross, 2nd Class, and summoned to regimental headquarters. The new commander, Lieutenant Colonel Engelhardt, congratulated them in his dugout and was in conversation with them when four of his company commanders arrived. Due to the lack of space, the enlisted men were asked to wait outside. They had not been out five minutes when a shell struck the dugout, killing or seriously wounding everyone inside. "It was the most terrible moment in my life," Hitler wrote to his former landlord. "We all worshipped Lieutenant Colonel Engelhardt."[30]

Called "Adi" by his friends, Adolf Hitler had at last found a home—in the headquarters of a combat infantry regiment. It was the first home he had known since his mother died and his first as an adult. In 52 months of service he took only 2 leaves of 14 days each: far less than what he was entitled to. He even turned down a promotion to corporal because it would have meant returning to his original company. Because there were no slots for a regimental runner above the rank of lance corporal, Hitler never advanced beyond that rank—although his lack of formal education would have barred his promotion above the rank of sergeant in any case. "The trenches . . . were his world," one of his companions recalled, "and what lay behind them didn't exist for him."[31]

The defeat at Ypres effectively ended the German offensive of 1914, and the war degenerated into a long period of static trench warfare. During this relatively quiet period, Hitler had time to paint, sketch, and read. His fellow soldiers admired him for his courage but also regarded him as an oddball with some strange ideas. He volunteered for dangerous missions (which they considered abnormal), refused to go drinking or womanizing with them, and lectured them on politics, the dangers of venereal disease, and about the evils of tobacco and alcohol. He never asked for leave, never wanted to go home, and refused to share the packages his comrades received from their families, because he could not reciprocate—he never received a package from home himself. He was also noted for his appetite. Adolf Hitler was considered the biggest "chowhound" in his unit and thoroughly enjoyed army food. He achieved a certain measure of local fame for the amount of marmalade he could stack on a single slice of bread. "He was just an odd character," Private Hans Mend commented, "and lives in his own world but otherwise he's a nice fellow." They liked him despite his peculiarities because he was reliable in a crisis and never abandoned a wounded comrade.[32]

Hitler fought in the trench warfare in Flanders and in the battles of Neuve Chapelle, La Bassee, Arras, and the Somme, where more than a million men became casualties. One of them was Corporal Adolf Hitler. On October 7, 1916, near Le Bargue, he was wounded in the left thigh by a shell fragment. Many men in all wars have prayed for such wounds—not bad enough to kill or cripple but serious enough to get them sent home for a prolonged period. Hitler, however, begged Fritz Wiedemann, his regimental adjutant, not to send him away. "It isn't so bad, Lieutenant, right?" he cried from his stretcher as the medics prepared to put him into an ambulance. "I can still stay with you, I mean, stay with the regiment. Can't I?"[33]

The wounded lance corporal was evacuated back to a field hospital at Hermies, where he heard a sound that almost made him jump from shock. Then he realized that it was the voice of a German nurse—the first woman's voice he had heard in two years.[34]

Hitler's wound was not serious but it was severe, so he was sent back to Germany, despite his objections. He spent three months in the Red Cross Hospital at Beelitz (just southwest of Berlin), where, he recalled in *Mein Kampf*, "I heard here for the first time something that was still unknown at the front: men bragging about their own cowardice!"[35] Hitler was thoroughly disgusted, but his contempt grew even greater when he was transferred to the 16th Bavarian's replacement battalion at Munich. Here, he wrote later, "the general mood was more than bad; shirking of duty was looked upon almost as a sign of higher wisdom, but faithful endurance as a sign of inner weakness and narrow-mindedness." Hitler blamed the Jews for this deterioration of morale on the Home Front. "The offices of the authorities were occupied by Jews," he wrote in *Mein Kampf*. "Almost every clerk a Jew and every Jew a clerk." He was so disturbed by what he saw, he professed later, that he "was glad to return to the front."[36] Like what he accepted from his readings, Hitler's personal observations were selective and tailored to suit his own prejudices. Later he would use the Jews as scapegoats for the German defeat and inflict a terrible vengeance on them, but this is getting ahead of our story.

As soon as he was out of the hospital, Corporal Hitler wrote to Lieutenant Wiedemann and asked him to expedite his return to the front. Wiedemann obliged, and Hitler rejoined the List Regiment on the Western Front on March 5, 1917. That year he fought in Flanders, Upper Alsace, and in the trenches north of the Ailette, as well as in the Battle of Arras and the 3rd Battle of Ypres. He was awarded the Military Service Cross, 3rd Class, with Swords, and the Wounded Badge in Black. Then came the climactic year of 1918. Corporal Hitler took part in the Ludendorff Offensives and received a regimental citation for outstanding gallantry in the Battle of Fontaine. He fought at Soissons, Arras, Chemin des Dames and Reims, in the Marne and Champagne offensive operations, in the trenches around the Aisne and Oise, and in the defensive operations in Flanders. On July 17 he saved the life of the commander of the 9th Company. Finding him severely wounded by an American shell, Hitler dragged him to the rear. On another occasion Hitler, carrying a message to a forward battalion, discovered 15 French soldiers who had recently been cut off in a forest by a sudden German attack. Armed with only a pistol, he ordered them to surrender, but they were reluctant to lay down their rifles. He shouted at them and fired a shot into their trench. The Frenchmen then dropped their weapons and raised their hands. Near the edge of the forest, Hitler spotted some men from the battalion staff. He delivered his message, borrowed a man with a rifle, and personally delivered his prisoners to his regimental commander. A few days later, on August 4, Adolf Hitler was awarded the Iron Cross, 1st Class—an extremely high decoration for an enlisted man in World War I. He did not receive this medal for any single incident but rather for his conduct over the previous four years, and he wore it with a great deal of pride for the rest of his life.

Hitler had a way of avoiding death that would frustrate and dismay his would-be assassins again and again from 1933 onward. "The man has the instincts of a rat," Colonel Count von Stauffenberg is said to have observed in 1944. His regiment, which had numbered only 3,600 soldiers when the war began, lost 3,754 officers, NCOs, and men killed during the war. Hitler himself spent 45 months at the front and fought in 35 major battles. According to the law of averages, there is no reason Adolf Hitler should have survived, but he did. One incident is fairly typical. Hitler was in a trench, eating dinner with a group of soldiers, when something told him to move on. He got up and moved about 20 yards down the trench. No sooner than he had resumed eating his meal than a stray shell landed on the spot he had just vacated, killing every man in the squad he had been dining with only moments before.

Corporal Hitler's luck ran out on the evening of October 13. He was near Ypres, only four miles from where he had undergone his baptism of fire four years before. Typically he was in a chow line when British high-explosive shells landed in the area. Cleverly, the British had mixed in some chlorine gas shells with them, and they landed undetected. Before Hitler and the others realized what had happened, they breathed in some of the gas. Several of the men died that night. Hitler's vision was affected. By morning, he wrote later, "my eyes had turned into glowing coals; it had grown dark around me."[37] Early in the morning of October 14 he joined a column of blind or partially blind gas victims, heading for the first-aid station at Linnselle, each holding on to the coattails of the man in front of him to keep from getting lost. For Adolf Hitler, the war was over.

After an initial treatment at the field hospital at Oudenarde, a temporarily blind Hitler was sent to the Prussian Reserve Hospital at Pasewalk in Pomerania, 17 miles from the Baltic Sea. Here Hitler regained his sight, but only very gradually. It was here on November 10 that a pastor informed him and the rest of the patients that the revolution had succeeded and the House of Hohenzollern had been replaced by a "republic." As the pastor, called a "dignified old gentleman" by Hitler, began to sob gently to himself, "everything went black before my eyes." He later recalled:

> I tottered and groped my way back . . . , threw myself on my bunk, and dug my burning head into my blanket and pillow. . . .
>
> And so it had all been in vain. In vain all the sacrifice and privations; in vain the hunger and thirst . . . , in vain the hours in which, with mortal fear clutching at our hearts, we nevertheless did our duty; and in vain the death of two million who died. . . .
>
> There followed terrible days and even worse nights—I knew that all was lost. Only fools, liars, and criminals could hope in the mercy of the enemy. In these nights hatred grew in me, hatred for those responsible for this deed.[38]

It was at this point, Hitler wrote later, that he decided to go into politics.[39]

5 Street Violence and Inflation

On November 19, 1918, Hitler was discharged from the hospital at Pase-walk and two days later reported to the 7th Company, 1st Replacement Battalion, 2nd Bavarian Infantry Regiment in Munich. This regiment was controlled by one of the "soldiers' councils," which Hitler found extremely repulsive. He and his wartime buddy, Ernst Schmidt, spent most of their time sorting military clothing and gas masks, for which they received three extra marks a day. Finally they voluntarily trans-ferred to the 2nd Demobilization Company (of the same regiment), lo-cated at Traunstein (60 miles east of Munich), where they guarded Rus-sian prisoners of war, until the camp was disbanded in March 1919. Then Hitler returned to Munich and was present when the Freikorps put down the Communist uprising.

In *Mein Kampf*, Hitler states that the Central (Soldiers') Council or-dered his arrest on April 27, and three "Reds" showed up at his barracks to take him into custody, but he frustrated this attempt by getting the drop on them with his rifle. If the Reds did attempt to arrest him, Hitler certainly did the right thing by resisting, for, as we have seen, they exe-cuted a number of their hostages in cold blood. We do know, however, that the Central Council could not have ordered his arrest on April 27, because it was dissolved on April 7. It seems more likely that the men who attempted to arrest Hitler were members of the Freikorps von Epp, and that they thought he was a Communist. He was, in fact, a spy, and his job was to identify who in the 2nd Bavarian Regiment supported the Reds. After the Freikorps captured Munich, Hitler was, in fact, arrested, but was soon released on the orders of the officers for whom he was working. Then he testified before the Commission of Inquiry, and, as a result, several Communist sympathizers faced firing squads—perhaps as many as 10. There is no doubt that Hitler the informant carried out his duties to the complete satisfaction of his superiors, for they sent him to a "special education" (that is, political indoctrination) course at the University of Munich. Here he met Professor Alexander von Mueller and his brother-in-law, Dr. Gottfried Feder, a qualified engineer who was regarded as an economic expert in certain right-wing circles. A member of the Thule Society and a man who gave the impression of deep practical and intellectual insight, Feder spoke of "interest slavery," for which he held the Jews largely responsible. Although he eventually came to reject most of Feder's ideas, Hitler was initially profoundly impressed with him and even adopted his mustache style—the "Charlie Chaplin" mustache, now so closely associated with Hitler. The 30-year-old corporal made a number of other right-wing contacts at this course and impressed and astonished both his professors and fellow participants with his anti-Semitic rhetoric. As a result, he was sent to the 41st Infantry Regiment in Munich as a *Vertrauensmann:* a low-level political agent for the Bavarian command. Hitler later called himself an "education officer." He was, in reality, a special agent and political indoctrination officer for Captain Karl Mayr's Section Ib/P, which was variously known as the Information Section, Propaganda Section, and Education Section for Headquarters, Group 4 of the Reichsheer. In this job, Hitler gave many speeches to the troops, the demobilizing soldiers and recently discharged prisoners of war concerning the dangers of Communism; many of his earliest supporters came from these gatherings. Hitler, to his secret delight, proved to be a fiery and dynamically effective speaker, capable of carrying away his audiences with his dialectic skill.

Another part of Hitler's job was to investigate the new political parties that were springing up in Bavaria like mushrooms. At this time there were more than 50 such parties and organizations in Munich, many of which received secret funds from the Reichswehr. In September 1919 Hitler was sent to investigate the German Workers' Party and to make a report. It received no money from the clandestine funds of the armed forces, but Captain Mayr thought that perhaps it should. Hence the reason for Hitler's visit.

An offshoot of the Thule Society, the German Workers' Party (*Deutsche Arbeiterpartei,* or DAP) was founded by Karl Harrer and Anton Drexler in January 1919. Its real history, however, began on September 12, 1919, when Gefreiter Hitler joined its meeting in the Leiber Room of the Sterneckerbraeu. The speaker that evening was Gottfried Feder, and his lecture was unremarkable—Hitler had heard it before. During the discussion session, however, a professor named Baumann stood up and advocated Bavarian succession from Germany and called for its incorporation into Austria. This was too much for Hitler, the rabid Pan-Germanist who hated Austria. Although he was sent to the meeting only to listen, he quickly seized the floor and leveled such a verbal tirade at Baumann that he "left the hall like a wet poodle" even before Hitler finished his oration.[1] The audience of 45 people was astonished and impressed. Anton Drexler followed Hitler out of the hall and handed him a copy of his political pamphlet, *My Political Awakening*.[2] Hitler read it the following morning at 5 A.M., while he fed bread crusts to the mice in his barracks. He found it interesting but thought no more about it until a few days later when he received a postcard announcing that he had been accepted as a member of the German Workers' Party. He was invited to express his opinion on the subject and to attend a committee meeting the following Wednesday.

Hitler, who had no intention of joining any established political party, recalled that he did not know whether to laugh or be angry. He was inclined to write them a curt letter of rejection, but his curiosity got the better of him, and he attended the meeting. Here he found clubism at its worst. Democratic procedure governed the most trivial proceedings, which were discussed at inordinate lengths. The party had no program—only vague ideas and no clues on how to realize them. Gradually it dawned on Hitler that this was an organization he could mold and dominate; he could provide it with his own brand of leadership and with the impetus to act. He therefore became the 55th member of the party (with membership number 555) and was promptly placed in charge of propaganda and named chief recruiting officer of the party.

In his autobiography, Hitler devoted an entire chapter to propaganda. In it he expounded on the lessons he learned in World War I from the British. Among other things, he wrote:

> It is a mistake to make propaganda many-sided. . . . The receptivity of the great masses is very limited, their intelligence is small, but their power of forgetting is enormous. In consequence of these facts, all effective propaganda must be limited to a very few points and must harp on these in slogans until the last member of the public understands what you want him to understand by your slogan. As soon as you . . . try to be many-sided, the effect will piddle away, for the crowd can neither digest nor retain the material offered.[3]

As propaganda chief, Hitler followed his own advice and kept his messages simple. Germany's current misery had been caused by the Jews and the November criminals, and only a strong leader, unrestricted by democratic institutions, could overcome these problems and restore Germany to greatness. Through the force of his oratory he linked anti-Semitism and love of country, and turned the DAP from a debating society into a *bona fide* political movement. His first step was to advertise his party's public meetings in right-wing newspapers and magazines. At the very first meeting 111 people attended—more than twice as many as the party had previously attracted. Hitler launched an "inflammatory" attack on the Jews that, he recalled later, "electrified" the audience. He then asked for donations and received 300 marks—a fortune to a party that had only 7 marks in its treasury when Hitler joined it.[4]

Emboldened by his success, Hitler decided to charge an admission fee of 50 pfennigs to his next performance. The DAP's executive committee was hesistant to take this step but was persuaded by Hitler. This meeting was attended by 129 people, and Hitler was on his way. By January 1920 the party grew to a strength of 190 members. On February 5 the party held its first really large meeting, which Hitler advertised in a unique and inflammatory way: He covered the streets of Munich in huge posters that were glaring red—the left's own color. Largely because of this deliberate provocation, the meeting was attended by 2,500 people, many of whom joined the DAP. By this time the party had already adopted the swastika as its symbol.

The growth of this young extremist party was indirectly aided by the Allies (Chapter 1), who demanded prompt reparation payments and, on February 4, demanded that nearly 900 Germans be handed over to them for trial as war criminals. The list included the Kaiser and his three sons; Ludendorff, Hindenburg, and the other three field marshals; Admiral Alfred von Tripitz; Crown Prince Rupprecht of Bavaria; and two wartime chancellors, von Bethmann-Hollweg and Michaelis. German pride was deliberately wounded and hatred stirred up for no good purpose. The German government delayed answering the demand for weeks and then offered a compromise: Certain individuals on the list would be arrested and tried—but by German judges in German courts. Seeing that they had little choice, the Allies accepted the compromise. In the end 16 people were arrested and 6 were actually convicted. However, as Charles Bracelen Flood wrote, "far from being regarded as a government victory, the entire matter increased the widespread dissatisfaction with what was seen as a spineless and ineffective administration."[5]

Meanwhile, on February 20, 1920, the German Workers' Party changed its name to the National Socialist German Workers' Party (*Nationalsozialistische Deutsche Arbeitpartei*, called the NSDAP or Nazi Party). Hitler did not like the addition of the term "Socialist" but acquiesced because the executive committee thought it might be helpful in attracting workers from the left.

While the Nazi Party was growing and Hitler was refining his propaganda techniques, the Weimar Republic was undergoing crisis after crisis. In February 1920 the Inter-Allied Control Commission ordered that the Freikorps be dissolved. The government complied and, on February 29, ordered two of the three naval brigade Freikorps to disband. The leader of the elite 2nd Naval Brigade, Captain Hermann Ehrhardt, refused to obey this order, and he was backed by the Wehrkreis (military district) commander, General Baron Walter von Luettwitz. After an angry confrontation, Defense Minister Noske relieved Luettwitz of his command.[6] Luettwitz and Ehrhardt responded by marching on Berlin. The army refused to fire on the Freebooters, and the police joined the rebels. The government declared a general strike early on the morning of March 13 and then fled to Dresden, and later to Stuttgart, while the Freikorps installed Dr. Wolfgang Kapp, a Prussian bureaucrat, agricultural official, and former Nationalist member of the Reichstag, as chancellor on March 13, 1920. The *coup* was badly planned from the beginning and eventually collapsed because of one of the most effective general strikes in history. Kapp capitulated at noon on March 17 and fled into exile in Sweden.[7] Only in Bavaria did the Putsch have a lasting effect. Here the pro-Weimar Wehrkreis commander, General Ritter Arnold von Moehl, assumed full governmental responsibility and politely dismissed the leftist minister-president, Johannes Hoffmann, and replaced him with Gustav von Kahr, a pro-monarchist who toyed with the idea of Bavarian succession.

Adolf Hitler's role in the Kapp Putsch was as inglorious as it was minor. Accompanied by Dietrich Eckart, he boarded an airplane for the first time in his life and flew to Berlin, where he intended to offer his services to the Putschists. He was airsick the entire trip and threw up continuously. The Nazis arrived only minutes after Kapp fled—in fact, it is likely that their cars passed as one raced to the Templehof Airport, and the other raced from it. Arriving at the chancellery, Hitler was warned to get out of the government quarter as quickly as possible—advice he took with audacity. However, he nevertheless spent a few days in the capital city, partially because he wanted to be driven back. He swore that he would never fly again as long as he lived (a pledge he did not keep). Incidentally, his pilot on this flight was Ritter Robert von Greim, a World War I ace, a future air fleet commander, and the last commander-in-chief of the Luftwaffe.

Meanwhile, with the Republic once again in chaos, the Communists again thought they saw an opportunity for revolution. With 50,000 armed workers they seized the demilitarized Ruhr, which was devoid of either French or German troops as a result of the Treaty of Versailles. They planned to use it as a base for a march on Berlin. Beginning on March 14 the Reds rapidly seized Dortmund, Remscheid, Hagen, Mulheim, and Duesseldorf, and slaughtered 300 people (mostly policemen)

when they seized Essen, the *de facto* industrial capital of Germany and the home of the Krupp Works, on March 19. To suppress this rebellion, the Ebert government had to undergo the indignity of rehiring the Freikorps, including the Ehrhardt Brigade, which had attempted to overthrow it only a few days before!

On April 3, under the overall command of General Baron Oskar von Watter,[8] 21 different Freikorps struck the Ruhr and annihilated the Red Army in 5 days. As in Munich and other cities the year before, hundreds of workers and suspects were "shot while attempting to escape" after they surrendered or were captured. "No pardon is given. We shoot even the wounded," a young member of the Freikorps von Epp wrote to his family.

> The enthusiasm is terrific—unbelievable. Our battalion has had two deaths; the Reds 200–300. Anyone who falls into our hands first gets the rifle butt and then is finished off with a bullet. . . . We even shot ten Red Cross nurses . . . because they were carrying pistols. We shot those little ladies with pleasure—how they cried and pleaded with us to save their lives. Nothing doing! Anybody with a gun is our enemy.[9]

After the reconquest of the Ruhr, the government ceased to pay the Freikorps, which were officially disbanded, but in reality merely went underground. The embattled government, however, faced other problems. On March 21, 1921, as mandated by the Treaty of Versailles, a plebiscite was held in the province of Upper Silesia, to determine if it would remain German or join Poland. Despite having been under French occupation since February 1920 (or perhaps because of it), it chose by a vote of 707,122 to 433,514 to remain German. On May 1, however, the Allied Plebiscite Commission announced that they would draw the boundary line and award almost half of the province to Poland. The Polish section would include most of Silesia's mines, mills, and furnaces, and 350,000 Germans. Berlin naturally protested—but to no avail. Then, on May 3, Polish volunteer forces under Wojciech Korfanty invaded Upper Silesia, attempting to take by force what they had been unable to win by plebiscite. The French regiments remained in their barracks, allowing the Poles to have their way, while Paris threatened to occupy the Ruhr if Germany sent the Reichswehr into Upper Silesia. By their threats and inaction the French were clearly aiding their Polish allies, while tying the hands of the German government.[10] But they could not tie the hands of the Freikorps. Acting on their own initiative, several of the disbanded units, consisting mainly of men working on large farms in the east, re-formed themselves and headed for the front. Other veterans joined individually. A Munich policeman and fu-

ture SS general named Joseph "Sepp" Dietrich, for example, took leave
from his job and paid his own way to Silesia to join the volunteers assembling to fight the Poles. The Freebooters chose General Hoefer as
their leader, but when he refused to attack, they followed Lieutenant
General Bernhard von Huelsen, who smashed the Poles at St. Annaberg
on May 23 and abruptly ended their attempt to annex the entire province of Upper Silesia.

The next day President Ebert yielded to Allied pressure and, under
Article 48 of the Weimar constitution, outlawed all Freikorps formations.
The Freebooters were stunned. Once again the government had let them
down. The Battle of St. Annaberg proved to be the last major act of the
organized Freikorps, but it was also their most selfless and patriotic.
They had saved more than half of the province for Germany.

Meanwhile, on April 27, 1921, even before the crisis in Upper Silesia
ended, the Allied Reparations Committee set the precise amount of the
German debt at 132 billion gold marks ($33 billion). Germany also had
to hand over 26 percent of her exports by value (in gold currency or
goods) to the Allies for 42 years. The final bill came to about 40–45
percent of the total value of the country. The Allies also declared Germany 12 billion marks in arrears and, on May 5, gave it 6 days to accept
their reparations burden unconditionally, or, they threatened, they
would seize the Ruhr. Faced with this threat, the German government
of Chancellor Fehrenbach fell and was replaced by yet another coalition
under Dr. Joseph Wirth.[11] Wirth and his highly respected foreign minister, Walter Rathenau, adopted the "Policy of Fulfillment"—that is, they
decided to pay the Allies what they demanded, or at least as much as
Germany could pay. The purpose of this policy was to win the good
will of the Allies and make them see the limits of Germany's capacity
to pay the reparations.

The decision to adopt the Policy of Fulfillment was announced on
May 10 and, of course, brought howls of protests from the right-wing
parties, especially in Bavaria, and most especially from Adolf Hitler and
his cronies. The Nazi Party, however, was one of the ultimate benefici-
aries of the policy, because it weakened both German and international
faith in the mark, led to a horrible inflation, and further demonstrated
the inability of the pro-democracy parties to provide effective leadership
in a crisis. It therefore drove more and more people into the arms of the
extremist parties of the right and weakened the people's faith in the
Weimar Republic to a point from which it never fully recovered.

The German inflation actually began during the war, when the Kaiser
and his governments met the need for increased expenditures by printing more and more marks. In the 1900s the typical rate of exchange was

4 marks per U.S. dollar. By the end of the war it took 7.45 marks to equal 1 dollar. The Weimar Republic continued and accelerated the process of printing more and more bank notes, rather than imposing additional taxes on the war-weary people and reducing the flow of currency. By the summer of 1919 the marks-to-dollar ratio stood at 15.5 to 1, but by the end of the year it had dropped to 35.45 to 1. The mark began to fall again the day the Policy of Fulfillment was announced, but by July it was rather stable at 60 marks per U.S. dollar. Then it began to fall again, and by September it took more than 100 marks to buy 1 dollar. By November 8, 1921, the exchange rate stood at +200 marks per dollar. The slide continued into 1922, and, by mid-July, the mark had less than 20 percent of the purchasing power it had 14 months before.

Like Hitler, Captain Ehrhardt and other right-wing Freikorps veterans held Rathenau primarily responsible for the inflation, mainly because he was Jewish. In July 1921 Ehrhardt and several members of his brigade formed a secret society known as the Organization Consul (OC). It was, in fact, an organization designed to engage in political assassinations, as was its counterpart, the *Feme*, named for an irregular tribunal that administered justice in medieval Germany at a time when the government was too weak to maintain order. The OC and *Feme* overlapped, and Captain Ehrhardt was involved in both groups.

The first major victim of the OC/Feme was Matthias Erzberger, who had been forced to resign as finance minister in 1920, after his involvement in some unsavory financial transactions had been exposed. Even though his political career was ruined by the scandal and was apparently over, Ehrhardt and his men still remembered him as the "November criminal" who signed the armistice and the Treaty of Versailles. Erzberger was gunned down by two OC killers on August 26, 1921, while on vacation at Bad Griesbach, Baden, in the Black Forest. He was shot eight times. The killers then made their way to Bavaria—a haven of right-wing extremist groups—and eventually escaped to Hungary, although seven of their accomplices were arrested. One of them was Hans Ulrich Klintzsch, a member of the Nazi Party.

The reaction of the left and center to the Erzberger murder was one of fury. On August 29 the Wirth government promulgated a decree designed to prevent political murders, but it was altogether inadequate. In Bavaria, Gustav von Kahr refused to take any action against the right-wing extremists and was forced to resign by the Diet. He was succeeded as provincial premier by the more moderate Count Hugo Lerchenfeld, but the atmosphere of lawlessness continued to pervade Bavarian politics and society.

"Are you aware that there are political murder gangs operating in Bavaria?" a worried citizen asked Ernest Poehner, the police president of Munich.

"Yes," replied the tall official, looking down through his pince-nez glasses, "but not enough of them."

With such an attitude as this, there can be little wonder why there were an estimated 400 political murders in the Weimar Republic from 1919 to 1922 alone. Most of these were never solved, and only a few of the assassins who were identified received punishment. Adolf Hitler was, of course, delighted with the murder of Erzberger. Even after the former minister's death, Hitler called him the nation's biggest *Judentzer* (Jew lover).

The Feme's next target was former Chancellor Philipp Scheidemann, who had declared the formation of the German Republic on November 9, 1918. He had resigned as chancellor rather than sign the Treaty of Versailles and became Lord Mayor of Kassel. On Sunday, June 4, 1922, he was out for a walk with his daughter and granddaughter when two OC assailants tried to squirt prussic acid into his face. Because of previous threats to his life, the distinguished-looking old gentleman always carried a pistol with him, even on Sunday walks. Although temporarily blinded, Scheidemann pulled his gun and fired twice, causing his attackers to run away. Then he collapsed. Scheidemann was very fortunate: His white goatee and a strong wind had deflected most of the acid, and he suffered no permanent damage.[12] Despite the widespread outrage this incident caused, the OC struck again less than three weeks later and claimed its most famous victim.

Walther Rathenau was born in 1867, the son of a rich and distinguished Jewish family. His father, Emil, had founded the German Edison Company, which grew into an international electrical complex known as AEG. Tall, handsome, brilliant, and vain, Walther considered himself a German first and a Jew second. During the war, he organized the War Materials Division, which kept the German field armies supplied with explosives during the critical campaigns of the war.

As a foreign minister, he went to Genoa in April 1922 and on the 16th signed the Rapallo Treaty with the Soviet Union, unexpectedly ending Germany's postwar diplomatic isolation. The *coup* was widely hailed in Germany, although far-right politicians such as Hitler denounced it as a *rapprochement* with Communism. (They had no way of knowing that General von Seeckt, the commander-in-chief of the Reichsheer, was using this pact to bypass the Treaty of Versailles and to build forbidden tanks and airplanes for the German army—but in the Soviet Union, far from the prying eyes of the Allied inspectors.)

What the reactionaries hated Rathenau the most for, however, was his Policy of Fulfillment. On the morning of June 24, 1922, he left his villa in a Berlin suburb and, alone in the back seat of an open car, was driven toward the foreign office by his chauffeur. He never made it. Gangland style, a touring car overtook him, and 24-year-old Erwin Kern, a former naval lieutenant and ex-member of the Ehrhardt Brigade, fired a nine-round burst into him with a machine gun. Hermann Fischer, another ex-officer, then lobbed a grenade into the back seat, killing Rathenau, if he were not dead already. Remarkably, except for his eardrums, the chauffeur was not injured in the attack.

This time the assassins did not reach Bavaria and safety. Trapped in a castle on July 17, Kern was killed in a gunfight with police, and Fischer committed suicide rather than be taken alive. They were hailed as martyrs by the right, and after Hitler came to power their death-site became a Nazi shrine.

A few days after Rathenau's death, the Reichstag passed a "Law for the Protection of the Reich" by a vote of 303 to 102. It provided the government with broad new powers to control political terrorism, including the right to shut down party newspapers, cancel meetings and political rallies, and ban certain organizations. Hitler promptly dubbed it the "Law for the Protection of Jewry."[13]

The new law also set Bavaria and Berlin on a collision course. The moderate minister-president, Count Lerchenfeld, tried to work with Berlin, but the Bavarian People's Party and the Bavarian branch of the Nationalist Party bitterly attacked the new legislation, stating that the Reich had no right to attempt to enact such a law in Bavaria. On November 8, 1922, they compelled Lerchenfeld to resign and replaced him with Eugen von Knilling, a member of the right-wing Bavarian People's Party.[14]

Rathenau's assassination also had a negative impact on the German mark, for it shook what little faith remained in domestic and international financial circles concerning the possibility of a viable future for Germany. The depletion of the Reich's gold reserves, her unpaid war debt, her reparations burden, the flight of private capital from Germany to avoid its attachment as reparations, and the government's deficit spending were all contributing factors to the fall of the mark, but the murder of the internationally respected Walther Rathenau broke the back of Germany's currency. On the day of Rathenau's death, the mark per dollar ratio stood at 272 to 1. By the end of July it had fallen to 670 to 1, and by August, 1 dollar could buy 2,000 marks. It was clear by now that the government could not control the inflation, which was climbing at triple-digit rates. The mark/dollar ratio stood at 4,500 to 1 by the end of October 1922.

Most people blamed the runaway inflation on the reparations payments and the Policy of Fulfillment. Chancellor Wirth attempted to regain financial stability by obtaining international loans, by securing a reduction in the reparations bill, by asking the Allies for a three- to four-year moratorium on reparations, and by increasing German productivity by extending the eight-hour day. Neither the Allies nor the Reichstag would cooperate with him. The Social Democrats, for example, considered the eight-hour day sacred. As a result of the lack of support for his programs in the Reichstag, Wirth resigned on November 14, 1922. He was replaced by 42-year-old Wilhelm Cuno, the head of the Hamburg-American shipping line, who put together a coalition cabinet of middle-centrist parties.

It was hoped that the suave Cuno, a businessman with no political affiliation, would have better luck in dealing with the Allies than did Wirth. Unfortunately, the French at this time were led by Premier Raymond Poincaire, a Germanophobe who refused to make concessions of any kind. On December 2 the German delegate to the Reparations Commission informed the Allies that Germany would be late in delivering 144,000 telephone poles and asked for an extension until April 1, 1923. This lag gave Poincaire the pretext he needed and, on December 27, Germany was declared in default. On January 11, 1923, over British and American objections, French and Belgian troops under General Degoutte marched into the Ruhr and occupied the industrial heartland of Germany, which produced 73 percent of Germany's coal and 83 percent of her iron and steel.[15]

Chancellor Cuno at once declared the French action illegal and adopted a policy of passive resistance. He believed that the French would find it impossible to run the mines and plants without German assistance, and in a sense he was right: Coal deliveries to France fell by 80 percent and Poincaire had to raise taxes in France to pay for the cost of the occupation. However, immensely worse effects were felt in Germany. The mark stood at about 10,000 per dollar when the Allies entered the Ruhr. By the end of that same month the ratio was almost 50,000 to 1 and falling.

The Reichsbank (the German national bank) attempted to intervene by buying marks in Berlin and from abroad in gold or with foreign currency, and by mid-February 1923 it had succeeded in driving the price of the mark down to 20,000 per dollar. This price held stable throughout March and into April, but the bank had to abandon this policy in the middle of the month, because it had already used up much of its gold and almost all of its foreign credits and could no longer artificially support the mark. In addition, the raw materials that had once been supplied by the Ruhr now had to be imported, and this also required foreign currency. As a result of the Reichsbank's admission of defeat, the mark collapsed again. By May 4 (that is, in less than three weeks) it had lost half of its value, dropping to 40,000 marks per dollar. By June 1 the ratio was 70,000 to 1, with no end to the crisis in sight. It lost more than half of its remaining value that month; by June 30, 1 dollar was worth 150,000 marks. By the end of July 1,000,000 marks could not buy 1 American dollar; and then the bottom dropped out of the German mark.

Dr. Rudolf Havenstein, the president of the Reichsbank, was an old-guard civil servant with his own economic theories. He believed that the answer to the monetary crisis lay in printing more money. During August, he proudly bragged that the Reichsbank was printing bills night and day and was issuing 46 billion marks every 24 hours. He was using 30 paper factories, 133 printing offices, 300 paper mills, and 2,000 printing presses. Eventually, to save time, the bills were only printed on one side. Bank clerks used the back of them as scratch paper, because the bills were literally worth less than the paper they were printed on. The British ambassador privately commented that any people who knew anything about money would have taken Havenstein out and hanged him.[16]

During the first week of August, the value of the mark fell to 3,500,000 per dollar. It had lost 99.3 percent of its purchasing power in 3 months; within the next 4 weeks, it lost another 93 percent of its value and continued to fall. In mid-August it was below 4,000,000 per dollar, and by September 1 the exchange ratio exceeded 10,000,000 marks per dollar. The inflation became so bad that the same amount of money that would buy a full dinner in the evening would barely buy a cup of coffee at breakfast. Students set out for universities with enough money to pay their tuition for a semester—funds their parents raised at considerable sacrifice. When they arrived at their destinations, they found that they could not even pay for a single book. Banks no longer counted money—they weighed it. People who had formerly been paid monthly were now paid twice a day. They then rushed to the market or store, to spend their checks before the New York Stock Exchange issued its 1 P.M. currency figures. People who were eating lunch at that time literally saw the price of their meals double while they were eating it.

Old people who had worked hard all of their lives saw the savings of a lifetime wiped out overnight. People on fixed incomes watched helplessly as their pensions—which some of them had worked 30 years to earn—became absolutely valueless. A fixed pension check, which would formerly allow an old couple to live comfortably for a month, was now not sufficient to purchase a single copy of a daily newspaper. There were hundreds of suicides all over Germany. Many of these were joint suicides—grandfathers and grandmothers taking the only way out that was left to them, other than starvation. Disabled veterans now had nothing. A typical German breakfast now consisted of turnip coffee, mildewed bread, and synthetic honey. Many could not even afford that. Thomas Mann, perhaps Germany's foremost author, now went hungry, as did his children. The children also went barefoot, because there were no shoes available. Malnutrition was widespread, but many farmers refused to sell their crops for worthless currency. Barter was the order of the day. In desperation many young women from respectable families turned to prostitution, just to feed themselves.

Those with foreign money could buy anything. Twenty American dollars could buy a house worth $50,000. Ernest Hemingway and three of his friends spent four days in a luxury resort for 20 cents a day each, including tips. Those with large debts or mortgages paid them off for almost nothing, and those with foreign assets became wealthy. A whole class of inflation profiteers arose, but the average German was devastated. An egg that cost 25 pfennings (¼ of a mark) in 1918 cost 80,000,000,000 (80 billion) marks in 1923. A beer that cost 17 pfennings in 1918 cost 150,000,000,000 (150 billion marks) in 1923; a newspaper that cost 40 pfennings (⅖ of a mark) in January 1922 cost 300,000,000,000 (300 billion) marks by late 1923. Based on the prewar mark/dollar relationship, an American postage stamp would have cost $11,900,000,000 if it had inflated at the same rate as the German mark.[17]

And the inflation was not yet over. By the end of September 1923 the mark stood at 60,000,000 per dollar. By November, 1 dollar was worth 4,210,500,000,000 (four trillion, 210 billion, 500 million marks). By this time, the total amount of German currency in circulation was about 750 quintillion marks, but it only had a value of 180 million U.S. dollars. "History," Wheaton writes, "knows of no similar currency depreciation."[18]

Is it any wonder that German confidence in democracy and the Weimar Republic collapsed? Is it any wonder that many people were seduced by the extremist propaganda of people like Hitler? After all, was what Hitler was saying any more fantastic than what was happening on the German streets, where people were picking up their half-day pay in wheelbarrows, and rushing to the store to buy a loaf of bread? Mothers and fathers lay in bed at night, listening to their children cry themselves to sleep because they were hungry. Hitler offered them hope. Is there any wonder that many became desperate enough to turn to him? Years later Robert Murphy, a U.S. diplomat stationed in Germany, would write: "Inflation, in my opinion, did more than any other factor to make Hitlerism possible."[19]

And what was Adolf Hitler doing during the 1920–1923 period while all of this was going on? Quite simply, he was building his party. On March 31, 1920, he signed out of the barracks for the last time, collected his 50 marks demobilization pay plus an issue of civilian clothing, and brought his military career to an end. He was a civilian for the first time in five and a half years.

Hitler rented a shabby pair of rooms over a store in a middle-class district of Munich, near the Isar River, at 41 Thierchstrasse. He made no attempt to get a job but rather devoted himself solely to his political activities, where he met with a great deal of success. From January to December 1920, the party's membership in Munich increased from 190 to 1,512, and 10 locals were established in other Bavarian towns, bringing the party's total membership to 2,000 or more. On December 17, in a move engineered by Hitler, the NSDAP bought its own newspaper, the *Voelkischer Beobachter.* Where he got the money from is a bit of a mystery, but most of it apparently came from secret Army funds, administered by Major General Ritter Franz von Epp and Captain Ernst Roehm, an early member of the Nazi Party who had recently replaced Captain Mayr as chief of Section Ib/P.

Ernst Roehm (born in 1887) was a native of Munich and a highly decorated, pudgy soldier whose face was badly scarred by his many war wounds. He was a man who delighted in the camaraderie of war and had no use for leftists, civilians, or women, and would later become a notorious homosexual. A strong nationalist, he eventually became the most famous of Hitler's Brownshirt commanders and the only member of the party who was allowed to call Hitler by the familiar German pronoun "du." For the present, however, Roehm was still an officer on active duty and a very influential one at that: He had direct access to the commander of the Wehrkreis and funnelled excess weaponry and secret money into the NSDAP.

Meanwhile, in the fall of 1920, Hitler created the *Ordnertruppen:* a group of muscular Nazis, ex-soldiers, and beer-hall brawlers, headed initially by Emil Maurice, a watchmaker and Freikorps veteran. Its job was to protect Hitler's speeches and to disrupt those of his opponents. Shortly thereafter, this group was given the cover name Sports Section *(Sportabteilung)* and came to be known by its initials, the SA. At first its members could not afford distinctive uniforms, so it wore the gray shirts of the Imperial Army. These were later replaced by cheap brown shirts, which were sold to the Nazis as army surplus. They had originally been manufactured for use by the German troops in colonial Africa, but World War I had made their delivery impossible. In late 1921 the SA became the *Sturmabteilung* (literally "Storm Detachment"), and its men became known as the Storm Troopers or Brownshirts.

In mid-1921 Adolf Hitler felt strong enough to force a showdown with the "old guard" party leadership, led by Anton Drexler, a chairman of the NSDAP. This bespectacled and unassuming locksmith had immediately recognized Hitler's value as an orator, partially because he lacked talent as a public speaker himself. In July he tried to merge the Nazi Party with the slightly larger German Socialist Party (Deutsch-Sozialistische Partei, or DSP). On July 11, the day after he learned that these negotiations were in progress, Adolf Hitler resigned from the Nazi Party. Realizing that the party would amount to little without Hitler, Drexler sent Dietrich Eckart to Munich to negotiate with the former corporal. Hitler responded with an ultimatum, demanding dictatorial power within the party for himself. Within the next two days the party's executive committee capitulated completely; Hitler rejoined the NSDAP on July 25, and four days later became the first chairman. He would be the *Fuehrer* (leader) of the party for the rest of his life. In return for his last-minute endorsement of Hitler, Anton Drexler was named honorary chairman for life.[20] Hitler then placed the party further in his control by naming Hermann Esser director of propaganda, and Dietrich Eckart editor of the *Beobachter,* and by hiring Max Amann, his former first sergeant, as business manager of the party.[21]

Three months later, on September 14, Hitler and his SA disrupted a speech by Otto Ballerstedt of the separatist Bavarian League *(Bayernbund).* The meeting ended with Hitler, Esser, and Oskar Koerner beating him to the floor with chairs and sticks. It took physicians 14 stitches to close the wounds in Ballerstedt's head. The three Nazis were arrested, tried before the People's Court of Munich, and sentenced to three months imprisonment for breach of the peace on January 12, 1922. After a series of legal delays, they were eventually incarcerated in Stadelheim Prison, Munich, on June 24 but were released upon the remission of their sentences on July 27. Hitler had served 33 days in jail.

Meanwhile, on September 17, 1921, the day the more liberal Count Hugo Lerchenfeld replaced Gustav von Kahr as premier of Bavaria, Hitler threatened violent street demonstrations against the "parliamentary parasites" and "slimy filth" that governed Berlin and Munich. To prevent him from disrupting Lerchenfeld's inauguration, the Munich police arrested Hitler again on September 20 and held him until the following day. They also closed the *Voelkischer Beobachter* until October 1. As soon as it was allowed to resume publication, the *Beobachter* launched a vicious attack on Chancellor Wirth and, as a result, was banned again on October 6.

Hitler's inflammatory speeches, propaganda techniques, and rabble-rousing tactics were highly effective in attracting people into the Nazi Party during the days of the inflation and panic, when everything in Germany that had previously been considered stable was collapsing. Hitler's own energy was also a factor in the rise of his party. His speeches were attended by more and more people, and he spoke more and more frequently. On November 30, for example, he spoke at five different beer halls in Munich. Two weeks later, he made 10 speeches in a single evening. Despite his appearance (several observers recalled that he looked like a waiter), he nevertheless kept his audiences spellbound. "Putzi" Hanfstaengl left a vivid description of a Hitler speech in his book, *Unheard Witness:*

He scored his points all round the compass. First he would criticize
the Kaiser . . . and then he rounded on the Weimar republicans
for conforming to the victors' demands. . . .

He stormed at war profiteers. . . . He attacked the Jews. . . .
Then he thundered at the Communists and Socialists.

As Hitler was carried away by his own oratory, he spoke more and
more rapidly, and he moved his hands in a manner designed to empha-
size and punctuate his words. "Sometimes," Hanfstaengl recalled,

he reminded me of a skilled violinist, who, never coming to the
end of his bow, always left just the faint anticipation of a tone. . . .

I looked round the audience. Where was the nondescript crowd
I had seen only an hour before? What was suddenly holding these
people. . . .

The audience responded with a final outburst of frenzied cheering. . . . It had been a masterly performance. I was really impressed beyond measure by Hitler. . . . With his incredible gifts as
an orator he was clearly going to go far.[22]

Hitler's speeches had a number of themes, but only two of them were
central: the necessity to replace the Weimar Republic and the "November criminals" with a strong dictator (that is, Hitler himself), and the
anti-Semitic message he had been harping on for years. This is as good
a place as any to digress in order to analyze why the second theme was
tolerated by the German people and actively embraced by a significant
minority of them.

Nazism would never have taken seed in Germany had not the Reich
(indeed all of Europe) had a long tradition of anti-Semitism. There is no
doubt that Jews in the Middle Ages were distinct from other Europeans
in terms of ancestry, religion, and culture; frequently they dressed differ-
ently as well. In an age that believed in magic and witchcraft, anyone
who was different was suspect. The Jews were different; therefore, they
were suspect. The illiterate, gullible, and superstitious populace of the
Medieval era believed the wildest stories imaginable: Jews participated
in ritual murders of Gentiles, Jews used the blood of Christian babies in
their religious services, and Jewish women frequently gave birth to pigs.
Even most of the relatively moderate Christians of that era believed that
Jewish stubbornness was the only reason that they refused to accept
Christ and baptism, and this stubbornness was the product of Satan and
his influence. Indeed, many Christians and so-called Christians believed
that the Jews and Satan had formed some sort of alliance. "Jews were

deemed treacherous, dealers in shoddy merchandise, blasphemers, dese-
crators of the hosts, traitors," Randall L. Bytwerk wrote. "Medieval
Christians believed that no manner of evil was beyond the ken of so
wicked a people."[23] The fact that Jews could engage in usury (the practice of loaning money for interest—an activity in which the Christians
of that era were forbidden to engage) did little to endear the Jews to the
Gentiles.

Martin Luther, the founder of the Protestant movement, has been
called the spiritual godfather of Nazism. Early in his career, Luther advocated tolerance and condemned persecution of the Jews; however,
when the Jews did not use the tolerance he offered for the purpose he
intended (that is, conversion to Christianity), he reversed his position.
In 1542 he wrote a pamphlet entitled *Against the Jews and Their Lies.* By
1543 he was writing that Jews "are nothing but thieves and robbers who
daily eat no morsel and wear no thread of clothing which they have not
stolen and pilfered from us by means of their accursed usury. . . .
[Jews] are our plague, our pestilence, and our misfortune."[24] He proposed that their synagogues and homes be burned, their legal rights
abolished, and their rabbis banned.

Luther further lay the groundwork for Nazism by expressing his conviction that all government is from God and that even bad rulers are
God-appointed, because they punish people for their sins. "Though Nazism cannot be tied directly to Luther," James D. Forman writes, "his
teaching of submission to one's ruler, even when that ruler is a tyrant,
preconditioned much of twentieth-century Germany to accept the Nazi
regime with unquestioning and unconditional obedience."[25]

The anti-Semitic spirit as verbalized by Martin Luther faded into the
background in the three centuries after his death, although it never van-
ished entirely. Even William Shakespeare, a shrewd judge of his public,
wrote an essentially anti-Semitic play entitled "The Merchant of Venice."
One character in this play states: "Certainly the Jew is the very devil
incarnal."[26] On the whole, however, the 300 years after Martin Luther
were ones of slow (if uneven) progress for the Jews, largely because the
Protestant and Catholic kings and princes of that era were too busy
fighting each other to worry about them. German Jews became fully
emancipated in 1869, and in 1871 the constitution of the Second Reich
(that is, Bismarck) gave the full right of citizenship to Jews. However, a
new wave of anti-Semitism struck Germany after the financial crisis of
1873, in which a number of Jews were involved. They were also "chosen
to play the scapegoat," Edmond Vermeil wrote, "so as to absolve the
Gentiles from responsibility for the disaster."[27]

Beginning about 1881, a new type of anti-Semitism evolved in Germany. This type was based on racial grounds rather than religious ones
and was called scientific or racial anti-Semitism. It was even more vi-

cious than religious anti-Semitism in that not even conversion to Christianity could "correct" a person's Jewishness. Judaism became "a crime of the blood" that could not be erased by the simple expedient of baptism.

Despite Bismarck's efforts to curb it, anti-Semitism was on the rise in the Second Reich for a number of reasons. One of these was that some of the leading German philosophers and intellectual leaders endorsed it. For example, Heinrich von Treitschke (1834–1896), perhaps the leading German historian of his era and an advocate of war *per se* as both a practical and theoretical necessity, wrote: "Even in the most educated circles, among men who reject any thought of religious intolerance or national arrogance, one hears as if from a single mouth: the Jews are our misfortune."[28] Later this phrase became Julius Streicher's motto, and it appeared on virtually every front page of his Jew-baiting newspaper, *Der Stuermer*. The philosopher Friedrich Wilhelm Nietzsche (1844–1900) had anti-Semitic views similar to Treitschke's, and there was a whole set of lesser lights too numerous to mention here. However, the most influential anti-Semite was Houston Stewart Chamberlain, a transplanted Englishman.

Born in 1855, the son of a British admiral, young Chamberlain was plagued by illness. He went to the mainland to regain his health, fell in love with Germany, and stayed there. In fact, he became an extreme German chauvinist—"more Catholic than the Pope" as the old saying went. His best-known work is *Foundations of the Nineteenth Century*, in which he proclaimed that race was the key to history. Among other things, he stated that "God builds today upon the Germans alone."[29] Furthermore, the Jew was not an "Aryan" (an unscientific racial term that alluded to what Hitler called the "superrace"—white, Gentile, Germanic people who were uncorrupted by Slavic or Jewish blood; the Anglo-Saxons were also "Aryans").

Chamberlain has been called "Hitler's John the Baptist."[30] A neighbor of Hitler's special friends, the Wagners, Hitler visited Chamberlain at his home in Bayreuth in 1923, and the pair were quite taken with one another. The *Voelkischer Beobachter* reported his death in 1927 in the most laudatory terms.

Hitler's hero, the composer Richard Wagner (1813–1883), also contributed to his anti-Semitism. "I hold the Jewish race to be the born enemy of pure humanity and everything noble in man," Wagner declared.[31] The Jewish writer Kurt Tucholsky (1890–1935) did not help matters with his literary retaliations, in which he lampooned the Germans and everything they held sacred; indeed, he helped confirm many Germans in their anti-Semitism.

Had Germany not lost the First World War and been subjected to the

Treaty of Versailles, the anti-Semitism of this era might well have become just an unpleasant footnote in history. But Germany did lose, and a disproportionate number of the leaders in the Bolshevik Revolution of 1917, the Revolution of 1918, and the subsequent Marxist uprisings were Jewish, as Hitler never tired of pointing out. Karl Marx was a Jew, he declared. Bela Kun, and 8 of his 11 commissars in the Hungarian Soviet Republic, were Jews. In Russia, Trotsky and several of Lenin's top lieutenants were Jewish. In Berlin, Rosa Luxemburg and Karl Liebknecht were Jewish. Matthias Erzberger was part Jewish—or so Hitler said. And in Munich, Kurt Eisner, Ernst Toller, Eugen Levine, Max Levien, and Tovia Axelrod were all Jews. These facts, according to Hitler, tied Judaism with Communism and proved that there was an international Jewish-Bolshevik conspiracy, whose aim was to dominate and enslave Germany and, indeed, the entire world. Hitler's assertions, of course, would not stand up to rational arguments, for one could point out that Lenin was not a Jew, nor was Ebert, Scheidemann, Noske, or most of the other founders of the Weimar Republic—and that included Erzberger, whose mother was not half-Jewish, no matter what Hitler claimed; however, no part of this counterargument mattered, because these were not rational times. Indeed, was the idea of an international Jewish-Bolshevik conspiracy any more farfetched than the fact that an egg cost 80 billion marks and that it took two bushel baskets full of million mark notes to buy a loaf of bread? Certainly not. The tenor of the times certainly made the fantastic appeals of Adolf Hitler and his cronies much easier to tolerate or even to accept.

Quite apart from his irrational hatred of the Jews, Hitler had some sound political reasons for attacking them. They were an easily identifiable minority, numerous and unique enough to be singled out but not numerous enough to retaliate effectively, because they only accounted for 0.9 percent of the population. Also they were more prosperous and successful than the average German, which excited jealousy and envy in certain circles. Hitler was a clever enough politician to harness these emotions and channel them for his own uses. His efforts to establish a common bond among all Germans (that is, the fact that they were not Jewish) would probably not have worked in better times; however, in the era of the Weimar Republic, his tactics succeeded to a remarkable degree.

It was during this, the Nazi Party's first growth period (1919–1923), that it recruited some of its most famous and influential leaders—people who would play pivotal and sometimes decisive roles in the days ahead. Foremost among these was Hermann Goering, a World War I flying ace who held the *Pour le Merite* and was the last commander of the "Red Baron's" famous 1st Fighter Wing, better known as the Richthofen Fighter Wing or the "Flying Circus." He succeeded Hans Ulrich Klintzsch, the former naval lieutenant from the Ehrhardt Brigade, as commander of the SA in 1923.

Hermann Wilhelm Goering was born in Marienbad Sanitarium at Rosenheim, Bavaria, on January 12, 1893, the son of Heinrich Ernst and Franiszha "Fanny" Goering. A headstrong and rebellious child, he was educated at various boarding schools, the Karlsruhe Military Academy, and the elite Gross-Lichterfelde Cadet Academy in Berlin. As a child, his hero was Ritter ("Knight" or "Sir") Hermann von Epenstein, a rich half-Jewish aristocrat who became Goering's mother's lover. In 1904, when the 11-year-old Hermann was attending the boarding school at Ansbach, in Franconia, he was required to write an essay about the man he admired most in the world. Goering wrote about Ritter von Epenstein. The following day the headmaster frigidly informed the children that Ansbach boys did not write compositions praising Jews. Young Hermann heatedly protested that his godfather was Roman Catholic, but to no avail—the headmaster was a racial anti-Semite. Goering was forced to frog-march around the grounds wearing a placard around his neck that read "Mein Pate ist ein Jude." He also had to write 100 times "I shall not write essays in praise of Jews" and had to copy all the names in the semi-Gotha (a book of Jewish names) from A to E. Naturally he was mocked and insulted by some of his peers, which led to a fistfight, in which three of them thrashed young Goering. Early the following morning he quietly slipped out of bed, cut the strings on every instrument in the school band, and walked to the railroad station, where he used the last of his money to buy a ticket home.[32]

At age 16, Hermann was sent to Karlsruhe, which had a reputation for taming the wildest teenagers. They certainly succeeded in Goering's case, and he gained admission to Gross-Lichterfelde, Imperial Germany's equivalent of West Point. Three years later (in 1912) he was commissioned into the Prince Wilhelm (112th Infantry) Regiment at Muelhausen.

Lieutenant Goering went to the Western Front with his regiment in the fall of 1914 and showed initiative and dash in fighting against the French. That winter, however, he fell ill with rheumatic fever and was sent back to the hospital at Freiburg. While there he was visited by a friend, 2nd Lieutenant Bruno Loerzer, a former officer of the 112th who was now undergoing pilot's training at Freiburg.[33] Goering was so excited by Loerzer's descriptions of the fledgling air service that he decided to join it as an aerial observer. His request for a transfer was denied, and he was ordered to rejoin his regiment; however, in direct disobedience of orders, Goering headed for the 25th Air Detachment at Ostend, Belgium, to join Loerzer as an aerial observer.

When he heard what Goering had done, the commander of the Prince Wilhelm Regiment demanded an immediate court-martial. However, Ritter von Epenstein had received his knighthood from Kaiser Wilhelm II and still had considerable influence at court. The legal proceedings against young Goering were quietly dropped, and he was soon officially transferred to the air service.

From the beginning, Lieutenant Goering proved to be an incredibly brave airman. "He was, quite literally, insensitive to physical danger," Manvell and Fraenkel wrote later.[34] In fact, the next four years were probably among the happiest of his life. He slept in a bed every night, had all of the food he could eat, had all of the champagne he could drink, and had plenty of the excitement and adventure he so ardently craved. For Hermann Goering, life would never be so simple again.

As a cameraman-observer, Goering soon earned the nickname "the Flying Trapezist" because of his ability to hang over the side of an airplane by his toes (without a parachute) and take photographs while under enemy fire. For his courage in doing this over the French fortifications at Verdun, under a huge concentration of enemy fire, he and Loerzer were both decorated with the Iron Cross, 1st Class, by Crown Prince Wilhelm himself.

In June 1915 he was sent to Freiburg, where he underwent pilot's training, and in October joined the 5th *Jagdstaffel* (Fighter Squadron) as a fighter pilot. Three weeks later he was shot down and severely wounded in the thigh by a British Sopwith. Curiosity seekers later counted 60 bullet holes in his airplane. Had he not crashed near a German field hospital, he would have bled to death.

Goering spent his convalescent leave at his godfather's Mauterdorf Castle, where he fell in love with Marianne Mauser, the daughter of a local landowner, to whom he quickly proposed. Their engagement had to remain unofficial, however, because her father objected to the match. He considered Hermann a young man with no prospects except that of an early death. It certainly appeared that he was right when the 23-year-old aviator returned to the Western Front in late 1916.

His new squadron was the 26th Fighter, led by his old friend, Bruno Loerzer. Here Hermann came into his own, shooting down 17 enemy aircraft and earning command of his own squadron, the 27th Fighter. For his leadership, Goering was awarded Germany's most prestigious medal, the *Pour le Merite* ("Blue Max"), after 15 kills instead of the usual 25.

The leading German ace was Captain Baron Manfred von Richthofen, the "Red Baron," commander of the 1st *Jagdgeschwader* (Fighter Wing).

Richthofen had 80 aerial victories when he was killed in action on April 21, 1918. He was replaced by Captain Wilhelm Reinhardt, who died in a flying accident on July 3. Most people expected Lieutenant Ernst Udet, a member of the wing and Germany's leading living ace with more than 50 kills, to succeed Reinhardt. Everyone was surprised when newly promoted Captain Hermann Goering received the prestigious command.

Goering led the 1st Fighter Wing "Richthofen" exceptionally well and made a series of lifelong contacts in the process, including future generals Wolfram von Richthofen, a cousin of the "Red Baron"; Udet; Karl Bodenschatz; and Kurt-Bertram von Doering. All except Doering played significant roles in the Luftwaffe in World War II. Meanwhile, Goering ran his victory total to 22 before the armistice. He and his pilots then smashed their aircraft at Darmstadt; next Hermann joined his widowed mother at Munich, where his engagement to Fraulein Mauser quietly ended. "What have you got now to offer my daughter?" Herr Mauser wrote to Goering. The unemployed ex-officer telegraphed back a one-word reply: "Nothing." And that was the end of that.[35]

With his engagement broken, Goering became a footloose adventurer. Embittered over the fall of the monarchy, the revolution, and the Treaty of Versailles, he had a brief career in the Freikorps before deciding to leave Germany forever. He then became a barnstormer and a pilot-for-hire in Denmark and Sweden. In the winter of 1920, he flew the African explorer Count Eric von Rosen from Stockholm to his castle at Rockelstadt, on the shores of Lake Baven, in central Sweden. The weather was suicidal, and three pilots had already turned down Rosen's request, but Goering accepted at once. After getting lost and almost hitting a tree, the German aviator managed to land on the frozen lake, right under the battlements of Rosen's family castle, in a snow storm just as night was falling. Inside Goering met Karin von Kantzow, a niece of Rosen's and the wife of a Swedish officer and aristocrat. Karin was a tall, beautiful, 32-year-old brunette with vivid blue eyes who was, despite her marriage, restlessly dreaming of and (perhaps subconsciously) searching for a mythical hero with whom to share her life. She found this man in Hermann Goering. Leaving her 8-year-old son behind, she left with Hermann when he returned to Germany. They were living together in Munich (on an allowance from her husband) when Goering, now a political science student at the university, attended a Nazi Party rally, accompanied by his mistress. Here they heard a speech by the party leader, and Goering found the second and last hero of his life. The first had been his half-Jewish godfather; the second was Adolf Hitler. He joined the NSDAP immediately and, on May 23, 1923, became commander of the SA. Karin, always ready to embrace the romantic myth, became an even more fanatical Nazi than Hermann ever was.[36] To his credit, Hermann never accepted anti-Semitism as an intelligent policy, and Hitler's hate-filled tirades against the Jews often left him depressed for hours.

Another young man to join the Nazi Party at this time was Rudolf Hess, the future deputy Fuehrer. Described as "tall, lantern-jawed, and looking perpetually in need of a shave," he was the buck-toothed son of Fritz Hess, a prosperous international merchant. Rudolf was born in Alexandria, Egypt, on April 26, 1894, and lived there until he was 12; then he was sent to a boarding school at Bad Godesberg, just south of Bonn. He very much resented his nickname, "the Egyptian." Later he attended schools at Neuchatel and Hamburg and was serving a business apprenticeship at Hamburg in 1914. Like Hitler, he had a tyrannical father and a passive mother. When World War I broke out, Fritz Hess ordered his son not to enlist. To his father's consternation, Rudolf rebelled. "Now it's not the merchants, but soldiers who are giving the orders!" he snapped.[37] On August 7, 1914, four days after Germany declared war on France, young Hess joined the Imperial Army. He entered the Battle of Ypres six days after Hitler did. Hess was awarded the Iron Cross, 2nd Class and promoted to corporal for bravery at Arras, where he successfully defended a position in savage hand-to-hand fighting. He also fought at Verdun, where he was wounded in the left hand and upper arm in June 1916. After he recovered, he was sent to the Eastern Front, were he fought against the Romanians. Here, as a sergeant and acting platoon leader, he was wounded in the upper arm. He was then assigned to the List Regiment and, on the Western Front, received his most serious wound in August 1917 when a rifle bullet caught him in the left lung. After four months in the hospital and two months on convalescent leave, he was declared medically unfit for further infantry duty. Not satisfied with rear area assignments, Hess applied for pilot's school. He completed his training, was commissioned second lieutenant, and was posted to the 35th Fighter Squadron on the Western Front. He was with this unit exactly one week when the war ended.

Incidently, both Hitler and Hess recalled seeing each other when they were both members of the List Regiment, but they did not meet until after the war.

In early 1919 Hess was studying economics at the University of Munich and earning his living as a furniture salesman. Until this time he was a patriot but without particular political convictions. Now, however, he was introduced into the Thule Society by his employer and became an anti-Semite after listening to Feder, Eckart, and Rudolf von Sebottendorff, the head of the society. After the Reds took control of Munich, Hess joined the Freikorps and was wounded in the leg when the Freebooters stormed the city in May 1919. A year later, on May 10, 1920, he was introduced to Adolf Hitler by Anton Drexler and was quickly converted. He joined the NSDAP on July 1, 1920.[38]

One of the most unusual young men to join the Nazi Party was Ernst Franz Sedgwick "Putzi" Hanfstaengl, a man of mixed German-American heritage who spent World War I in the United States. His grandfather had founded one of the first and best firms specializing in the photographic reproduction of paintings and other works. The family business soon had branches in Rome, Paris, Berlin, New York, and London.

Putzi's grandfather, who was named Wilhelm Heine, fled from Germany after the Revolution of 1848 collapsed. Later he changed his name to William, became a Union general in the American Civil War, and was a pallbearer for President Abraham Lincoln in 1865. Lieutenant General John Sedgwick, a famous Union corps commander who was killed in 1864, was the cousin of Hanfstaengl's maternal grandmother.

Despite the failure of the Revolution of 1848, the family continued to maintain branches in Germany. Putzi was born in Munich in 1887 and educated at the Royal Bavarian Wilhelm-Gymnasium (high school), where his form master was Heinrich Himmler's father. Hanfstaengl was given the nickname "Putzi" ("little fellow") by a family servant, and it stuck with him, despite the fact that he grew into a very big man who stood 6'4" tall.

Putzi was chosen to take over the Fifth Avenue branch of the family business in New York City, so he was sent to Harvard for his education. A very strong young man, he was a member of Harvard's oar crew and also a gifted pianist. His friends included Theodore Roosevelt, Jr.; Walter Lippmann; T. S. Eliot; and others. He graduated from college in 1909. Disappointed at not being able to serve his fatherland in World War I, he returned to Germany in July 1921. He found that "Germany, politically speaking, was a madhouse."[39] He was soon attracted to the Nazi Party and became the unofficial court jester for Adolf Hitler, who was quite impressed with Hanfstaengl's wife, Helene. Putzi was the only truly cultured member of Hitler's inner circle, and the Fuehrer loved to listen while Hanfstaengl pounded out the more difficult passages of Wagner or Liszt with his huge hands. Hanfstaengl was much less successful in his efforts to convince Hitler that the side that allied with the United States would win the next war. Putzi's official job with the party was foreign press secretary.[40]

Julius Streicher, the principal Jew-baiter in the Nazi era and whose favorite hobby was collecting pornography, was born in Fleinhausen,

Bavaria, a small village 15 miles west of Augsburg, on February 12, 1885, the ninth child of the village schoolmaster. As a child he absorbed the predominantly anti-Semitic attitudes of his district, listening as the local priest described how the Jews bitterly opposed Christ and eventually crucified him.

Streicher followed his father into the teaching profession and, after completing a five-year course, started out as a substitute teacher in January 1904. Although his childhood was a happy one and he was brought up with a strongly Catholic background, he had trouble with local priests (who had supervisory authority over teachers in Bavaria) throughout his academic career.

He taught in various villages from 1904 to 1907 and then served a year in the Bavarian Army, where he was a disciplinary problem, had to serve company punishment, and was judged unfit for officers' training as a result. In 1909 he was in trouble again, this time for throwing a priest out of his classroom. Then he got a job in Nuremberg—an island of Protestantism in this Catholic region—and actually became a good elementary school teacher. In 1913 he married (slightly above his station); his bride was Kunigunde Roth, the daughter of a prosperous baker. She proved to be a patient and long-suffering wife, ignoring Streicher's constant infidelities and giving him two sons: Lothar (who later wrote for *Der Stuermer*), born in 1915, and Elmar, born in 1918.

When World War I began, Streicher promptly rejoined the army and found that he relished combat. He won the Iron Cross, 2nd Class on the Western Front in 1914. In 1915 he was selected for officers' training and was eventually commissioned second lieutenant of reserves. (The combination of wartime demand and heavy casualties among officers had forced the German army to lower its standards by 1915.)

Lieutenant Streicher was assigned to a machine gun company and fought in Romania (1916), Italy (1917), and France (1918), winning the Iron Cross, 1st Class in the process. When he returned home after the armistice, however, he had changed. Prior to the war, he had been a member of the Democratic Party, a moderate-right organization. Now he became more active in politics, and his views were more extreme, revolving around the idea that the Jews were a sinister, racially distinct people who were plotting to rule (or at least dominate) the world. By January 1919 Streicher was attending meetings of the anti-Semitic *Schutz und Trutz Bund* (Protection and Defense Society), and in January 1920 he established the Nuremberg branch of the *Deutschsozialistische Partei* (German Socialist Party). He was the Nuremberg delegate to the first DSP national convention in April 1920.

Streicher's most important asset to the DSP was his ability as a propagandist. He founded the *Deutsche Sozialist* newspaper in June 1920 but came under increasing fire from his party for the Jew-baiting. Unable to move the DSP in what he thought was the correct direction, he joined the *Deutsche Werkgemeinschaft* (German Working Community) in 1921 and changed the name of his newspaper to *Deutscher Voelkswille.* On its pages he accused the Jews of committing ritual murders to obtain Christian blood for their religious ceremonies, among other things. When he stated that several Nuremberg children disappeared each year because of Jewish perversions, he was brought to trial for malicious slander, convicted, and forced to pay a small fine. His relentless Jew-baiting continued, however.

As was the case with the DSP, Streicher was unable to gain a leadership position in the Werkgemeinschaft, although it also valued his ability as a propagandist. Finally recognizing that he would not be Germany's anti-Semitic savior—he had already tried to dominate two insignificant right-wing splinter groups and failed miserably—he decided to become a follower of Adolf Hitler, with whom he was highly impressed. On October 22, 1922, Streicher and 2,000 of his Franconian supporters met and established the Nuremberg branch of the NSDAP. This move solidified his position with Hitler, who remained Streicher's friend for the rest of his life.[41]

Two Balts also joined the party during this period: Dr. Erwin von Scheubner-Richter and Alfred Rosenberg. Scheubner was a shadowy adventurer who had been a spy in Turkey during the war. His "doctor" (supposedly in engineering) was suspect, as was his aristocratic "von." A bit of a clandestine "operator," he had connections with the House of Wittelsbach and with the White Russian émigrés, and he was involved in the Kapp Putsch. He was also on good terms with certain church groups and was apparently able to raise funds for the NSDAP from right-wing industrialists.

Alfred Rosenberg, the "philosopher" of the Nazi Party, was born in Reval (now Tallinn), Estonia, on January 12, 1893, the son of an Estonian mother and a Lithuanian father, both of German extraction. He received his engineer's diploma from the Riga *Technische Hochschule* (literally "technical high school," but more correctly translated in today's English as "college of technology"). He also studied architecture at the University of Moscow but fled to Paris and then to Munich after the Russian Revolution of 1917. Like Scheubner-Richter he was active in White Russian circles. He was also a member of the Thule Society, which reinforced his obsession concerning the alleged Jewish-Bolshevik conspiracy. He joined the Nazi Party in 1919 and was introduced to Hitler by Dietrich Eckart. Rosenberg impressed the Fuehrer with his seemingly vast storehouse of knowledge, especially when he reissued the *Protocols of the Elders of Zion,* a demonstrable forgery that both Rosenberg and Hitler accepted as an accurate transcript of a meeting of Jewish leaders who were plotting to rule the world. Because of Hitler's faith in Rosenberg's genius, the Baltic émigré succeeded the seriously ill Eckart as editor of the *Voelkischer Beobachter* in 1923.[42]

Hans Frank, who was born in Karlsruhe on May 23, 1900, was the son of a lawyer who had been disbarred for corruption. Frank served in the army at the end of World War I and then joined the Freikorps and fought at Munich. He was a member of the DAP before it was absorbed by the Nazi Party. Frank joined the storm troopers in September 1923, but he would achieve his greatest fame after he passed the bar exam and became a lawyer in 1926. In the next 7 years he defended the party in several hundred cases (and the Fuehrer himself in some 150 legal actions) and became the party's star lawyer and the head of its legal office in 1929.[43]

Another invaluable man in the Nazi Party at this time was Wilhelm Frick, one of Hitler's closest collaborators during his rise to power. Frick was born in Alsenz, in the Palatinate, on March 12, 1877, the son of a schoolteacher. He matriculated from a Gymnasium in Kaiserslautern and studied law from 1896 to 1901 in Goettingen, Munich, Berlin, and Heidelberg, where he received his doctorate. He had worked for the Munich police department since 1904 and became head of its political section in 1919. Here he helped Feme murderers to escape. An early convert to Nazi ideology, he was Hitler's contact man and an NSDAP spy at police headquarters.[44]

Several minor Nazis who were already members of the party at this time included Ulrich Graf and Emil Maurice, Hitler's bodyguard and bodyguard/chauffeur, respectively. Both were very loyal, but neither was particularly bright. Two minor party members who would not remain minor were Heinrich Himmler, the future chief of the SS, and Joseph "Sepp" Dietrich, a Great War tank crew member who later became commander of an SS panzer army.[45]

6 The Beer Hall Putsch

At the end of 1922, Hitler claimed that the Nazi Party had 40,000 members. This figure is probably too high, but, in the days of the inflation, there is no doubt that it was growing by hundreds every week. Hitler was further strengthened by the fact that he had formed an alliance with General Erich Ludendorff, the "national commander" in World War I and still one of the most respected figures in the Reich.

Meanwhile, a crisis was brewing between Berlin and Bavaria—one that had the potential to end in a full-scale civil war. It had been developing for some time. On August 11, 1920, the national Disarmament Law took effect, disbanding the Civil Guards, which had been established by the Freikorps. Bavaria flatly refused to comply—the first time a province had defied Berlin to this degree since the time of Bismarck. In addition (as we have seen) the political leaders in Munich exhibited a marked tendency to look the other way while assassins of Republican officials escaped. Now, with the currency on the verge of collapse, inflation out of control, and hunger everywhere, there was open talk of secession in Bavaria—the very act the French were encouraging in the occupied Rhineland. Germany was clearly threatening to disintegrate, to break up into a number of small, weak states, just as Paris wanted it to. In fact, the French were even threatening to march on Berlin if the Republic did not give up passive resistance in the Ruhr.

General Hans von Seeckt, the commander of the Reichsheer since the failure of the Kapp Putsch, believed that a further Allied advance to the east would be the end of Germany. He therefore disposed the bulk of his small but highly professional army to counter such a threat. Seeckt also became afraid that General Ritter Arnold von Moehl, the Reichsheer commander in Munich, was too pro-Bavarian, so he replaced him with General Otto von Lossow.

Lossow proved to be a very bad choice from Seeckt's point of view. The commander of the Bavarian Military District occupied a unique position in the German military hierarchy. He was not only the commander of Wehrkreis VII and the 7th Infantry Division, he was also *Landeskommandant:* the commander of the provincial forces of Bavaria as well. As such, he was subordinate to Minister-President Eugen von Knilling and his cabinet in Munich, as well as to Seeckt, Cuno, and Ebert in Berlin. Although he gave no indication of it prior to his appointment, Lossow quickly came under the control of the right-wing government of Bavaria, once he arrived in Munich.

To make matters worse, Chancellor Cuno suffered a series of minor nervous breakdowns. Totally unable to deal with his awesome responsibilities, he predictably lost a vote of confidence in the Reichstag and, on August 13, was replaced by Gustav Stresemann, who simultaneously became foreign minister.[1] The Weimar Republic had its seventh chancellor in five years.

Meanwhile, back in Munich, Adolf Hitler was in fine oratorical form. "Germany's hope lies in a Fascist dictatorship, and she is going to get it . . . ," he cried. "What Germany needs is a revolution—not reform. The printing presses must stop. . . . This can only be effected by a government not bound by republican slogans. This government must rule by force."[2]

With a single bread roll selling for 20,000,000 marks and quarts of milk selling at 300,000,000 marks each,[3] this kind of revolutionary rhetoric did not seem at all out of line.

The fact that Germany might be ripe for revolution was not only clear to Hitler; it was clear to others as well. In the fall, a military auxiliary force called the Black Reichswehr plotted to overthrow the government. General von Seeckt, however, had thoroughly infiltrated this body with his own agents (including Major Fedor von Bock, a future field marshal), so he was able to crush the rebellion with regular Reichsheer troops (at Kuestrin on September 30) before it had a chance to succeed.

The revolutionaries in Moscow also recognized that a Bolshevik uprising in Germany might well be victorious. Using diplomatic pouches, Lenin funnelled thousands of American dollars to the Communist Party in Germany, giving it tremendous purchasing power, which it used to buy support. By mid-October, it had been able to install its members in key positions in the provincial governments of Saxony and Thuringia. The Reds planned to begin their revolution in early November, but once again Seeckt learned of their plans beforehand. On October 20, with the consent of Chancellor Stresemann, he forced their hands by ordering General Alfred Mueller, the commander of Wehrkreis IV, to seize control of the Saxon government. Mueller marched in with regular army troops, but no one manned the barricades, and an attempt at a general strike fizzled. Only in "Red" Hamburg, the most Communist of all German cities, did the revolution experience some success, although it was transitory. The rebellion began at 2 A.M. on October 23, but the Reichswehr reacted quickly, and the Communists were suppressed on October 25.

Meanwhile, events in Bavaria raced to a head. Recognizing that the policy of passive resistance in the Ruhr had failed, Chancellor Stresemann ended it on September 24, 1923. This act brought howls of fury and protest from Munich. The next day six representatives of the *Kampfbund* (Battle League), a heavily armed right-wing extremist group made up mainly of veterans, met with Adolf Hitler. The Fuehrer was in peak form that day, and by the end of the meeting, most of them were actually crying. Overwhelmed by Hitler's emotional appeal, they named him political leader of the Kampfbund. Captain Ernst Roehm, also in tears, decided to resign from the Reichswehr the next day, so he could serve Hitler's cause full-time.

This alliance shocked the provincial government to its core. The following day, September 26, fearing a Hitler-Ludendorff grab for power, the von Knilling cabinet issued an emergency decree and named Gustav von Kahr state commissioner and, in effect, dictator of Bavaria. Kahr's first act was to ban 14 mass meetings Hitler had scheduled for the following night.

The Berlin government knew that Kahr was a strong monarchist who wanted above all to restore the House of Wittelsbach to the Bavarian throne in Munich, under the leadership of Crown Prince Rupprecht. Stresemann therefore demanded that von Knilling revoke the emergency decree. When Knilling refused to do so, he invoked Article 48 of the constitution, which handed emergency executive powers over to Defense Minister Otto Gessler. This move, made on September 27, had the effect of making General von Seeckt the *de facto* dictator of Germany.

Hitler lost no time in provoking Seeckt. That same day the *Voelkischer Beobachter* published a vicious personal attack on Stresemann and Seeckt, pointing out that both of their wives were Jewesses and that Seeckt's wife influenced him politically. (Seeckt's wife was, in fact, half Jewish, but he was not dominated by anyone. The Nazi newspaper may have come closer to the truth when it accused Seeckt of wanting to be dictator of Germany.) In any event, Seeckt was furious at this personal attack, so he ordered General von Lossow to shut down the *Beobachter* until further notice. Instead of carrying out this order, however, Lossow met with Kahr and, in effect, asked his permission to close the Nazi publication.

Gustav von Kahr had no love for Adolf Hitler or his movement; however, he had no intention of letting Berlin shut down any newspaper in his province—not even a Nazi one. He flatly forbade Lossow to touch the *Voelkischer Beobachter*. Torn by divided loyalties, Lossow did nothing. Again outraged, General von Seeckt invited Lossow to submit his resignation. When he failed to do so, President Ebert, acting in his capacity as commander-in-chief of the Reich, relieved him of his command on October 20 and appointed Major General Baron Friedrich Kress von Kressenstein to succeed him. Lossow, however, refused to step down— in effect refusing to recognize the authority of Berlin to interfere in a Bavarian matter. Lossow had, in fact, crossed the line from insubordination to high treason, for he and Kahr were actively plotting to lead Bavaria's secession from the Weimar Republic. In preparation for this step, Kahr required every soldier in the Wehrkreis to swear a new oath of allegiance, this time to the Bavarian state alone. The nation as a whole was not mentioned.

Bavaria was now, in reality, ruled by a triumvirate of Kahr, Lossow, and Colonel Ritter Hans von Seisser, the commander of the Bavarian State Police. Rumor, conspiracy, and the political double cross was the order of the day, and no one knew what anyone else planned to do. The value of the mark was falling by as much as 60 percent a day, and the Reich was becoming more unstable politically every day. Kahr heightened the tension by sending two regiments of paramilitary troops (under Captain Hermann Ehrhardt of Freikorps fame) to the Bavaria-Thuringia border, causing many to speculate that he intended to march on Berlin, duplicating Mussolini's famous march on Rome of the year before. This prompted Seeckt to reinforce General Mueller in Thuringia and send Kahr a warning not to cross the border. Marching on Berlin was, in fact, exactly what Adolf Hitler wanted to do. Never an advocate of Bavarian secession, he wanted the forces of the right to take over all of Germany—preferably under himself. Hitler was disgusted when Kahr failed to act and obliquely warned him (Hitler) not to move out of Bavaria with his Kampfbund.

During the evening of November 6 Hitler met with Goering, Scheubner-Richter, Ludendorff, and Lieutenant Colonel Hermann Kriebel, the military leader of the Kampfbund. Also present was Dr. Friedrich Weber, commander of the Bund Oberland, a Freikorps-like organization that had several thousand members. Ernst Roehm, now commander of the *Reichskriegsflagge* (Reich War Flag), another paramilitary extremist group, was probably there as well. They decided to end the Berlin-Munich stalemate by taking over the government of Bavaria themselves. Then they would proclaim Hitler ruler of Germany and march on Berlin with all available forces. They originally planned to strike on November 11, the fifth anniversary of the armistice. Then Hitler learned that Kahr planned to hold a mass meeting at the Buergerbraeukeller (a Munich beer hall) on the evening of November 8. Fearful that Kahr might use this occasion to declare the restoration of the House of Wittelsbach and/or the independence of Bavaria, he moved the date of the *coup* forward. He would seize power in the beer hall itself and then march on Berlin.

Hitler need not have worried about von Kahr. His speech of November 8, as Hanfstaengl recalled, was "incomprehensible and boring,"[4] just a dull rehash of some of his own earlier anti-Berlin, anti-Communist remarks, made doubly dull by the fact that he read them word for word, without looking at his audience, which consisted of about 3,000 beer-guzzling Munichers.

On November 8, 1923, Hitler had the support of about 4,000 Brown-shirts (from the 55,000 members of his own party); perhaps 2,000 allies from the Kampfbund; the 200 or so men from the Reichskriegsflagge; and about 300 officer cadets and officer candidates from the Reichswehr Infantry School, led by the notorious 1st Lieutenant Gerhard Rossbach, a Freikorps adventurer who would later introduce Ernst Roehm to the world of homosexuality. Hitler also had some supporters in the military, such as 1st Lieutenant Eduard Dietl, commander of the 1st Company, 19th Infantry Regiment. His opposition was potentially much stronger: the bulk of the 7th Infantry Division; the Bavarian State Police (called the Green Police because of the color of their uniforms); and the Munich City Police (the "Blue Police"). However, Hitler was counting on the element of surprise. In Munich, a city of more than 600,000 souls, the alert of a few thousand storm troopers did not go unnoticed, but it did not cause particular alarm, either. They did not assemble until nightfall or after, which helped to camouflage their plans. The fact that several paramilitary units were attending the Reichskriegflagge party at the Loewenbraeukeller also allayed police suspicions. A few officers apparently did report this activity to police headquarters, but Inspector Wilhelm Frick, head of the political section, told them there was nothing to worry about. Also, security at the Buergerbraeukeller was very weak; Kahr wanted to project the image of a man in charge, not a commissioner who had to be protected by battalions of police. There were only about 30 Blue Police on duty at the beer hall that night: few enough for a beer-drinking crowd of 3,000; certainly not enough to prevent a *coup* attempt by several hundred veterans of the trenches.

At 7 P.M. the men of the *Stosstrupp* (Shock Troop) Adolf Hitler formed up in the bowling alley of the Torbraeu Hotel, in full battle gear. This elite formation of 100 men had been organized to serve as the Fuehrer's elite special operations unit and was the forerunner of the SS. Led by Josef Berchtold, a former army lieutenant, it existed outside the SA chain of command and was the best trained and disciplined of the Nazi paramilitary formations. In battle dress, it looked almost exactly like a Reichsheer unit, except that its men wore black caps with the skull-and-cross-bones insignia on the front.

The Stosstrupp's job on November 8 was to begin and spearhead what was to go down in history as the "Beer Hall Putsch." It began at 8:30 P.M.—exactly on schedule—with the Shock Troop rolling up to the entrance of the Buergerbraeukeller and overwhelming the 20 to 30 Blue Police on guard there. All the police knew was that 100 uniformed men, armed with machine guns and rifles with fixed bayonets, were suddenly on top of them, demanding that they surrender. They did. Inside, Kahr was still speaking, unaware of what was going on outside. Then Hermann Goering marched into the hall. He was an impressive sight: helmeted, with a pistol in one hand and a sword in the other, his Pour le Merite dangling from his neck, and his uniform covered with his many decorations. He was followed by Berchtold and his heavily armed storm troopers.

Everything happened at once. Some stood up and shouted, while others dove for cover. Women screamed, beer mugs were overturned, and pandemonium threatened to break out in the hall, as 3,000 excited voices all rose at once.

Meanwhile, Adolf Hitler mounted the podium and said something to Kahr but could not make himself heard, even though they were only two feet apart. He climbed on a chair and fired a shot into the ceiling. All noise ended abruptly.

"The national revolution has begun!" he shouted. "This hall is occupied by 600 armed men, and no one may leave. The Bavarian government and the Reich government are deposed. The Reichswehr and the State Police are marching from their barracks under the banners of the swastika!"

Almost none of this was true: Hitler was trying a bluff. Furthermore, he did not look very impressive when he said it. He was pale, sweating profusely, and his hair was falling over his forehead. He was also wearing a badly fitted cutaway morning coat, which did nothing to enhance his appearance. Some witnesses thought he was mad, and others guessed he was drunk. To Paul von Hintze, a former ambassador and admiral of the Kaiser, he merely looked ridiculous. "Poor little waiter," he thought.[5]

Hitler harshly ordered Kahr, Lossow, and Seisser to come with him. Then, as an afterthought, he personally guaranteed their safety.

"Hermann, watch your step," Putzi Hanfstaengl said to Goering. "Lossow is going to double-cross us."

"How do you know that?" the SA commander asked.

"One look at his face is enough," Hanfstaengl replied.[6]

He was right. "Put on an act!" Lossow hissed to Kahr and Seisser, just before they were hustled into a small side room that Rudolf Hess had reserved for just this purpose.

The room was bare and cold. Hitler paced up and down, waving his Browning automatic pistol and trembling, sweat pouring off of his face in spite of the temperature. He warned the three not to try to talk to each other, or they would be shot. He asked the triumvirate to forgive him for breaking an earlier promise that he would not launch a coup, but he was doing it for Germany. He then informed them that Bavaria was a springboard to Berlin and announced his appointment for the new government. He, Hitler, would be in charge of the national government. Poehner, the former police-president of Munich, would be minister-president of Bavaria, with dictatorial powers. Kahr was named provincial administrator, Ludendorff would command the national army, Lossow would be Reichswehr minister, and Seisser would be minister of police. When the triumvirate said nothing, Hitler said that he had taken this step to make it "easier for you gentlemen to make the jump" (that is, to march on Berlin). "Each of you is to take his place; if he does not, then there is no justification for his existence. You must fight with me, be victorious with me, or die with me. If the undertaking fails, I have four bullets in my pistol. Three for you, my colleagues, if you fail me. The last one is for myself," he said, pointing the pistol at his own head for dramatic effect.[7]

The three captives were still uncertain and as resentful as they dared to be; they refused to commit themselves. General von Lossow asked where Ludendorff stood on this matter. Hitler replied that the national commander was available and ordered Scheubner-Richter to fetch him immediately. He then left the trio in the unheated room, guarded by Rudolf Hess and Ulrich Graf.

Back in the main hall, trouble was brewing. Some of the 3,000 patrons were offended and getting more restless and disorderly—especially the government officials and the 70 or so Jews in the hall. Cries of "Theater!" "Mexico!" "Side Show!" and "Banana Republic!" were heard. Hesitantly, Hitler approached the podium. To Putzi Hanfstaengl, he still seemed awkward and frightened. Then he began to speak, and in moments the crowd was electrified, like so many before it.[8] Again Hitler proclaimed a new government and his intention to oust the "November criminals" in Berlin. He made a rousing speech in which he said that the next day would find a new national government in Berlin or them dead. By the time Hitler finished, the audience had been completely won over, and shouts of "Heil!" rocked the walls. The ovation also had an effect on the prisoners in the side room.

Then General Ludendorff entered the beer hall, dressed in an old tweed hunting jacket. He and Hitler disappeared into the side room and did not emerge for an hour. In the meantime, Rudolf Hess stood on a chair in front of the podium and asked for several gentlemen to go to the main entrance of the hall. The crowd grasped the implications of this request at once: The arrests were already beginning. Of the seven names Hess called, four surrendered without resistance; one tried to hide but was turned in and captured; and the other two were not present. The new prisoners included Premier von Knilling; Interior Minister Franz Schweyer; and Count Josef von Soden, advisor and chief aide to Crown Prince Rupprecht.

Meanwhile, Hitler and Ludendorff made a deal with Kahr et al. after considerable negotiation. Kahr would be named royal governor, acting for the crown prince, until the House of Wittelsbach could be formally restored. Hitler knew that this was the kind of deal Kahr could never resist, although it is extremely doubtful that Hitler ever had any intention of restoring the royal house, especially in view of the fact that he had already placed the crown prince's chief aide under arrest. In any case, Kahr returned to the hall with Hitler and announced that he was to be royal governor and that he, Lossow, and Seisser were cooperating with Hitler and the Nazis. Cheers and applause swept the hall; then the evening ended for most of those present.

Most, but not all. To get out of the hall, every member of the crowd had to stop at an SA checkpoint and show identification. Jews and members of trade unions were roughly shoved to one side; they would be detained in the hall all night long.

All over Munich, the news of the revolution was being hailed with enthusiasm. People were sick of inflation, food shortages, and the inability of the government to do anything positive or constructive. Crowds cheered SA detachments, Roehm and his followers occupied the Wehrkreis headquarters, and the police seemed to be cooperating with Hitler's forces. Back at the beer hall, however, Hitler received conflicting reports about a disturbance at the Engineer Barracks, between elements of the 7th Engineer Battalion and the Bund Oberland. Hitler decided to go see what was wrong. He left the Buergerbraeukeller shortly after 10 P.M.

This was the typical reaction for a corporal who had been a dispatch runner for four years: Go and see for yourself. Hitler, however, was now the man in charge of a revolution. He should have ordered a subordinate to handle this relatively trivial detail. By leaving his post at this critical time, Hitler unwittingly initiated a chain of events that would lead to disaster. Almost as soon as he had gone, Kahr, Lossow, and Seisser asked Ludendorff's permission to leave, having given their words of honor that they would cooperate with the putschists. Ludendorff, who wanted to go to the Wehrkreis headquarters and who felt uncomfortable holding top-ranking German officials prisoner anyway, promptly consented. Only Dr. von Scheubner-Richter objected. He was in the process of explaining that they would have no way of holding the triumvirate to their agreements if they released them without guards, but Ludendorff cut him off. "I forbid you to doubt the word of a German officer," he snapped.

Scheubner-Richter was absolutely correct. As soon as they were outside, the trio decided that promises made at gunpoint were not binding. They went to their respective stations, intent on crushing the rebellion.

The rest of the night unfolded as a series of disconnected but related events. Hitler was unable to reach the Engineer Barracks, where seven men under the command of Captain Oskar Cantzler managed to trap 400 men from the Kampfbund in the drill hall and lock them in.[9] Meanwhile, Major General Jakob von Danner, the city commandant of Munich, made a personal reconnaissance in civilian clothes. Determining that a rebellion was definitely in progress and that Wehrkreis headquarters was in enemy hands, he returned to his own HQ and started telephoning every Reichswehr unit in Bavaria, telling them to converge on Munich at once. Some time later Lossow himself arrived, and they were soon joined by Kress von Kressenstein and another general. The four commanders decided to concentrate all the army forces they could against the putsch, but to keep the news of Lossow's defection secret as long as possible to prevent Hitler and Ludendorff from organizing countermeasures. Then, deciding that their HQ was too deep inside enemy-held territory, they decided to relocate to the headquarters of the 19th Infantry Regiment. From here they set up an anti-Putsch command post (CP).

Meanwhile, Colonel Ritter von Seisser was out in the city, organizing police units for use against the putschists. Gustav von Kahr went to his headquarters, the Generalstaatskommissariat, where he was joined by Seisser around midnight. The pair were almost recaptured by Lieutenant Rossbach, who was leading 350 officers and cadets from the Infantry School, but they managed to escape because the soldiers refused to fire on a small defending detachment of Green Police, many of whom were also combat veterans. Following this near disaster, Kahr and Seisser joined Lossow at his CP about 1 A.M. United again, the triumvirate worked in harness to put down Adolf Hitler's "national revolution."

And what were the Nazis doing while the provincial government was trying to organize itself and regain control of the situation? They were busy giving a preview of what Nazi rule would be like.

On Hermann Goering's orders, Josef Berchtold and the Stosstrupp Adolf Hitler seized the *Muenchener Post,* a Social Democrat newspaper that had frequently attacked Hitler in print. The Stosstrupp attacked it in person; they broke every window in the place and demolished or burned desks, equipment, newstype—everything except the typewriters. They stole the typewriters.

Emil Maurice led a gang to the home of Erhard Auer, the leader of the Social Democrats and editor of the *Post*. Fortunately for Auer, he had wisely decided not to sleep at home that night. At a critical cabinet meeting some months before, Auer had persuaded the government not to deport Hitler, on the grounds that freedom of speech applied to everyone—even irresponsible fanatics like Hitler. A frustrated Maurice showed the Fuehrer's "gratitude" by terrorizing his family, smashing the house, and taking Auer's son-in-law as a hostage. Other armed groups roamed Jewish neighborhoods, vandalized homes, and beat the fire out of any Jew who looked at them crossly. Back in the beer hall, SA men beat their hostages at random and speculated aloud as to when they would receive permission to cut their throats.

Elsewhere, a special SA detachment seized a money printing plant that was producing 14 quadrillion marks a night (about U.S. $22,000). The smallest bill the plant printed was a 50 billion mark note, worth 8 cents in American money. With this money the Nazis planned to pay each man involved in the putsch 2 trillion marks, or $3.17. As the Nazis were about to leave, one of the plant's owners, who happened to be Jewish, stepped up to the Nazi commander and demanded a receipt for the money. Naturally, one was written out for him at once. This was Germany![10]

At 2:50 A.M. on November 9, Kahr issued a proclamation dissolving the Nazi Party, the Reichskriegsflagge, and their allies. Word of this decree, however, did not reach the rebels for hours. Meanwhile, Hitler and his cronies began to realize that something was going wrong. The NSDAP-Kampfbund forces dispatched to seize the cities of Augsburg, Regensburg, Nuremberg, and Wuerzburg had not reported in; most of these forces had, in fact, been captured or dispersed by the Reichswehr. Even now the Munich telegraph building and central telephone exchange were unguarded, but the Nazis failed to seize them. Everyone seemed to be waiting for word as to whether Kahr, Lossow, and Seisser were going to cooperate with them or not. By waiting, the putschists surrendered the initiative to the government.

Shortly after 3 A.M., Wilhelm Frick, who had been effectively neutralizing the police, was arrested in the headquarters of the Munich Police Department. Ernst Poehner, Hitler's minister-president of Bavaria, was arrested at about 4:45 A.M., when he came to police HQ to speak to

Frick. The coup was clearly coming unraveled. When dawn broke at the beer hall, the enthusiasm of the previous night had evaporated. Outside it was cold, and a light snow was falling. There was nothing to eat or drink in the hall, except beer, and some of the SA men drank it for breakfast. By now government forces had occupied the western side of the Isar River and held the western sides of the bridges. Eastern Munich belonged to the Nazis. An uneasy truce reigned between the forces on either end of the various bridges. The middle of the bridges was a no-man's land. Headquarters, Wehrkreis VII, where Ernst Roehm was, became increasingly isolated. Ludendorff, however, had ordered him to hold it at all costs, and that is exactly what the scarfaced ex-captain was determined to do.

At about 10 A.M. it became clear that Reichswehr units were converging on Munich, and that the Green and Blue Police were becoming increasingly hostile to the Nazis. No one had heard anything from Wilhelm Frick for seven hours. Around 11 A.M. Hermann Goering suggested that they retreat to Rosenheim, a NSDAP stronghold, to regroup. Colonel Kriebel, the military commander of the Kampfbund, agreed. Ludendorff, on the other hand, advocated a great march into the city. Public opinion was still on the side of the putschists, and the former national commander was certain that no soldier would fire on him. Hitler did not share Ludendorff's enthusiasm, but he did not want to abandon Munich either. Another half an hour passed with no decision. Word arrived that a detachment of 30 Green policemen had crossed the Isar and occupied the eastern side of the Ludwig Bridge, nearest the beer hall. Then, just before 11:30 A.M. news arrived that strong police and Reichswehr units were converging on the Wehrkreis HQ, and even now Roehm might be surrounded. Ludendorff reacted as if he had been stung by a bee. "Wir marschieren!" he cried. The decision had been made.

Roehm was, in fact, surrounded, and by overwhelming forces: two infantry battalions, three artillery batteries, an engineer battalion, plus several companies of *Landespolizei* (state police), trench mortar units, and armored cars. Nevertheless he refused to surrender, even when pro-Nazi Major General Ritter Franz von Epp (recently retired) arrived under a flag of truce and told him that his situation was hopeless.

At noon the NSDAP/Kampfbund units forces formed up and marched toward the Wehrkreis HQ, 12 men abreast. Hitler was in the first rank, with Ludendorff on his left and Scheubner-Richter on his right. Also in the first rank were Ulrich Graf, Hermann Kriebel, Friedrich Weber, Julius Streicher, and Hermann Goering. Gottfried Feder and Alfred Rosenberg were among those in the second rank. Rosenberg, for one, was reluctant. He considered the entire march a suicide mission. All totalled, there were between 2,000 and 3,000 in the ranks. The 30 Green Police on the east side of the river could not bring themselves to fire on Ludendorff. They were taken prisoner by Berchtold and his Stosstrupp. Across the river the marchers were greeted by large and joyous crowds who hailed them as heroes. It seemed for a brief time that Ludendorff's gamble was about to work; however, on the Residenzstrasse, just in front of the Feldherrnhalle (the Hall of Generals), they were blocked by Lieutenant Max Demmelmeyer's state police company. Seeing this, Adolf Hitler instinctively locked arms with Scheubner-Richter. Again the putschists called out that General Ludendorff was with them, but this time it had no effect; the police stood firm. Nevertheless the Nazi column marched right up to the police, and there was pushing, shoving, and bayonet fighting.

No one knows which side fired the first shot, but the police clearly fired the first volley. A regular firefight ensued, lasting 20 to 30 seconds. One of the first bullets went through Scheubner-Richter's heart, killing him instantly. He fell to the street, carrying Hitler with him. Despite the fact that Hitler was only a few feet from the policemen, he was not touched by a bullet; however, his left shoulder was dislocated when he hit the pavement. Ulrich Graf, the faithful bodyguard, threw himself on top of his master, just before the police fired bullet after bullet at the immobile Nazi leader. In all, Graf was wounded by 11 bullets. Remarkably enough, he survived.[11]

On Hitler's left, Ludendorff also threw himself to the ground. Unlike the case with Hitler, no one particularly wanted to kill him, so he got up and surrendered to the Green Police a few minutes later. His orderly, Kurt Neubauer, was not as lucky. He was fatally wounded. Hermann Goering was hit in the thigh and groin by a policeman's bullet and was critically wounded. Unable to walk, he crawled to cover behind the statue of a lion. Oskar Koerner, one of Hitler's earliest supporters and his cellmate during his first imprisonment, was among the dead, as was Theodor von der Pfordten, a court councillor. In all, 16 putschists and 4 policemen were killed. Scores of seriously wounded were rushed to the University of Munich hospital, where surgeons were busy all afternoon and into the night.

As soon as the firing stopped, Dr. Walter Schultze, the physician of the Munich SA Regiment, saw the injured Hitler staggering to the rear. He assisted him into a car, which sped away but was twice brought under machine-gun fire before it could get out of the city. In the back Dr. Schultze had Hitler take off his shirt and found a severely dislocated shoulder. Hitler was in great pain, but it was decided to take him to Putzi Hanfstaengl's house in Uffing, a village 3.5 miles south of Munich, before treating him. They arrived at 4 P.M. and found Putzi gone, but Frau Hanfstaengl took him in at once.

Back in Munich, the police were rounding up SA and Kampfbund men. They arrested 216 men; many of the rest they merely disarmed and sent home. At least 20 officers were taken into custody. Friedrich Weber of the Bund Oberland was arrested, as was Wilhelm Brueckner, the commander of the Munich SA Regiment. Dietrich Eckart was arrested, but Rudolf Hess released his captured cabinet ministers at the last moment and went into hiding. Gerhard Rossbach, Hermann Kriebel, and Gottfried Feder escaped to Austria, as did Putzi Hanfstaengl, who never dreamed that Hitler was hiding in his home.

Some SA men found Hermann Goering and carried him into the home of a Jewish furniture dealer. This man's wife, Frau Isle Ballin, had wartime experiences as a nurse. She knew who Goering was and what the Nazis stood for, but nevertheless she and her sister removed his breeches, cleaned the wounds as well as they could, and tried to stop the flow of blood with towels. Even though they knew Goering was a wanted man, they did not summon the police. That night Goering was carried to the clinic of Professor Ritter Alwin von Ach, a Nazi sympathizer; his terrible wound was still bleeding when he arrived early in the morning of November 10.

There was, of course, no escape for Ernst Roehm, who capitulated at 1:30 P.M. His men were allowed to go out the back door, but Roehm himself was taken to Stadelheim Prison, where he was charged with high treason. At 2 P.M. a large police force surrounded the Buergerbraeukeller, where the Nazi command post surrendered without resistance, and the last of the hostages were freed. At 3 P.M. that afternoon Lossow reported to Gustav von Kahr that the putsch had been suppressed. This did not give either of them much satisfaction; their careers were ruined.

At 4:20 P.M. on November 11, Colonel von Seisser's office telephoned Police Lieutenant Rudolf Belleville, the officer in charge of the Landespolizei company at Weilheim, the headquarters of the district in which Uffing was located. The order was brief: Adolf Hitler was at the Hanfstaengls; arrest him and carry him to the maximum security prison at Landsberg. Belleville did not care for this duty, because he was a Nazi sympathizer and a former gunner/observer for Rudolf Hess in the last days of the war; nevertheless, he did as he was told. Unfortunately, the order did not specify which Hanfstaengl, so a dozen heavily armed policemen with dogs showed up at Putzi's mother's villa. As a result, Hitler learned that the police were on the way some minutes before they

arrived. His reaction was one of hysteria. He pulled a pistol, began waving it wildly, and said he would shoot himself rather than submit to arrest. Helene Hanfstaengl walked up to him, grabbed the gun, and took it away from him. Obviously surprised, the weakened Hitler did not resist, but slumped, exhausted and utterly defeated, into a chair, while Helene threw his gun into a flour barrel. She then lectured him on his duty to his party and his country. Apparently her words struck a responsive cord, because Hitler jumped up and dictated one short message after another to Frau Hanfstaengl. The most important one was to Alfred Rosenberg, naming him head of the Nazi movement. This was a shrewd move on the part of Hitler, the master politician, especially under the circumstances, for it ensured that no strong and capable leader would take his place during his imprisonment. In fact, by giving this post to a dreamer and pseudo-philosopher like Rosenberg, the ex-Fuehrer virtually assured that the movement would divide and perhaps fragment. Hitler did not care; he was confident that he could always put it back together, once he got out of prison.

A few minutes later, Belleville arrived and arrested Adolf Hitler for high treason.

Hitler's depression returned as soon as he got into the police car. When he was placed in his relatively luxurious cell at Landsberg, a fortress-prison about 35 miles west of Munich, he announced that he was going to starve himself to death. "A man doesn't deserve to live who is responsible for so great a fiasco as I am,"[12] he said. This hunger strike lasted two weeks. Apparently Hans Knirsch, a member of a Nazi group in Czechoslovakia, was the man who talked Hitler out of his severe depression. He ended his strike and ate a bowl of rice. Then he began to think about the future and to plan for his trial.

On the day of his arrest, Hitler's political career appeared to be ruined. He was a laughing stock, a cartoon figure, and the subject of ridicule in the newspapers worldwide. Imagine launching a coup in a beer hall! Hitler, however, pulled off a miracle. He turned his trial into the Adolf Hitler Show: a propaganda performance of the highest order and an international platform from which he heeped scorn on Kahr, Lossow, Seisser, and the government of the Weimar Republic.

The trial began on February 26, 1924. There were 10 defendants, chief of whom were Hitler, Ludendorff, Roehm, Weber, Kriebel (who had returned from Austria and turned himself in), Frick, and Poehner. The others were Heinz Pernet, who had served as a liaison man between Ludendorff and the Nazis; Wilhelm Brueckner, the commander of the Munich SA Regiment; and Lieutenant Robert Wagner, who had played a leading part in convincing the officer cadets and candidates of the infantry school to join the Putsch. The trial was held in a "People's Court," which had a bench of two professional judges and three lay judges (two insurance salesmen and the owner of a stationery store). German courts at this time had a strong bias in favor of right-wing and voelkische defendants, and this court was no exception. It allowed Hitler to dominate the proceedings from the opening gavel. Franz Guertner, the Bavarian minister of justice and an old friend of Hitler's, had seen to it that the presiding judge, Georg Niethardt, was indulgent. Hitler was allowed to speak as much and as often as he wanted to, and his opening remarks alone consumed four hours. The lay judges, who obviously had never heard him speak before, were completely won over on the first day of the trial. "But he's a colossal fellow, this man Hitler!" one of them declared after Hitler's opening oration.[13]

None of the regular courtrooms in Munich was large enough to hold this trial—it took two police battalions just to control the crowds, and there were more than 100 newspaperpeople and correspondents present from every part of the world. The trial was held in the huge assembly hall of the Infantry School (or rather the former Infantry School; General von Seeckt was so angered by its mass defection to Hitler that he closed it down and transferred its functions to Doeberitz, a suburb of Berlin).

Hitler never made the mistake of trying to hide or deny his guilt; instead, he capitalized on it. He freely confessed to the deed but denied that it was high treason; rather, he said, he was trying to undo the treason of November 1918. He only wanted what was best for the German people, he proclaimed. Later he commented that he did not intend to make the same blunder as the Kapp putschists, who later claimed that

> they knew nothing, had intended nothing, wished nothing. That was what destroyed the bourgeois world—that they had not the courage to stand by their act . . . to step before the judge and say, "Yes, that was what we wanted to do; we wanted to destroy the state."[14]

"I alone bear the responsibility," Hitler cried in front of the representatives of virtually every newspaper in Germany. "But I am not a criminal because of that. If today I stand here as a revolutionary, it is as a revolutionary against the revolution. There is no such thing as high treason against the traitors in 1918."[15]

After whipping the audience and judges into a state of patriotic fury, he turned his oratorial guns on the prosecution's three star witnesses: Kahr, Lossow, and Seisser. If he was guilty of treason, he cried, then these three should be on the dock with him, for they were as guilty as he—they also wanted to overthrow the government in Berlin. The triumvirate squirmed uncomfortably, for everyone knew he was right: Kahr, Lossow, and Seisser had conspired against the Weimar Republic, which was why Kahr had been stripped of his office and Lossow had retired in disgrace.[16]

At several times during the trial, Hitler was asked by what right he, a man without origins, title, or education, had to govern Germany, pushing aside hundreds of experienced public figures, diplomats, presidents, ministers, and generals. Hitler confessed that he intended to do just that.

> This was not overweening or immodest of me. On the contrary, I am of the opinion that when a man knows he can do a thing, he has no right to be modest. . . . The man who is born to be a dictator is not compelled; he wills; he is not driven forward; he drives himself forward. . . . The man who feels called upon to govern a people has a duty to step forward.[17]

At various points in the trial Hitler hit all of the right themes that stirred most of the German people and made them long for revenge. He spoke of the stab-in-the-back; the November criminals; Versailles; reparations; Silesia; inflation; hunger; the Marxist rebellions; the Ruhr occupation; and how the weak, ineffective, and cowardly government in Berlin was responsible for so much misery among the German people. By the end of Hitler's final speech many of the reporters were moved to tears. "As though by an explosion, our ideas were hurled over the whole of Germany," Hitler recalled.[18]

Hitler was scheduled to be sentenced on April 1. Dozens of women arrived hours early, carrying bouquets for the Nazi leader. Several of them asked permission to bathe in the guardhouse tub Hitler had used. There is no doubt that Hitler had a strangely compelling effect on women throughout his career. They were not allowed to soak in his tub, however.

As expected from the beginning, General Ludendorff was acquitted. Brueckner, Roehm, Pernet, Wagner, and Frick were sentenced to 15 months in prison for abetting high treason but were immediately paroled by the court and released. Hitler, Weber, Kriebel, and Poehner were found guilty of high treason and sentenced to five years' imprisonment, but they would be eligible for parole in six months. The court also decreed that Hitler was not to be deported to Austria. It also noted that all of the defendants were "genuinely patriotic, noble and selfless."[19]

"Prison was no more than a comfortable interruption in the career of Adolf Hitler," Hanser wrote later. He was certainly *the* favored prisoner at Landsberg, and by the time he left, virtually the entire prison staff had been converted to National Socialism, warden and all. Prisoners were allowed to have visitors for six hours per week, but the warden could extend this time, and Hitler would sometimes receive visitors for six hours per day—including his Alsatian dog and a large number of women. Putzi Hanfstaengl commented that one could open up a fruit and flower stand and a wine shop with all of the gifts in his cell. Hitler later referred to his days in prison as "my university [education] at state expense."[20] As in his youth, he devoured books during his incarceration; and he began writing one of his own to help defray his legal expenses. His planned title was "My Four and a Half Years Struggle against Lies, Stupidity and Cowardice." His publisher later shortened it to *Mein Kampf* (My Battle). Most of it was dictated to Rudolf Hess, who had surrendered and was one of the 40 minor putschists convicted in various trials. It is part memoir, part propaganda, part historical fiction, part blueprint, and almost all disorganized and rambling. Certain passages were brilliant and others frightening, but the vast majority of it was very heavy, dull reading. It was also a warning to the world. It was ignored.

At Landsberg, Hitler drew some significant conclusions. One was that Germany did not support revolutions; he must therefore defeat democracy with the weapons of democracy. Outvoting his opponents might take longer than outshooting them, he told his followers, but the results would be more certain. He often expressed his determination to attain power legally, and he never again deviated from this course.

Within a few months of his confinement Hitler was enthusiastically recommended for parole by the warden of Landsberg, but the Bavarian Ministry of the Interior opposed it, so it was denied. Meanwhile, however, Hitler's fears of being deported were at last put to rest, because Austria revoked his citizenship and declared that they would not accept him if Germany tried to deport him. Hitler was now in reality a stateless person, but this did not bother him; he would be able to stay in Germany.

A second round of parole negotiations began in December, and this time parole was granted, largely because the three lay judges who had been so impressed with him during the trial threatened to make a public appeal for his release if he were not paroled at once. Thirteen months and one week after his arrest for high treason, he walked out of Landsberg on December 20, 1924, a free man.

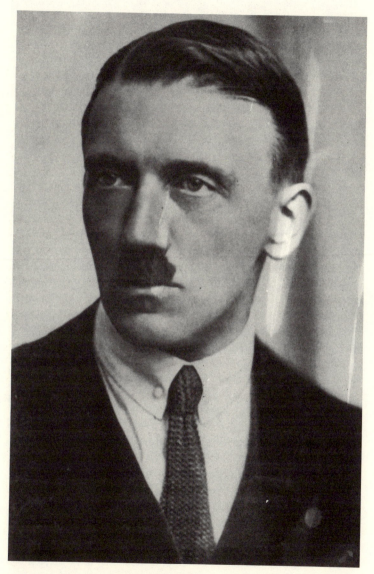

Adolf Hitler as he appeared in 1923, shortly before the Beer Hall Putsch. From a private collection

The last photograph ever taken of Hitler's jail cell at Landsburg.
After this photo was taken by Colonel Williams, the U.S. Army's
commandant of the prison in 1945, it was filled with rocks and ce-
ment and sealed. According to the plaque, Hitler occupied the cell
from November 11, 1923 until December 20, 1924. From a private
collection

Hermann Goering in the uniform of a Storm Trooper. This photograph was apparently taken in the late 1920s. From a private collection

Paul Joseph Goebbels on the campaign trail, Berlin, circa 1932.
From a private collection

Left to right: Franz Schwarz, treasurer of the Nazi Party; Rudolf Hess, deputy Fuehrer and personal secretary to Hitler; and Dr. Robert Ley, leader of the German Labor Force. This photo was taken in 1933, when all three were members of the Prussian Landtag. From a private collection

Hitler with unidentified admirers near Berchtesgaden, circa 1933. From a private collection

Hitler the picnicker, near Berchtesgaden, circa 1933. From a private collection

Hitler feeds a deer, Berchtesgaden, 1933. From a private collection

Hitler's house on the Obersalzberg in Berchtesgaden, near the Austrian border. From a private collection

Hitler with an unknown woman. The Fuehrer's amorous adventures caused more than one death in his career and caused him more than one problem during the 1920s and 1930s. Courtesy of National Archives

Eva Braum with a pair of children. This photo was taken during World War II.
Courtesy of U.S. Army Military History Institute

Adolf Hitler in the uniform of a Brownshirt. Courtesy of National Archives

7 Political Stability and the Nazi Party's Slow Growth Period, 1924–1929

While Adolf Hitler was in jail, the German national economy stabilized itself. The principal engineer of this remarkable recovery was Dr. Hjalmar Horace Greeley Schacht, who was named national currency commissioner *(Reichswaehrungskommissar)* on November 12, 1923, only three days after the collapse of the Beer Hall Putsch.

Dr. Schacht, the son of an American citizen of Danish extraction, was as brilliant as he was arrogant and ambitious. Born in Tingleff, Schleswig (now Denmark), on January 22, 1877, he was raised in the United States but matriculated from a Berlin Gymnasium; then he studied medicine in Kiel, philosophy in Berlin, political science in Munich, and economics at the University of Berlin, where he took his doctorate. He worked for the Dresdner Bank from 1903 to 1914, when he joined the staff of the economics section of the German occupation forces in Belgium. In 1916 (at the age of 39) he became director of the National Bank for Germany, which he merged with the Darmstadt Bank in 1922. Despite his monarchist sympathies, he had helped found the German Democratic Party in 1919.

Schacht realized that the only way to halt the inflation was to abandon the old currency entirely. This he did on November 15, 1923, when he issued the *Rentenmark,* which was pegged to the price of gold and had an exchange rate of 4.2 marks per U.S. dollar. The final exchange rate of the old mark was 4,200 trillion per dollar.

Schacht was aided in his efforts to return to the gold standard and to stabilize the currency by the timely demise of Havenstein, the President of the Reichsbank, who died on November 20. President Ebert promptly named Schacht to this post as well. Using his contacts and his good reputation in international financial circles, Schacht secured the public support of the extremely prestigious Bank of England, which made foreign credits available to him. Schacht did not actually have to borrow the money the British offered, but the fact that it was available boosted public confidence in his efforts and made it possible for his financial program and new currency to survive the difficult transition period.

With the economy stabilized, a new period of prosperity began in Germany. The next five years (1924–1929) constituted the golden age of the Weimar Republic, during which the causes that spawned the Nazi Party and contributed to its early successes ceased to have national importance. Ironically, Chancellor Gustav Stresemann, who had successfully dealt with crisis after crisis while simultaneously presiding over the "Rentenmark Miracle," fell victim to the parliamentary system when his government lost a vote of confidence in the Reichstag by a vote of 231 to 156. He was overthrown because the Social Democratic Party withdrew its support from him on the grounds that they felt that he had dealt more severely with the leftist revolts in Saxony and Thuringia than with the Kahr-Lossow revolt in Bavaria. By far the best chancellor in the history of the Weimar Republic, and the only one to exhibit a touch of greatness, he had been in office only three months. He was succeeded on November 30, 1923, by Dr. Wilhelm Marx.

The situation in Bavaria had also stabilized. Kahr was removed as state commissioner, Lossow retired in disgrace, and General von Seeckt outlawed the Nazi, Communist, and Racist parties on November 25. By February 28, 1924, conditions in Germany had improved to the point where the military state of emergency could be abrogated, and Seeckt's *de facto* dictatorship in Germany came to an end.[1]

In the meantime, the German situation also improved in the diplomatic sphere. French Premier Raymond Poincaré had had to raise taxes 20 percent to finance his adventures in the Ruhr. This led to his defeat in the elections of 1924 and his resignation in May. He was succeeded by the Radical Socialist Edouard Herriot, who pursued a more conciliatory policy toward Germany. As a result, Marx, Schacht, and Stresemann (who was now foreign minister) were able to negotiate a lower reparations payment rate with the French, British, and Americans. Although by no means lenient for Germany, the new arrangement was certainly better than the old. Germany would be required to pay 2.5 billion gold marks a year, beginning in 4 years. Before then she would make lower payments, to give her economy time to fully recover from military defeat and financial collapse. Dubbed the Dawes Plan, after U.S. reparations representative Charles G. Dawes, it included a loan to Germany worth 800 million marks, mainly from British and American banks, to further stabilize the German economy. The right-wing parties, led by Ludendorff and former Grand Admiral Alfred von Tirpitz, opposed the plan, because it failed to set any specific reparations total; it just required Germany to pay the victors the equivalent of $600 million a year indefinitely. Also, to ensure payment, it would give the Allies partial control of the German railroad system, plus the tax revenues on beer, alcohol, tobacco, and sugar. Nor did the plan provide for the immediate and total evacuation of the Ruhr by the French and Belgians. Despite its flaws, however, many Reichstag delegates thought it was the best deal Germany was likely to get. The Dawes Plan gained the approval of the Reichstag on August 29, 1924, and, with the signing of the London Accord the following day, became a formal agreement between the Republic and the Allies. As a result of this new rapprochement, the French and Belgians evacuated Dortmund on October 20 and reduced the size of their garrisons elsewhere. They finally evacuated the Ruhr completely in July 1925, thus further contributing to Germany's economic recovery. They did not leave the Rhineland, however, until June 30, 1930.

Meanwhile, Adolf Hitler was released from Landsberg prison on December 20, 1924, and returned to his old apartment at 41 Thierschstrasse in Munich, a free man with a new plan. He had decided to reestablish the Nazi Party, this time based upon the principle of legality. Prior to the failure of the Beer Hall Putsch, the NSDAP had been a purely revolutionary movement and, as such, had disdained participating in elections. Now Hitler was determined to secure power by legal means—via the ballot box. After consulting with Ernst Poehner, he began his political comeback on January 4, 1925, when he met with Dr. Heinrich Held, the new minister-president of Bavaria. Held greeted Hitler coldly; it is unlikely that he would have received him at all, had it not been for the appeals of Franz Guertner, the provincial minister of justice, who had protected Hitler prior to the Beer Hall Putsch and had worked for his early release afterwards. Hitler had to all but prostrate himself before Held, promising to support the authority of the state in all respects and saying that he regretted launching the putsch. His one desire was to fight Marxism, he said, and he promised to have nothing more to do with the increasingly unstable Ludendorff, who had offended the premier and many other Bavarians with his anti-Catholic remarks. In return for this performance, Hitler got what he wanted: The ban on the NSDAP was lifted and the *Voelkischer Beobachter* was allowed to resume publication. "The wild beast is checked," Held told Guertner. "We can afford to loosen the chain."[2] One wonders if Held really believed what he was saying, however, because the chain did not remain loosened very long. On February 27, 1925, Hitler made his first speech since his release from prison. Delivered at the Buergerbrauekeller in front of 4,000 followers, it was not particularly provocative, as Hitler speeches go, but it did prove that he had lost none of his overwhelming oratorical powers. At the end of two hours, he had the audience whipped into an emotional frenzy. Also, one or two of his remarks could be interpreted as anti-State and anti-democratic. The government was alarmed by Hitler's renewed popularity and seized on these comments to ban Hitler from speaking in public in Bavaria—a ban that was soon extended to every other province in Germany except Thuringia, Brunswick, and Mecklenburg. This ban remained in effect in Bavaria until May 1927 and was not lifted in Prussia (the province that contained two-thirds of Germany's population) until September 1928. As an ex-convict out on parole, Hitler dared not violate the provisions of this order. He had been deprived of his greatest asset.

As a result of the public speaking ban, Hitler devoted himself to two tasks: completing the second volume of *Mein Kampf* and reuniting the movement under his personal leadership. That summer he rented the *Haus Wachenfeld*, a villa on the Obersalzberg ("Upper Salt Mountain") in the Bavarian Alps, overlooking the small city of Berchtesgaden, several hundred feet below. He had first visited the place with Dietrich Eckart and his wife three years before; eventually Hitler would buy the villa that, after extensive rebuilding and remodeling, would become known to the world as the Berghof. Here in the summer of 1925 he dictated the second volume of *Mein Kampf* to Max Amann and to a secretary.[3] Then he set out to accomplish the second task.

During the spring elections of 1924, while Hitler was still in prison, the Nazi-Voelkisch block scored two significant triumphs. After the provincial elections it emerged as the second largest party in the Bavarian Landtag. Next, largely because of Hitler's performance at his trial, the National Socialist German Freedom Movement (NS *Deutsche Freiheitsbewegung*) polled almost 2,000,000 votes in the national elections and captured 32 seats in the Reichstag. Among those elected were Ludendorff, Feder, Roehm, Frick, and Gregor Strasser, a druggist who rapidly became the Nazi-Voelkisch leader in northern Germany. Then, to Hitler's secret delight, the movement fell apart. Rosenberg, as Hitler had foreseen, was unable to provide effective leadership, and Streicher and Hermann Esser broke away to form their own party, the *Grossdeutsch Volksgemeinschaft* (GVG), in open opposition to the more moderate Strasser. Roehm also went his own way, establishing the *Frontbann*, a paramilitary organization that he formed despite Hitler's objections. Ludendorff, chief of the Voelkisch bloc in the Reichstag, also proved to be ineffective in his new role, but he would not cooperate with or submit to the leadership of anyone else. All of these quarrels fragmented the movement. In the elections of December 1924 the Nazi-Voelkisch vote fell by more than half, from 1,918,300 to 907,300, and they were reduced to 14 seats in the Reichstag. As a result, Ludendorff and Strasser dissolved the National Sozialistische Freiheitsbewegung shortly thereafter.

Losses had been heavy, but to Hitler they were worth it: No powerful personality had emerged to challenge his leadership of the Nazi movement. Streicher and Esser remained loyal to the Fuehrer and dissolved the GVG on February 27, 1925—the night of Hitler's return speech. Amann, Feder, and Frick returned to the fold that same evening, but the rest were conspicuous by their absences. Hitler and Roehm broke over the new policy of attaining power by legal means and over the role of the *Frontbann,* as the proscribed SA was now called. Hitler insisted that it be reconstituted strictly as a political force—not as a neo-Freikorps. As a result, Roehm resigned in disgust in April and headed for South America, where he became a mercenary in Bolivia. Brueckner left the party at the same time. Meanwhile, Dietrich Eckart died; Ernst Poehner was killed in an automobile accident; Kriebel left Germany; Goering was still in exile; Scheubner-Richter was dead; and Rosenberg, who was of little use anyway, was offended by Hitler's previous lack of support and did not rejoin the movement for some time.

The Hitler-Ludendorff relationship had also soured, largely because of the general's increasingly outspoken hostility to the Catholic Church (and Christianity in general), which Hitler considered a politically foolish position to take. Their rupture became permanent after the presidential primary of 1925, in which Ludendorff received only 200,000 out of almost 27,000,000 votes cast. Incredibly, in spite of this awful showing, Ludendorff wanted to stand for election in the second primary, but Hitler and the NSDAP endorsed Hindenburg instead. This caused the final breach between the ex-corporal and the former national commander, who developed a fierce hatred for Hitler. Ludendorff, who was strongly influenced by his second wife, established the Tannenberg Bund, which advocated the formation of a new German religion, dedicated to the worship of the old Nordic pagan gods. In his last years the old general became increasingly unstable, even to the point of becoming an extreme pacifist. He lived long enough to see the despised Hitler become Fuehrer of Germany; he died in bitter loneliness in Tutzing, Bavaria, on December 20, 1937.

The presidential election of 1925 would be a significant one in the Nazi rise to power, although this fact would not become apparent for years. In a sense, like so many other events in the history of the Weimar Republic, it had its genesis in a scandal. The culprits were the Barmat brothers, Julius, Herschel, Solomon, and Isaak, who had emigrated from Poland to the Netherlands in 1907. They established an import-export business and, after the war, shipped food to the hungry Germans, whose own ports were still under the Allied blockade. The already wealthy brothers, with an ample and ready supply of foreign currency, got even richer during the inflation. After Schacht stabilized the currency, and money was tight in Germany, the Barmats acquired some 46 companies by loaning their owners money and then taking them over when they ran into financial troubles. The Barmats' holdings included banks, mills, and metalworks. The brothers, however, also spent lavishly and did not know when to stop. As a result they overextended themselves financially, and, early on New Year's Eve morning, 1924, the police arrested Julius in his elegant villa on Schwanenwerder, a wooded island on the Havel River, on the western outskirts of Berlin. Then the investigation began. It revealed that their bankruptcy involved defaults on millions of dollars, most of it borrowed from the National Post Office or the Prussian State Bank. It also revealed that politicians at all levels of the Social Democratic Party were involved—they had taken bribes from the Barmats. (Lacking the experience in corruption and shady dealings of the pre-1995 U.S. Congress, the German politicians had neglected to legalize bribery under the term "consulting fees.") Among those implicated in the scandal were former Chancellor Gustav Bauer, now an influential Reichstag delegate; Friedrich Ebert, Jr., the son of the president of the Republic; President Ebert's own secretary; members of the board of directors and other officers of the Prussian State Bank; the police president of Berlin; and members of the Social Democratic press, who had accepted thousands of dollars in gifts from the brothers. It was even discovered that President Ebert's office had issued Julius Barmat a permanent visa, so he could go in and out of Germany any time he pleased. The scandal reached such proportions that the Prussian Landtag set up a special fact-finding commission, the Barmat Committee, to investigate the scandal.

In the end, Julius Barmat was convicted and sent to prison for 11 months for bribery. The Berlin police president was dismissed, and Gustav Bauer was forced to resign from the Reichstag, his political career ruined.[4] It was never proven that President Ebert was guilty of anything except bad judgment; however, he was suffering terrible abdominal pains in early 1925 but refused to listen to his doctors' recommendations that he have surgery. "I cannot go away [from my office]," he told his old friend, Gustav Noske, on February 23. "Do you know what is happening today? In the Barmat Committee they want to establish today whether I have had sexual relations with one of my office secretaries. . . . The filth which surrounds me! Disgusting!"[5]

Five days later, at the age of 54, Fritz Ebert died of appendicitis and peritonitis. Near the end he consented to the surgery, but he had waited too long, and the doctors could not save him.

Following Ebert's death, the chief justice of the supreme court, Dr.

Walter Simon, assumed his office until a special election could be held to choose his successor.[6] At first it appeared that Defense Minister Dr. Otto Gessler, the former Lord Mayor of Nuremberg, would easily win the election; however, his candidacy was torpedoed by Foreign Minister Stresemann and Dr. Leopold von Hoesch, the ambassador to Paris, both of whom pointed out that Gessler's election would be offensive to the French. A nationalist-circulated rumor that he was having a love affair with a Berlin society woman also contributed to the collapse of Gessler's candidacy. As a result, the various political parties all nominated separate candidates. They included Prussian Premier Otto Braun of the Social Democrats; Wilhelm Marx of the Catholic Center; Dr. Karl Jarres, the mayor of Duisburg, who was endorsed by both the Nationalist and People's parties; Dr. Held of the Bavarian People's Party; General Ludendorff of the NSDAP; Premier Dr. Willy Hugo Hellpach of Baden from the Democratic Party; and Reichstag delegate Ernst Thaelmann of the Communist Party.

On the first ballot, Jarres led with 10,700,000 votes, followed by Braun with 7,800,000, Marx with 4,000,000, and Thaelmann with 1,800,000. Hellpach, Held, and Ludendorff trailed the field of major candidates with 1,500,000; 1,000,000; and 200,000 votes, respectively. Because no candidate received a majority, a second ballot was necessary.

The Weimar Republic's Presidential Election Law was borrowed from the French and contained three provisions for the second ballot: The successful candidate needed only a plurality, not a majority, to win; no candidate was eliminated, merely because he only received a few votes; and new nominations could be made, even if the nominee did not appear on the first ballot. The second ballot, then, was not a runoff in the American sense, but rather an election system designed to encourage compromises from all sides. The election procedure certainly worked as the law intended, for the top two vote-getters were quickly eliminated. The parties of the moderate left (the Social Democrats, Democrats, and Centrists) lined up behind former Chancellor Wilhelm Marx, who seemed a cinch to defeat the less-well-known Dr. Jarres in the second ballot. The parties of the right, however, proved that they could compromise as well. For their second ballot nominee, they selected Field Marshal Paul von Hindenburg. Their problem was that Paul Ludwig Hans von Beneckendorff und von Hindenburg was not the least bit interested in seeking the office.

Hindenburg was born in Posen, East Prussia (now Poznan, Poland), on October 2, 1847. Commissioned second lieutenant in the elite Prussian 3rd Foot Guards Regiment at the age of 19, he fought in the Austro-Prussian War of 1866 and distinguished himself by storming an enemy battery at the Battle of Koeniggraetz. He also fought in the Franco-Prussian War (1870–1871), joined the General Staff in 1879, and grew old in

the service of the Kaiser. He assumed command of the 4th Army in
Magdeburg in 1903 and went into retirement in 1911, three years before
World War I broke out. Recalled to the colors in 1914, he assumed command of the 8th Army and was charged with saving East Prussia from
two invading Russian armies, while Germany's other seven armies dealt
with the French and British. The German 8th Army smashed the Russians in the battles of Tannenberg and Masurian Lakes and inflicted
more than 300,000 casualties on them in the process—about ¼ of their
total mobilized strength. Czarist Russia never really recovered from this
defeat. As his divisions pushed the Russians out of Prussia and pursued
them into Poland, Hindenburg was named supreme commander of the
Eastern Front and was promoted to field marshal on November 27, 1914.
Almost overnight he became a major hero of the German people, partially because he *looked* like a field marshal: 6'5" tall, thick set, a face that
looked as if it were chiseled out of granite, close-cropped hair, and a
large curving mustache. Considered the epitome of solidness, the people
called him "der eiserne Hindenburg"—the Iron Hindenburg. After further victories in the east, the field marshal replaced General Erich von
Falkenhayn as chief of the General Staff and supreme military commander on August 29, 1916, and held this post until the end of the
war. Then, after presiding over the German withdrawal from France and
Belgium, he retired to his home at Hanover in 1919.

Basing their conclusions upon his political record, certain authors
have implied that Hindenburg was a bit stupid and a charlatan. He was
not stupid, but he was old. Already 77, he suffered from the normal
ailments associated with a lifetime of active campaigning and only
wanted to be left alone in his retirement. Furthermore, he had little experience in politics and considered himself utterly unfit for the presidency. The first conservative delegation to visit him was sent away
empty-handed. Only the heartfelt appeals of his old friend, Grand Admiral Alfred von Tirpitz, the mastermind behind the German U-boat
campaign of World War I, persuaded Hindenburg to change his mind.
Even then he would not engage in electioneering or make even one
campaign trip.

Although certainly no genius, Hindenburg possessed a certain crafti-
ness that belied his physical appearance and his popular image as a
simple soldier. He had a talent for receiving credit for other men's successes and for escaping responsibility for his own failures. The lion's
share of the credit for the victories of Tannenberg and Masurian Lakes
should have gone primarily to Hindenburg's chief of staff (Ludendorff)
and to his brilliant chief of operations, Colonel Max Hoffmann. When
defeat stared the German Army in the face in 1918, it was Ludendorff
who was dismissed, not Hindenburg. Although Hindenburg had urged
the Kaiser to abdicate, it was left to General Groener to persuade the

monarch that he must go, and Groener who received the blame for what followed. In 1918 Hindenburg recognized and admitted that the war was militarily lost. After the war Hindenburg became the leading spokesman of the "stab in the back" legend and publicly proclaimed that the German Army had never been defeated in the field. Finally, it was left to Matthias Erzberger to sign the armistice, not Hindenburg. He emerged from the war a father figure to his people, his reputation unscathed.

Hindenburg agreed to run for president on April 7. He was quickly endorsed by the People's Party, the Nationalists, and the Nazis. On April 26 he received 14,600,000 votes to 13,700,000 for Wilhelm Marx. Thaelmann, the Communist candidate, received 1,900,000 votes, and Paul von Hindenburg became president of the Weimar Republic. It is ironic to note that had the Communists withdrawn their candidate and had only half of their voters cast their ballots for the moderate ex-Chancellor Marx, he would have been elected, and there would have been no President Hindenburg to appoint Adolf Hitler chancellor in 1933. The stubborn Communists, who had no realistic chance of winning the presidency on the second ballot, were thus indirectly responsible for the election of the very conservative field marshal to the presidency—an election that was a major victory for revived militarism and later worked to the advantage of Adolf Hitler.[7]

Meanwhile, Hitler was taking his ban on public speaking much as he took his imprisonment: After a brief period of hysteria, he became philosophical and used this period as a time to reorganize and restructure his party and to purge "disloyal" elements (that is, those who refused to accept the Fuehrer Principle of unquestioned obedience to the leader). One group he definitely wanted to keep in the party, however, was the Strasser faction, which included Gregor Strasser, his brother Otto, his secretary, Dr. Paul Joseph Goebbels, plus an entire group of north German *Gauleiters* who would later achieve infamy in the second rank of Nazi rulers. They included Robert Ley of Cologne, the future chief of the Reich Labor Force; Bernhard Rust, the leader of the party in Hanover and later Nazi Minister of Education; Hans Kerrl, the future minister of Ecclesiastical Affairs; Karl Kaufmann, the future Gauleiter of Hamburg; Erich Koch, one of the most vicious Nazis who, in time, became Gauleiter of East Prussia and Reichskommissar of the Ukraine, where he was responsible for the murders of hundreds of thousands of innocent people.[8] Their leader was Gregor Strasser, an early Nazi who, at that time, was the most important man in the party after Hitler. Born in Geisenfeld, Lower Bavaria, on May 31, 1892, he fought in the war, emerging with both classes of the Iron Cross and the rank of lieutenant.

After the war, he opened a pharmacy in Landshut, Bavaria, and led a group of volunteers in the Beer Hall Putsch. During Hitler's imprisonment he had been an indefatigable organizer and worker for the Nazi cause, especially in northern Germany. He founded the first Nazi newspaper in the north, the *Berliner Arbeiteszeitung* (Berlin Workers' Paper), which was edited by his brother, Otto. Big, powerful, and with a strong personality, he stressed the anticapitalist segments of the Nazi platform and, at that time, his working-class views were more readily accepted by the north German masses than those of the more conservative Hitler.

From Hitler's point of view, the problem with Strasser and his group was that they refused to give him the unconditional obedience he demanded and that they took the term "National Socialist" seriously. Most of the Strasser people were, in fact, anti-Semitic socialists—what the SA men would call "Beefsteak Nazis": brown on the outside and red on the inside. They actually wanted to nationalize heavy industry; Hitler wanted financial contributions from the industrial magnets and, in time, to control them, but he did not want government ownership of the factories. After all, who could imagine a Nazi politician producing more and better artillery or running the munitions plants any better than Gustav Krupp?

The Strasser faction went into open rebellion on November 22, 1925. At a meeting of the northern leaders in Hanover, they voted that the property and possessions of the former royal house should be expropriated by the state. At that time Hitler was receiving 1,500 marks a month (75 percent of his income!) from the Duchess of Sachsen-Anhalt and was trying to recruit certain members of the House of Hohenzollern to his cause; he did not want the royal estates confiscated. Also, the northerners officially rejected the Fuehrer Principle. "The National Socialists are free and democratic men," Bernhard Rust declared. "They have no pope who can claim infallibility."[9] It was during this meeting that Joseph Goebbels is said to have jumped to his feet and cried: "I demand that the petty bourgeois Adolf Hitler be expelled from the National Socialist Party!"[10] This story was later spread in an unreliable account of the meeting by Otto Strasser, who published the story in 1940. Two distinguished German historians of that period, Roger Manvell and Heinrich Fraenkel, deny that Goebbels ever said any such thing,[11] and it is highly doubtful that he did. Dr. Helmut Heiber, who wrote the best biography of Goebbels this author has seen, wrote: "There seems little doubt that whatever happened, it did *not* happen like that," although he goes on to speculate that "it may well be that Goebbels did say something along this line when in a small group of friends."[12] Goebbels' diary of these days survives (he kept a journal religiously, although much of what he wrote has unfortunately been lost), and no such comments are mentioned. It makes a good story, though.

Even though Goebbels was not demanding his expulsion from the party, Hitler had a very delicate problem on his hands, for he had to suppress the Strasser faction without splitting the party, and one must admit that he handled the problem with considerable skill. The standard historic version of this meeting comes from comments that the Strassers made later and from the book Otto published. Their account goes like this. First, Hitler made the position of Gauleiter a salaried office in southern Germany. This left the south German leaders free to work solely on party business, unlike their counterparts in the north, who had to have regular jobs. Then Hitler called a party conference for February 14, 1926—a weekday—in the south German town of Bamberg. By choosing a day other than Sunday, he knew that most of Strasser's Gauleiters would be unable to attend. When Hitler and Strasser fought out the party platform in Bamberg, Hitler had a solid majority and was thus able to defeat the Strasser program point by point.

This is all pure historic nonsense. First of all, Bamberg was geographically closer to many of the northern Gaus than was Munich. Secondly, Hitler felt no need to have a solid majority in his confrontation with the Strassers. Thirdly—and most importantly—February 14, 1926, *was* a Sunday. The historians and biographers who have reported otherwise (and there are dozens of them, including some of the best people in the field) have simply accepted the Strasser version at face value and have not thought it necessary to consult a calendar. Certainly Otto's story sounds plausible; it just is not truthful. Finally, all of the important north German Nazi leaders *were* there, because Hitler *wanted* them there. What good would it do to defeat Strasser if nobody knew about it? Besides, Hitler's objective was to win over the northern leaders, and that could best be done in person, face to face. Hitler was not counting on a majority, solid or otherwise; to achieve his goals, he was relying on his own skills of oratory, debate, and persuasion to convert the rebels. In this his faith was not misplaced: He was totally successful. Strasser tried to object a number of times, but he was awkward and hesitant. Hitler was self-assured and forceful. Certainly Strasser was no match for Hitler dialectically, and he was verbally overwhelmed every time he opened his mouth. Halfway through the concave, Hitler won over Joseph Goebbels, who stood up and proclaimed that, after listening to the Fuehrer, he was convinced that he and the Strassers had been wrong, and the only proper thing to do now was to admit their mistakes and support Hitler. The north German faction was routed. Strasser was defeated on every issue: confiscation of the royal property, capitalism, the idea of gaining power legally, the Fuehrer Principle, and the role of the working class in the party.

Having crushed his opponent in front of his own people, Hitler turned on the charm in an effort to keep him in the party. "Listen, Strasser," he said, putting his arm around Gregor's shoulders, "you really mustn't go on living like a wretched official. Sell your pharmacy, draw on party funds and set yourself up properly, as a man of your worth should."[13]

Hitler's tactics worked; the breach was sealed, and the party remained unified. Hitler, however, believed in the political principle of divide and rule. He therefore decided, almost instinctively, that it was time to set up another powerful leader in the north, to split and further weaken Strasser's support and thus make it easier to keep him in line. At Bamberg he found his man: Paul Joseph Goebbels.

Joseph Goebbels, the future Reichs minister of enlightenment and propaganda, was born in Rheydt, a town in the textile district of the lower Rhineland, on October 29, 1897, the son of a manual laborer/textile worker and his wife, who was the daughter of a blacksmith. During his early childhood they lived in working-class rowhouses in Rheydt. Joseph Goebbels was apparently born with a clubfoot. (After the Second World War, members of his family gave two different versions for his deformity. One was that he had infantile paralysis about the age of four. The other was that at age seven osteomyelitis made it necessary for doctors to operate on his left thigh, and as a result his left leg failed to grow properly and was eight centimeters shorter than his right leg. It seems likely that the family was trying to explain away his handicap as something other than an inherited genetic malformation.)[14]

Goebbels' family was very supportive of their unfortunate son (he was the third of five children) and sacrificed so that he could have a good education. At home the atmosphere was one of love and harmony; however, it could not make up for his physical handicap or his sickly, puny body. Even as a man he probably never weighed more than 130 pounds. This ever-present sense of physical inferiority probably accounts for the energy and determination with which he threw himself into his studies and also explains many of his personality traits. He disliked large men, especially if they were handsome; he was a passionate woman-chaser and a whoremonger; and he was faithless, mean, suspicious, and malicious. Even his party comrades referred to him as Mephistopheles, partially because of his disordered personality and partially because the devil also had strange feet. Goebbels was a very unhappy young man. "Life is shit," he concluded in his diary.[15] More than anything else, he wanted to be a hero and to find a hero to idolize. And he wanted power. He wanted to be able to manipulate and control others, to rise above all of those men who were physically superior to himself, and to sexually possess as many beautiful women as possible. This he could accomplish only through the force of intellect, which could be obtained through education and training.

No one could ever deny that Paul Joseph Goebbels was intelligent.

He graduated at the top of his gymnasium class in 1917 and enrolled in the University of Bonn as a student of classical philology almost immediately thereafter. Within a month he changed his major to German philology. After one semester he was called up for three months' active duty as a desk soldier—his only military service—although he later encouraged the rumor that his limp was the product of his war wounds. He had, in fact, volunteered for combat duty, but the examining physician took one look at him and sent him home in tears. This inability to serve his country in time of war also left its mark on Goebbels' already scarred psyche. In any event, Goebbels returned to school and, from 1918 to 1922, restlessly pursued his studies at a whole series of universities: Bonn, Freiburg, Wuerzburg, Freiburg again, Munich, Freiburg a third time, and then Heidelberg, where he received his doctorate in literature on April 21, 1922, at the age of 24. Despite his wanderings, he completed his degree in the shortest amount of time possible, a testimony to both his brains and his intensity. Much of the money Goebbels used to pay for his studies came from interest-free loans from the Albertus Magnus Society, a Catholic organization. Later, after he was wealthy and famous, but shortly before the Nazis came to power, the Society had to sue him to get its money back.

Goebbels did not seek a job after obtaining his degree; rather, he went home to his parents, where he wrote articles, plays, and a semiautobiographic book entitled *Michael.* It is rather pathetic, for it obviously portrayed Goebbels as he would like to have been: heroic, physically masculine, a war veteran of distinction, etc. It was not published until after the Nazis came to power—and it never would have been had not Goebbels attained such prominence.

Goebbels eventually went to work at the Cologne branch of the Bank of Dresden. This job was obtained for him by his fiancée at the time. He went through several, including one who was half-Jewish. Goebbels did not become an anti-Semite until he felt it was in his interest to do so; then he became one overnight. In any case, Goebbels hated his job and quit after nine months. He applied for a position with the *Berliner Tageblatt,* a major newspaper, but was rejected. He tried to find employment as a director at various theaters, with a similar lack of success. Finally in 1924, Fritz Prang, an old school friend who had joined the Nazi Party in 1922, introduced him into the world of *voelkisch* politics, and he found employment as the editor of the *Voelkische Freiheit,* the weekly paper of the National Socialist Freedom Movement. He had found his niche in life—as a propagandist. In early 1925 he linked up with Gregor Strasser, who made him business manager of the Rhineland-North Gau of the NSDAP, headquartered in Elberfeld. At the time of the Bamberg conclave he was also editor of the *National Socialist Letters,* a biweekly Strasser publication.

Initially, Goebbels thought that Strasser might be the hero he was seeking, but this illusion was shattered when Hitler humiliated him at Bamberg. Then Hitler began to woo Goebbels. He hosted the clubfooted doctor in Munich for two days in April, where Hitler let him speak before a large crowd at the Buergerbraeuhaus. Despite his appearance, Goebbels turned out to be an excellent speaker, so the Fuehrer took him to dinner and confirmed him as co-Gauleiter of the Ruhr. Extracts from Goebbels' diary entry of April 13 reveal the success of Hitler's efforts to seduce him away from the Strasser camp. "Hitler . . . speaks for three hours. Brilliant. . . . We are moving closer. We ask. He gives brilliant replies. I love him. . . . He is a man. With this sparkling mind he can be my leader. I bow to his greatness, his political genius." [16]

Hitler completed his recruitment of Goebbels by inviting him to Berchesgarten at the end of July. "The Fuehrer gave him a thorough brainwashing," Heiber wrote, "and subjected him to all his hypnotic magnetism." [17] Goebbels was completely won over. Then Hitler offered him a new job: Gauleiter of Berlin. After thinking it over for several weeks, Goebbels accepted the post, broke his latest engagement, and headed for the capital, where the Nazi organization was in chaos.

When Goebbels arrived on November 7, 1926, the Berlin branch of the NSDAP was down to 600 members. Until that time, the people of Berlin had looked upon the Nazis as harmless cranks and malcontents, not worthy of being taken seriously. Goebbels' first goal was to get people talking about the National Socialists. In this he was completely successful, for he was a born agitator. In February 1927 he held a meeting in Wedding, a solidly Communist district of Berlin. This deliberate provocation ended in a riot, just as Goebbels intended. After that the Berliners took him seriously and began to listen to the Nazi message. Goebbels started his own newspaper, *Der Angriff (The Attack)*, in 1927, in direct competition with the Strassers' publishing house, Kampf Verlag. By now Goebbels and his former mentor were becoming bitter enemies. Despite this friction, the party made considerable gains under his stewardship, and on May 1 he was able to invite 5,000 Nazis to hear Hitler give a private address at the Clou entertainment center (the meeting was closed because Hitler was still banned from speaking in public). Goebbels, however, finally overdid it three days later. He was addressing a meeting in the Veterans' Association Hall when a heckler shouted an insult. Goebbels ordered his SA men to beat up the agitator and throw him into the street. Unfortunately, the white-haired man turned out to be a pastor of the Reformed Church. True, he was not exactly a sterling example of the men of that profession, because he had lost his position in the Nazareth Church due to a predilection for the bottle, but he was a clergyman nevertheless. As a result of the public outcry over this incident, the party was banned from conducting public meetings in Berlin and throughout Brandenburg. This was a major blow for Goebbels, for the ban lasted until April 13, 1928—five weeks before the Reichstag elections. Goebbels could not make up for lost time and the party did poorly in Berlin, receiving only 16,478 votes (1.4 percent of the ballots cast in the city).[18] Hitler nevertheless awarded Goebbels a seat in the Reichstag, via the party's national list. (Under the Republic's intricate proportional representation system, some seats were awarded on the basis of having received a sufficient number of votes in individual election districts; the rest of the seats to which a party was entitled were assigned based upon its national list.) Goebbels joked to his supporters that all the seat meant was that he would draw an extra 750 marks a month and could attend Reichstag sessions without paying the amusement tax. However, when Adolf Hitler spoke at the party's election central in Munich that evening, he did not joke, for it was clear that the National Socialist Party had suffered a major defeat.

In the election of 1928 the Nazi Party received only 810,127 votes—2.6 percent of the total (see Table 7-1). It had received 100,000 votes less than its cover-name parties had gotten in December 1924, and more than 1,000,000 less than its block had gotten in May 1924 when it captured 6 percent of the national vote. Since 1924, its representation in the Reichs-

Table 7-1
Reichstag Election of May 20, 1928 (4th Reichstag)

Party	Votes (Percentage)	Delegates
Social Democrat	9,152,979 (29.8%)	153
Catholic Center	4,657,796 (15.2%)	78
Nationalist	4,381,563 (14.2%)	73
Communist	3,264,793 (10.6%)	54
People's	2,679,703 (8.7%)	45
Democrat	1,479,374 (4.8%)	25
Nazi	810,127 (2.6%)	12
Splinter Parties	4,326,912 (14.1%)	51
Total	30,753,247	491

75.6% of those eligible voted.

Sources: Dr. Christian Gneuss, comp., *The Path to Dictatorship, 1918–1933* (New York and Washington: Frederick A. Praeger Publishers, 1967), pp. 206–7; Wilhelm Dittmann, *Das politische Deutschland vor Hitler* (Zurich and New York: Europa Verlag, 1945).

tag had declined from 32 to 12.[19] Analysis of the voting pattern, however, revealed some surprising facts. First of all, it had done very poorly in the cities—where it was best organized; where it concentrated its best speakers, its strongest efforts, and the bulk of its campaign money. In the rural districts, which the party treated as backwater areas, it had done surprisingly well. For example, in the Norderdithmarschen area of Schleswig-Holstein, the party received 18.1 percent of the vote, as opposed to 2.6 percent in Hamburg. It received only 1.6 percent of the ballots in Cologne and only 1.3 percent in the entire Ruhr district. It had done much better in the rural areas of Weser-Ens (5.2 percent), South Hanover-Brunswick (4.4 percent), Franconia (8.1 percent) and Upper Bavaria-Swabia (6.2 percent), where none of the party's major figures had spoken. The only city were the NSDAP did well was Munich, the party's headquarters, where it received 10.7 percent of the vote, but even this was a major decline from the election of May 4, 1924, when the Voelkische Bloc received 28.5 percent of the ballots.[20] (In the Beer Hall Putsch trial and after, General Ludendorff made a number of highly inflammatory anti-Catholic statements that deeply offended the members of that church. The Nazi movement did not fully recover in the Catholic areas until after Hitler came to power.)

After analyzing the election results and after considerable discussion with his subordinates, Hitler abandoned his urban focus and shifted to what Dietrich Orlow called the "rural-nationalist" plan. He redrew the boundaries of the Gaus to correspond roughly to those of the 34 Reichstag electorial districts,[21] replaced several of his "Old Fighters" (that is, veteran Nazis who had joined the party prior to the Beer Hall Putsch) with younger Gauleiters who were more-capable administrators and campaign managers, and gave the Gauleiters unquestioned authority over the district and local leaders.[22] To oversee the restructuring of the party and the rural-nationalist plan, Hitler named Gregor Strasser Reich Organization Leader and, in a sense, party campaign manager (although without full powers). Strasser was an administrator and organizer of unusual talent, and he soon had the party's campaign apparatus functioning like a well-oiled machine. The party was now, in fact, on the political campaign trail full-time—and would be until 1933.

Hitler (aided by Heinrich Himmler, his propaganda assistant) also reorganized the propaganda department in accordance with the new rural-nationalist plan and sent Nazi "experts" on farming and agriculture into the towns and villages. They spoke to farmers' groups and convinced many that only the Nazi Party understood their serious financial troubles and their fears of an agricultural depression, and that only the Nazi Party could solve their problems.

A few weeks before the election of 1928, Fritz Reinhardt had set up a correspondence school for would-be party speakers.[23] After the election,

Hitler institutionalized it as the School for Orators of the NSDAP. Reinhardt's instruction was as simple as it was highly effective. The student would memorize standard speeches, practice them in front of a mirror, write his own speeches (which were corrected by Reinhardt), and then prepare answers for questions members of the audience might ask. These mass-produced, unpaid speakers concentrated their efforts at the local level, thus demonstrating the party's concern for the villages, towns, and neighborhoods that were too small, remote, or isolated for major party speakers to visit. Although generally not polished or sophisticated, they were nevertheless highly successful, largely because of their sincerity. They gave Adolf Hitler an army of volunteer orators who would saturate Germany in the days ahead.

Above them, two other types of orators existed. The Gau speakers were those skillful enough to handle major rallies, but who lacked the prominence to attract large crowds outside their provinces. The other category—the Reich speakers—included only the best and most prominent of the NSDAP speakers. They only addressed the largest audiences at major rallies, usually in large cities.

Once the reorganization of the propaganda department was completed, Hitler handed it over to Dr. Goebbels, who also retained his post as Gauleiter of Berlin.[24] Hitler's former propaganda assistant, a slightly built, bespectacled desk worker named Heinrich Himmler—a man who looked like a born clerk—received a promotion that would someday be one of immense importance: On January 6, 1929, he was named Reichsfuehrer-SS and replaced Erhard Heiden as commander of the *Schutzstaffel* or SS—the former Stosstrupp Adolf Hitler, which had become Hitler's personal bodyguard and a highly disciplined and reliable counterweight to the undisciplined SA. In the days ahead, it would become considerably more than that.

In addition to Strasser's organization branch and propaganda department, the NSDAP had a major branch under retired Colonel Konstantin Hierl, which was charged with building up in advance cadres of administrators for the new National Socialist state. This branch consisted of several sections and subdivisions and included Dr. Otto Dietrich (press); Walter Schumann (new party cells); Walter Darre (agriculture); Hans Nieland (foreign affairs); Helmut Nicolai (ministry of the interior); Otto Wagener (economics); Hans Frank (law); Gottfried Feder (technical questions); and Walter Schulz (labor service). In addition, other organizations within the party were established or changed. For example, the Hitler Youth (which had existed since 1922) tried to broaden its appeal by changing from an SA recruiting organization into a real youth group, aimed at presenting an alternative to the "moral decay" of the Weimar

Republic and thus attracting lower-middle class parents into the NSDAP. The National Socialist Student Organization (now under Baldur von Schirach) ceased to be an isolated, revolutionary propagandist group. Now it became much more cooperative with the traditional campus groups and fraternities and sought to reach the mainstream student body with its message of fervent nationalism and anti-Semitism. In this attempt it was remarkably successful: The idealistic young people joined the party in droves. Other newly organized Nazi groups included the Order of German Women, the National Socialist Teachers' Association, and the bunds of Nazi lawyers and physicians.[25]

Meanwhile, Hitler's own dislike for paperwork and administrative detail had become a problem. He seldom visited party headquarters and could not sit at his desk for more than an hour at a time, often would not read reports, and frequently would handle his correspondence by simply ignoring it. As the party grew, this procedure became increasingly harmful, and Hitler knew it. He therefore made his devoted private secretary, Rudolf Hess, *de facto* chief of staff of the party, in charge of day-to-day party affairs, thus freeing Hitler for the all-important task of pursuing votes and political power. Of course, Hitler continued to make all of the major decisions himself and meddled in the trivial affairs of his subordinates whenever the mood struck him.

Despite the new and improved efficiency and organizational structure of the party, it still lacked one essential ingredient before it became a serious contender for political power: It lacked an issue. No longer could railing against the "November criminals" and Hitler's anti-Semitic ranting deliver support and votes. For the NSDAP, times were too good in Germany. The inflation was over; money from foreign loans was pouring in for both the business and public sectors; there were plenty of jobs; the people were prospering; and even waiters became rich, playing the stock market. Few people realized that, by accepting these large, high-interest, short-term loans, the German governments (national, provincial, municipal, and local) were heading for disaster, as were many businessmen. Among those who saw the chasm yawning before the German economy was Hjalmar Schacht, the financial genius most responsible for ending the inflation. When his warnings were ignored, Schacht resigned, but the borrow-and-spend spree continued.[26] New government and municipal buildings, parks, and theaters sprang up like mushrooms all over Germany; new social welfare programs were adopted; and the governmental policy of reckless borrowing for any conceivable purpose continued. Corporations were hardly less irresponsible than governments. They borrowed money to build new plants, factories, and assembly lines, where unionized workers were paid more than ever before. Even churches secured foreign loans to build new churches, confident that they could repay them with increased donations from their ever more prosperous congregations. Germany even borrowed foreign money to pay its reparations debt (largely because its government had spent much of its money on nonproductive projects, such as new offices, nature parks, and opera houses). Meanwhile, citing Germany's inability to pay its reparations bill (but without spelling out why), Gustav Stresemann went to The Hague in 1929 and negotiated a new reparations agreement, the so-called Young Plan. Germany regained full control of its railroads and got its reparations debt reduced from 2.5 to 2 billion marks a year, but committed itself to paying this bill for 59 more years in exchange.[27]

Many Germans did not care about the Young Plan, one way or the other, especially in the capital of the Reich. It was the Roaring Twenties, and the heyday of the Weimar Republic. Morals were loose in many places, but Berlin was especially decadent. Here little boys and girls were painted in lipstick and rouge and sent out as prostitutes. The Republican capital became a haven for sexual perverts of every taste. There were "pleasure houses," which featured nothing but old women, homosexual bathhouses, bordellos that catered to child molesters, nightclubs for lesbians, and one bathhouse that specialized in black male prostitutes. Women, dressed in leather and carrying whips, patrolled certain districts of Berlin, where they beat their customers—for a price. Beer and champagne flowed like water, and contraceptive manufacturers and clandestine abortioners grew wealthy as sexual freedom became the order of the day. Transvestite bars, cabarets, and strip joints operated in blatant openness and were even on the regularly scheduled tourist stops, while the mayor of Berlin, a Social Democrat named Gustav Boess, paid two of his friends more than $2 million for uniforms that were never delivered. When he was caught, he was forced to resign— and to pay a fine of $750. "Once we had an unsurpassed army," Klaus Mann (Thomas's son) proclaimed. "Now we have unsurpassed perversities!" Small wonder that Adolf Hitler called Berlin "the great Babylonian whore."[28] But there was nothing he could do about it yet, except bide his time.

8 The Great Depression and Political Chaos

Extremist parties such as the NSDAP rarely come to power in good economic times. For the sake of convenience, most historians date the start of the Great Depression as October 24, 1929, the day the New York Stock Exchange crashed. This date, as they know, is not strictly accurate: The depression hit the agricultural sector much earlier, both in the United States and Germany. The German peasant had never benefited from the foreign loans, and poverty and unemployment were growing in the rural areas, as the already low market prices of agricultural commodities declined. This is why the Nazi Party had done relatively well in the farming districts in the election of 1928, in spite of its lack of effort there. The Wall Street crash, however, woke up everybody. Germany's foreign indebtedness stood at between 28,500,000,000 and 30,000,000,000 (30 billion) gold marks,[1] most of it in the form of short-term loans. The foreign investers soon started calling them in, which resulted in a flow of capital out of Germany. Also, Americans and other foreigners no longer had money to purchase German exports. Many German companies could not repay their loans and were forced into bankruptcy. Others, faced with a shrinking market, cut back production, laid off workers, and closed branch plants. By the start of 1930, unemployment had jumped from about 650,000 to 1,500,000. By the end of the year it stood at 2,500,000. And this figure excludes hundreds of thousands who lost part-time jobs, farmers who lost their farms, shopkeepers who lost their shops, and students who graduated, only to lose themselves searching for jobs that no longer existed. Soon the government was having a difficult time meeting its unemployment relief obligations, which entitled workers to $17 a month. Even the workers who still had jobs had to take pay cuts. The average salary for a miner, for example, was reduced from $47 a month in 1930 to $39 a month the following year.[2] Crime rose at an alarming rate, but there was less and less to steal. In Berlin alone, a city of 4,000,000, there were 750,000 unemployed. Tent colonies sprang up on the edge of the city, populated largely by middle-class and working families who had been unable to meet their mortgages. Foreign observers were amazed by the cleanliness and orderliness of these camps, but, after all, these were Germans, and they were just exhibiting their national characteristics. The foreign visitors were also struck by the silence that hung over these camps. Inside, as Otto Friedrich wrote, "The women cooked turnips, the children played in special playgrounds, and the men sat in sullen despair." Nearby, armed peasants guarded their potato fields against incursions by desperate family men who were no longer able to feed their families.[3]

The government, of course, was unable to cope with the problem. By early 1930 its unemployment fund showed a deficit of almost $100 million, and it was unable to secure any more short-term, high-interest foreign loans. In March 1930 the last "great coalition" of the Weimar Republic collapsed, because those on the left wanted to increase the taxes of the employers and those on the right wanted to reduce unemployment payments. As a result, the Social Democrats (SPD) withdrew from the coalition, and the government of Hermann Mueller fell.[4] With him went the last truly democratic government in the history of the Weimar Republic.[5]

Mueller was succeeded by Dr. Heinrich Bruening of the Catholic Center Party.[6] President von Hindenburg hoped that he could form a majority in the Reichstag. This Bruening was unable to do so he reluctantly asked Hindenburg to invoke Article 48 of the Constitution, allowing him to rule via emergency decree, without a majority in the Reichstag. To his credit Hindenburg complied with this request only with the greatest reluctance and only because it was clear that there was no possibility of anyone forming a working majority in the fragmented, multiparty national parliament. For the next three years the aging Prussian field marshal would work toward the return of government ruling by parliamentary majority.[7]

Chancellor Bruening, meanwhile, worked out a policy of economic retrenchment that led to disaster. On the unemployment issue, he compromised by increasing taxes on employers and simultaneously cutting benefit payments to the unemployed. Unwilling (and to a large extent unable) to finance reparations payments with American loans, which were drying up at their source, Bruening sought to meet the debt with increased exports, a dramatic reduction in imports, new taxes, and an austerity program that featured massive cuts in public spending. Civil servants, for example, found their pay cut 25 percent. As a result Germany was able to both balance her budget and meet the reparations payments; also, unemployment reached unheard of levels, and Bruening became known as "the Chancellor of Hunger."

Even before the stock market crashed, Adolf Hitler was making some significant gains, aided by Alfred Hugenberg, the bigoted and domineering chief of the Nationalist Party. A former Krupp director, Hugenberg had made a fortune during the inflation and converted it into a media empire of newspapers, film companies, and news agencies. In 1929, at the age of 63, he organized a committee to defeat the Young Plan via a national plebiscite. He got the support of the Stahlhelm, the nation's largest veterans' organization; of the Pan-German League; of Dr. Schacht of the Reichsbank, one of the German delegates to the Young Committee; and of powerful and influential industrial and financial interests. What he needed now was a speaker to arouse the masses. He arranged to meet with Adolf Hitler at the Deutscher Orden, a nationalist club in Berlin. Hitler agreed to spearhead the anti-Young campaign, but at a high price: complete independence in waging the campaign, and huge financial payments that would allow him to do it. Hugenberg acceded to Hitler's demands, and the campaign began in September 1929. It was destined from the beginning to fail miserably. Hitler, however, gained immeasurably from it. The massive amounts of free publicity he and the other Nazi leaders received from the Hugenberg news agencies and newspapers made them national political figures; he put his party on a sound financial footing; he had the opportunity to prove his potential as a propagandist; and he attracted the notice of the representatives of German heavy industry and big business, who were always willing to fund pro-business parties. It is indeed ironic that Hitler gained all of this at the expense of his shortsighted political opposition, which foot the entire expense of the referendum campaign. With part of the money he received, Hitler purchased the Barlow Palace on the Briennerstrasse in Munich, which had housed the Italian embassy in the nineteenth century (when Bavaria was independent). Hitler had it remodeled and turned it into the Brown House. When it opened at the start of 1931, it was the new national headquarters of the NSDAP. Meanwhile, from October to December 1929, the party was able to score some impressive gains in the provincial and municipal elections in Baden, Luebeck, Prussia, Thuringia, Saxony, and Brunswick. Most of these gains took place at the expense of the Nationalist Party, which split over the Young Referendum and Hugenberg's high-handed leadership. In

Berlin, for example, the party's vote increased from 39,052 (1.5 percent of the total) in 1928 to 132,097 (5.7 percent of the total) in 1929—a 400 percent increase. In Saxony the Nazis became the second largest party in the provincial diet. In Thuringia, Hans Frick became provincial minister of the interior and the first Nazi to assume public office.

The anti-Young referundum was defeated at the polls at the end of December 1929 when it received the support of fewer than 6,000,000 voters. President Hindenburg signed it into law on March 13, 1930. Hitler promptly blamed the Nationalists for the defeat of the referendum, because they had failed to give it undivided support. He then broke off his alliance with them as quickly as he had made it.

To Adolf Hitler and his newly reorganized Nazi Party, the Depression had created a new political environment that they could not help but regard as a godsend. From 27,000 at the end of 1925, the number of dues-paying members rose slowly but steadily: to 49,000 in 1926; 72,000 in 1927; 108,000 in 1928; 120,000 by the summer of 1929; and 178,000 by the end of the year.[8] Then the full force of the Depression hit Germany. In July 1930 the Reichstag passed a motion nullifying Bruening's retrenchment decrees, whereupon he asked Hindenburg to dissolve the Reichstag and set new elections for September 14, 1930.

Bruening's decision to hold new elections flew in the face of all political wisdom and was a blunder of the first magnitude. How he hoped to win a parliamentary majority by advocating a severe austerity program in a time of hunger, economic depression, and massive unemployment is unclear. Perhaps he hoped that the voters would reward him for the diplomatic successes that Stresemann had achieved, such as getting Germany a seat in the League of Nations or securing an agreement from the Allies to evacuate the occupied Rhineland in 1930. On the other hand, he may have hoped that economic conditions would improve prior to the elections. If so, he was very much disappointed, because they grew worse instead. Unemployment reached the 3,000,000 mark in September 1930. Meanwhile, Hitler and his army of speakers tirelessly saturated the Reich with their propaganda, appealing to all classes to join the National Socialists. Hitler personally delivered 20 major speeches in the last 6 weeks of the campaign, and Goebbels organized an incredible 6,000 meetings nationwide. Many of the Nazis' appeals were similar to the Communists—"Freedom, Work and Bread!" was a slogan used extensively by both—but Hitler aimed his appeals at all classes except the Jews; the Reds targeted only the workers. Hitler courted the farmers by advocating a concrete program originated by Richard-Walter Darre, his agricultural advisor, but published under Hitler's own name. It called for state credits, higher tariffs on foreign produce, cheaper fertilizer, cheaper power, and reduction and remission of taxes. To the voelkisch groups, he used the anti-Semitic approach. To the workers he also offered the hope of employment. When speaking to audiences from the educated classes, he clearly avoided anti-Jewish comments but instead offered them hope for a better future. "He was learning how to appeal to the basic needs of the average German," John Toland wrote later.

> No longer was he the voelkisch fanatic, the frightening revolutionary of the Munich Putsch, but a reasonable man who sought only the welfare of the Fatherland. His "basic values and aims" were as reassuring as they were acceptable. His listeners could not possibly know that the "reasonable" words were a mask for one of the most radical programs in the history of mankind.[9]

The crudity of his Bavarian days was gone—or at least hidden. When he addressed the middle-class groups, Hitler blamed the corrupt Republic that had left them unemployed without the prospect of getting jobs. Even some of the conservatives and a number of the former elite were drawn to Hitler, who denounced the "November criminals" and offered the business and industrial classes protection from the Communist menace. Even the Kaiser's youngest son, August Wilhelm ("Auwi") and Prince Philip von Hessen, a grandson of Queen Victoria, supported Hitler.

The Nazi Party was able to unite such diverse groups under its standards because it was not really a political party at all in the American sense of the term; it was a political movement. It had few philosophical underpinnings and advocated action, not thought. The Nazis, A. J. P. Taylor wrote, "were action without thought, the union of all those who had lost their bearings and asked only a change of circumstances no matter what."[10] Into its ranks came Germans of every description: Freikorps mercenaries who never really returned from the war; officers who never found a place in civilian life; the unemployed workers; the bankrupt businessmen; the students without job prospects; and the disillusioned from every class.

The mood of many of the German people in 1930 was one of resentment. They had been through war, defeat, civil war, inflation, and now the Depression. They had lost faith in the Weimar Republic, which they regarded as the tool of dishonest, self-serving politicians. On election day, 35,000,000 Germans voted—four million more than 1928. Hitler originally hoped to win 50 or 60 seats, but his expectations increased as the campaign progressed. On election day the Nazi Party received 6,371,000 votes—more than 18 percent of the total. It increased its representation in the Reichstag from 12 seats to 107, vaulting from the ninth largest party in the Reichstag to the second party in the Reich. The Communists also gained substantially, receiving 4,592,000 votes and increasing their representation in the national parliament from 54 to 77. This meant that nearly ⅓ of the German voters had cast their ballots for extremist parties whose avowed aim was to overthrow the Republic. The big loser was the Nationalist Party, whose deputy total fell from 107 to 41. The Democratic, People's, and Economic parties also lost votes. The exact results are shown in Table 8-1.

This election proved that Hitler's shift to the rural-nationalist plan was fully justified. The Nazis' most impressive gains took place in the lower-middle-class districts of rural and Protestant northern Germany, although gains were also registered in Catholic and middle-class areas, as well as in virtually every city.

It should be noted here that one group that did not support Hitler to any important degree prior to January 1933 was big business. It is true that after the election of 1930 Hitler did receive financial contributions from industry, but only in token amounts. Most of big businesses' political contributions went to the Catholic Center Party and the nonsocialist parties of the right. To finance its election campaigns, the Nazi Party

Table 8-1
Reichstag Election of September 14, 1930
(5th Reichstag)

Party	Votes (Percentage)	Delegates
Social Democrat	8,575,244 (24.5%)	143
Nazi	6,379,672 (18.3%)	107
Center	5,185,637 (14.8%)	87
Communist	4,590,160 (13.1%)	77
Nationalist	2,457,686 (7.0%)	41
People's	1,693,878 (4.9%)	30
Democrat[1]	1,205,521 (3.4%)	20
Splinter Parties	4,868,673 (14.0%)	72
Total	34,956,471	577

82% of those eligible voted.
1. State Party after 1930.

Sources: Dr. Christian Gneuss, comp., *The Path to Dictatorship, 1918–1933* (New York and Washington: Frederick A. Praeger Publishers, 1967), pp. 206–7; Wilhelm Dittmann, *Das politische Deutschland vor Hitler* (Zurich and New York: Europa Verlag, 1945).

demanded and received financial sacrifices and contributions from its members, even if they were unemployed. For the most part the NSDAP financed itself and was broke by the end of 1932.[11]

In his landmark article, "Big Business and the Rise of Hitler," Professor Henry Ashby Turner of Yale University concludes that, as a whole, big business did not finance the Nazi Party to any significant extent during the last years of the Weimar Republic. It is true that certain industrialists (most notably Fritz Thyssen, heir to one of the great Ruhr steel corporations) did contribute to the NSDAP. "If, however," Turner writes,

> one examines the political record of big business, it quickly becomes evident that these pro-Nazis are conspicuous precisely because they were exceptions. The failure to recognize this basic fact has led to great exaggeration of their importance, as has the reliance on untrustworthy sources. . . .
>
> A number of legends about industrial support for the Nazis have been perpetuated . . . and, largely by the virtue of repetition, have come to be accepted as fact.[12]

In this context, one of the most widely cited and highly inaccurate sources for the entire Nazi era is the book *I Paid Hitler*, published under the name of Fritz Thyssen but not written or approved by him. It was written by Emery Reves, a British journalist of Hungarian origin who interviewed Thyssen in France in the spring of 1940, after the industrialist had fled Germany and denounced Hitler. Although Thyssen did see and approve a few chapters (written in French), the work was interrupted when the German Army overran France in June. Reves fled the country, but Thyssen remained until the government of Vichy France handed him over to the Nazis. He and his wife spent the rest of the war in jails or concentration camps. Meanwhile, Reves finished the book (in English), and it was published in the fall of 1941. Thyssen never got to see or approve the chapters dealing with his financial relationship with the Nazi Party. According to Dr. Turner (who compared the stenographic records of the Thyssen-Reves interviews with the original draft chapters), even that part of the book approved by Thyssen "contains numerous spurious and inaccurate statements."[13] Wolfgang Koch, another prominent historian of the Nazi era, agrees with Turner's assessment and also points out that Reves assisted Hermann Rauschning in the fabrication of the book *Hitler Speaks*.[14]

After the Second World War, it was in the political interests of the Communists to link big business and National Socialism, which led to the publication of an entire collection of highly colored and downright fictionalized accounts of the alleged Nazi–Big Business alliance, most notably by Soviet and East German historians. In fact, Hitler repeatedly sought funds from big business, but his efforts were repeatedly compromised by both the rhetoric and actions of the left wing of his own party. The basic problem was that the entrepreneurs did not seem to believe Hitler, the Fuehrer of the National Socialists, when he told them that he was not a socialist.

There were, of course, industries that did contribute to the NSDAP after they became a national political force in 1930, but these generally contributed to several other parties as well. This type of gift giving is not uncommon even in America today, where a corporation, industry, or interest group might contribute to all of the candidates in a given election, so that—no matter who wins—their influence is maintained. "On the balance," as Dr. Turner wrote, "big business money went overwhelmingly against the Nazis."[15]

Nothing of the above analysis is meant to imply that big businesses' role in the Weimar Republic was exemplary or even praiseworthy. German big business did indirectly contribute to the rise of the Third Reich but mainly through its support of reactionary political groups and figures (notably Hindenburg and Papen) and due to its failure to support the Republic rather than due to any direct financial contributions to the Nazis, at least before Hitler became the chancellor of Germany.

One organization that provided Hitler with a lot of assistance and publicity—good and bad—was the SA, whose ranks swelled during the Depression. Many of these men would never have considered joining the Nazi Party, much less the Storm Troopers, in better times. Otto Friedrich wrote:

> The economic crisis had provided Hitler with an ideal political climate of discontent and bitterness; it had also provided him with an equally basic ingredient for political success—manpower. Every week, thousands of men lost their jobs, their pay, and, no less important, their sense of self-respect. They stood in line for hours to get their semiweekly dole and then wandered through the streets or sat sullenly in some Bierstube. To these outcasts, Hitler now offered a sense of purpose and fraternity and the brown uniform of his SA. . . .
>
> They gathered in their "storm centers," which were generally the back rooms of beer halls. "There sat the unemployed," according to one chronicler, "in their coarse brown breeches and discolored yellow shirts for many hours of the day over their half-empty beer mugs; at mealtimes they were fed for a few pfennigs from a great iron kettle that simmered in the laundry room. . . . But when the

whistle blew, . . . when the squad leader cried 'Attention!' then these men rotting in inactivity sprang up, formed ranks, and stood at attention. . . . And they marched off. For wherever they might be marching, it could only be better." Day and night, the Storm Troopers tramped through the streets of Berlin, singing, shouting their slogans, looking for fights.[16]

Fight they certainly did. One Brownshirt recalled that "we made it our maxim that 'terror must be broken by terror'; furthermore, we felt that all opposition had to be stamped into the ground."[17] This they did with the greatest enthusiasm whenever possible; and, if a Communist or Reichsbanner man (that is, a member of the Social Democrat's paramilitary group) occasionally died of his injuries, they felt it was perhaps not to be regretted too greatly.

One of the main duties of the Storm Troopers was that of disrupting opponents' meetings, which they would do by starting a brawl or directing a well-aimed chair, beer mug, or table leg against the head of the opposition's main speaker, and their aim improved with practice. If they went to jail as a result of such an incident (as Adolf Hitler did in July 1923), they could rest assured that they would be welcomed back to the SA as heroes. They were instructed, however, not to start *small* brawls; only *large* ones would do. Preferably they would end in full-scale riots. The Nazis wanted people to feel that they were risking their lives (or at least their health) by attending anti-Nazi rallies and political meetings—an impression that came closer and closer to the truth from 1929 on.

If it was not possible to break up an opposition meeting by a large brawl or riot, other tactics were used. Sounding a fire alarm in a crowded hall was sometimes effective, as was an anonymous threat to kill the main speaker if he attempted to address a particular rally. Other tactics included having four or five Nazis infiltrate a meeting and, at a predetermined signal, set off tear-gas bombs. Dropping mice, rats, or small snakes down the dresses of women in attendance was another method sure to cause confusion and consternation.

The SA also had the responsibility of guarding Nazi speakers not only from physical assault and violence but against hecklers and hostile questioners. If a questioner became too insistent or pointed, Dr. Goebbels instructed the party speakers to reply: "Someone seems to have gone off his rocker. You, Mr. Contemporary, you don't seem to realize that you're at a National Socialist meeting. If you have the gall to disturb the peaceful and reasonable course of the meeting once more, I'll not be able to guarantee that you will not be turned back into a usable member of the human race by a suitable head massage."

If this warning did not quiet the heckler, an SA man would immediately carry out the threat. Then, more often than not, the bleeding and unconscious dissident was carried out of the hall and thrown into the street. Finally, Goebbels instructed, one of the Nazis would ask the audience: "Would anyone else like to address the speaker?"[18]

This type of political violence was not all one-sided, of course. Frequently the Nazis were on the receiving end. One Brownshirt recalled being showered with flower pots, beer bottles, and even the contents of chamber pots.[19] Occasionally, Storm Troopers would be severely beaten. When he was giving a performance, Goebbels liked to have these "victims" sit in the front rows, accompanied by their young and appropriately concerned Nazi nurses. Early in the Nazi movement, there were not always enough injured Brownshirts to make an impression. No matter: Suitably bandaged, healthy men would serve just as well, as long as they did not forget and applaud with hands that were supposed to be broken. By 1931 this type of subterfuge was no longer necessary, because there were always plenty of SA men who really were injured to attend Nazi speeches.

What the Nazi Party really needed in the late 1920s, Dr. Goebbels decided, was a martyr. The best one they had to date was Albert Leo Schlageter, a young Freikorps veteran and idealist who engaged in sabotage against Allied occupation forces in the Ruhr. He was caught trying to blow up a train and executed by the French in Golzheim meadow on May 26, 1923. The NSDAP certainly made maximum use of Schlageter's brief association with it, and his grave became a Nazi shrine. The men who were killed by the police gunfire in Munich on November 9, 1923, were also good for propaganda mileage, Goebbels thought, but this was not good enough. What he needed was a recent victim, killed by the Communists, not by the police. He found him in Horst Wessel, the 21-year-old son of a Protestant military chaplain.

Wessel was born in Bielefeld on September 9, 1907. As a student he rebelled against his middle-class upbringing, dropped out of school, and began hanging out in flophouses and bars of the worst sort. He joined the Nazi Party in 1926 and became an SA-Sturmfuehrer (platoon leader) in the heavily Communist slum district of Friedrichshain in Berlin. He was also a very effective NSDAP speaker and even wrote a simple but catchy marching song, "Die Fahne Hoch!" ("Raise the Banners!"). The words were his, but the melody he stole from a Communist songbook. Apparently he earned his modest living as a pimp. In 1929 he fell in love with a prostitute named Erna Jaennicke and moved in with her in an apartment owned by a widow named Salm. Frau Salm had moved out, but for some reason decided to move back in. The lovers, however, refused to leave. Frau Salm lacked the legal grounds to have them evicted, but, on January 14, 1930, she came up with an alternative plan: She would ask the Communist comrades of her late husband to eject them. They replied that they would be delighted to do her this favor, and several of them, led by a highly tattooed cabinetmaker named Albrecht ("Ali") Hoehler, set out to do just that.

Unknown to his comrades or Frau Salm, Hoehler had ulterior motives. He was also a pimp and a criminal with several convictions, and he was the former procurer for Erna Jaennicke, Wessel's live-in lover. He had recently been released from his latest prison sentence, only to find Erna living with Wessel. Frau Salm let the Reds into the apartment and, when Horst opened the door to his room, Hoehler shot him right in front of his lover.

While Wessel lay seriously wounded in a Berlin hospital, Goebbels published daily bulletins on his condition in *Der Angriff*, along with highly fictionalized accounts of his career and how he came to be hovering between life and death. The propaganda wizard elevated Wessel to the status of a socialist Christ, who abandoned his family and studies to preach the Nazi gospel to the downtrodden people of the slums. His shooting, Goebbels said, was an act of pure political terrorism by a ruthless Communist gang. The German public, cleverly manipulated by this master propagandist, poured out its sympathy for the heroic idealist, so brutally struck down in the flower of his youth. Then Goebbels had a great piece of luck: Horst Wessel died of his wounds on February 23, 1930.

After delivering a touching funeral oration (which the Communists obligingly tried to break up), the Goebbels publicity machine skillfully turned the former pimp into the Nazi Party's greatest martyr. "Die Fahne Hoch," now called the Horst Wessel Song, became the official anthem of the Nazi Party and the marching song of the SA. Five years later, along with "Deutschland ueber Alles" ("Germany Above All"), it became the national anthem of Nazi Germany.

As for Ali Hoehler, he was sentenced to life imprisonment. After the Nazis came to power, he was checked out of prison by Rudolf Diels, the first chief of the Gestapo. The hard-drinking Diels was tough by any standards; he liked to end his many drinking binges by literally chewing up his beer steins. After Diels picked him up, no one ever saw Hoehler alive again. Several weeks later in Mecklenburg, some picnickers were hunting for mushrooms and discovered a hand sticking out of the ground. They had found the body of Ali Hoehler.[20]

The SA, for the most part, never accepted the rural-nationalist plan or the concept of attaining power by legal means. The views of a great many Brownshirts were verbalized by Otto Strasser, who advocated an alliance with the Communists and opposed all parliamentary and electoral activities. However, unlike his brother Gregor, Otto had no organizational skills and was not well liked within the party. When he would not accept Hitler's views, the Fuehrer expelled him from the party with no major repercussions in July 1930.[21] A month later, Hitler forced the resignation of Captain Franz Pfeffer von Salomon, the commander-in-chief of the SA, who demanded more freedom to train the SA as a core for a new German Army. Then, in late August 1930, Walter Stennes, the SA commander in Berlin and eastern Germany, called a Storm Trooper strike in that region because of a financial dispute with Goebbels, his theoretical boss. They seized the party's city headquarters, and Goebbels had to seek police protection from his own Brownshirts! Hitler personally had to make emotional appeals at various SA beer halls—were he occasionally burst into tears—before the Storm Troopers agreed to return to guard duty at Nazi meetings.

All of this activity made the Reichswehr nervous, and Hitler knew that he had to both reassure the army and bring the SA back into line. On September 1, 1930, therefore, he announced that he personally would be the new commander-in-chief of the Sturmabteilung. This move virtually left the SA without effective central leadership, under the caretaker administration of the uninspiring Otto Wagener, chief of staff since early 1930.

Hitler did not need the German Army in order to rise to power, but he knew that he could not attain office if the army opposed him. Also, Nazi relations with the generals had been bad since Roehm left the SA in 1925, and the Reichsheer even forbade the employment of Nazis as civilian workers in arsenals and supply depots. In September 1930 Hitler took advantage of the trial of three lieutenants to improve this relationship and to help discredit the Defense Minister, General Groener, at the same time.

Several months before, Lieutenants Richard Scheringer, Hans Ludin, and Hans-Friedrich Wendt of the 5th Artillery Regiment at Ulm had been arrested and charged with spreading Nazi propaganda within the army—a direct violation of military regulations. General Groener was inclined to handle the entire matter at the disciplinary level, but Lieutenant Scheringer, an ardent revolutionary, demanded a public trial. Accordingly, a week after the September 1930 elections, the three young men were arraigned before the Supreme Court at Leipzig on charges of high treason. The prosecution also accused the Nazi Party of being a revolutionary organization intent on the violent overthrow of the government. The trial began on September 23. Two days later, as previously arranged, defense attorney Hans Frank called Adolf Hitler to the witness stand.

Hitler quickly made it clear that he was there to defend the party, not the revolutionaries. His real objective was to impress the army (and especially its generals) and to assure it that the NSDAP was not a threat to them; in fact, he said, it was really quite the opposite. He stated that the SA had been set up exclusively to protect the party, not to fight or replace the Army. "I have been a soldier long enough to know that it is impossible for a party organization to fight against the disciplined forces of the army," he said.[22] Furthermore, Hitler declared, "I have always held the view that any attempt to replace the army was madness."[23] He reiterated his position that the NSDAP intended to attain power by constitutional means; then there would rise a larger, stronger German Army, but it would be created under the direction of the present Officers' Corps, not the Brownshirt leadership.

Although he gave a masterfully deceitful performance, telling the conservative senior officers exactly what they wanted to hear, his attitude was not entirely nonviolent. After the Nazis took power, he said, the "criminals of November 1918," who had so treacherously stabbed the German Army in the back, would be hauled before National Socialists courts of justice. Then, he said ominously, "heads will roll."

Hitler had once again used a highly publicized trial to make his points, and the army was duly impressed. Alfred Jodl, the chief of operations of the High Command of the Armed Forces during the Second World War, later told the tribunal at Nuremberg that Hitler's statements at Leipzig changed the attitudes of the senior officers about Hitler and his party. Even General von Seeckt (now retired) completely changed his mind about Hitler, allied with him, and publicly denounced Groener's decision to try the young officers. Their regimental commander, Colonel Ludwig Beck, a rising star in the Reichsheer, even took the witness stand on behalf of the lieutenants and, in effect, testified for them and against Groener.

By his testimony Hitler had, of course, disavowed and sacrificed the three National Socialist lieutenants for what he considered to be the good of the party. They were convicted of conspiracy to commit high treason and given a mild sentence: 18 months' fortress detention. Their reactions were varied and interesting. Lieutenant Scheringer, the ringleader, considered himself betrayed by the Fuehrer. In prison he renounced the Nazi Party and became a strong Communist. He was later on one of the death lists during the Night of the Long Knives (June 30, 1934) but managed to elude his executioners and even survived the war. Lieutenant Ludin, on the other hand, remained a fanatical Nazi and was rewarded for his fidelity with a seat in the Reichstag in 1932. Later rising to high rank in the SA and SS, he was a German minister in the puppet state of Slovakia during World War II. After the war he was executed by the Czechs.

After the Leipzig trial, Hitler announced his choice for the post of permanent chief of staff of the SA: Ernst Roehm, the former captain whom he had forced out of the party in 1925.[24] Roehm had gone to South America and served as a lieutenant colonel in the Bolivian Army, but he had returned to Germany in 1928 and had reestablished contact with the NSDAP. He was an outstanding staff officer, and his relations with the Reichswehr (at that time) were excellent. Furthermore, he was a friend of the influential General von Schleicher.

Roehm assumed command of the SA in January 1931 and immediately reorganized it along military lines into 21 districts, with an SA-Obergruppenfuehrer (General of SA) in charge of each. He set up an SA general staff and an SA officers' training school at Munich. Within 9 months, SA membership increased from 70,000 to 170,000. The SA was soon the most efficient of all party armies in Germany, and Adolf Hitler was quite satisfied, even though complaints about Roehm's homosexuality and that of the Brownshirts with which he surrounded himself did the NSDAP no good. Hitler countered the charges against Roehm with the sharp remark that the Nazi Party was "not a school to educate the daughters of the upper classes."[25] His defense of Roehm lay Hitler himself open to charges of homosexuality—charges that were absolutely false. Hitler was, in fact, not homosexual, but he was remarkably tolerant of homosexuality or of sexual deviance of any kind, as long as the person or persons in question served his purposes. He only became sickened and disgusted by their behavior when he felt the need to get rid of them, as he finally did during the "Night of the Long Knives" in the summer of 1934.

Another rift with the SA occurred in March 1931. Walter Stennes, now the SA Deputy Commander-in-Chief, East, approved of Army-Brownshirt cooperation in the eastern marchlands, both for patriotic reasons (that is, the possibility of a Polish invasion) and because it gave the SA a chance to spread its propaganda within the service. Hitler, however, forbade this cooperation for strictly political reasons. A successful Polish attack would automatically increase Nazi representation in the Reichstag by 80 to 100 delegates, he predicted. Stennes was repelled by this selfish attitude, but he did not break with Hitler until March 28, 1931. That day the Bruening government issued an emergency decree to curb political violence in the country. In keeping with his policy of legality, Hitler at once ordered all party officials and agencies to obey the decree. Stennes immediately rebelled. He denounced Bruening for issuing the decree and Hitler for obeying it. The next day, Hitler expelled him from the party. Contrary to Stennes's expectations, very few Brownshirts followed him out of the party, and he disappeared into political obscurity. Years later he turned up again in China, as commander of Chiang Kai-shek's bodyguard. Meanwhile, a few days after sacking Stennes, Hitler appointed Hermann Goering (now returned from exile and living in Berlin) to the temporary post of Higher Political Commissar East *(Politischer Kommissar Oberost)* and ordered him to purge the SA of all Stennes influences. He also named Wilhelm Loeper, the Gauleiter of Halle-Mecklenburg, to the new post of party personnel manager. Loeper, an early and bitter personal enemy of Stennes, was given the power to screen all appointments for Gauleiter, deputy Gauleiter, and provincial SA leader posts, to ensure that they were personally loyal to Hitler and committed to his policy of legality. It is significant that Ernst Roehm was left out of the process entirely.[26] In any case the Storm Troopers and their leaders were completely united behind Hitler—at least for the time being.

With the Brownshirts back in line, Hitler again turned his attention back to the political arena, where the election of 1930 had made him a national figure for the first time. He had hoped that he could attain some measure of power immediately by forming a Nazi-Center coalition, and he probably thought his requests were extremely modest: only three ministerial portfolios. Bruening, however, turned him down, so a disappointed Hitler returned to the campaign trail. Meanwhile the party bureaucracy, capably directed by party treasurer Franz Xaver Schwarz and business manager Philip Bouhler, had to hire special clerks who worked from 6 P.M. to 11 P.M. to process membership applications and applications fees.[27]

After the election of 1930, Bruening was largely discredited and real power devolved on the three men closest to President Hindenburg: Otto Meissner, the head of the chancellery; Colonel Oskar von Hindenburg, the president's son; and Lieutenant General von Schleicher, chief of the *Ministeramt* (Ministrial Office) of the Defense Ministry. Schleicher's power extended far beyond his rank or position, however. He was the real power broker in the Presidential Palace and the most influential man in the Reich.

Kurt von Schleicher was born in Brandenburg on April 7, 1882. He entered military service at the age of 18 as a *Fahnenjunker* in President Hindenburg's old regiment, the 3rd Foot Guards, where he became a close friend of Oskar von Hindenburg. He was a frequent visitor at the Hindenburg home and made contacts that would serve him well in later life. Later he attended the Kriegsakademie, where he attracted the attention of Wilhelm Groener, then an instructor at the War Academy. When Groener was named head of the Transport Section of the General Staff, he arranged to have Schleicher transferred to his command. John W. Wheeler-Bennett described him as good looking, "charming of manner and witty of speech, with no doubts as to his own capabilities, he let no opportunity slip . . . to make acquaintance with the great ones who surrounded him. . . ."[28]

Schleicher served briefly on the Eastern Front and was awarded the Iron Cross. For most of the war, however, he was a *Schreibtischoffizier*— a desk officer—and a very efficient one at that. He was Groener's adjutant at the end and played a major role in the suppression of the Communist revolutions in Berlin in 1919 and in the formation and arming of the Freikorps and Black Reichswehr. Later, as a protégé of Seeckt, he was a secret liaison officer to the General Staff of the Red Army. A dandy ladies' man and a born intriguer, he was an unscrupulous military politician who wanted to shape events and to rule behind the scenes, without having to take personal responsibility for his actions. Already Schleicher had played a role in the forced retirement of General von Seeckt (whom he could not dominate) and was a major force behind the appointments of General Groener (whom he could dominate) as defense minister and of Heinrich Bruening as chancellor. Now, in late 1930, Schleicher made his first contacts with the Nazi Party through Colonel Franz Halder, who introduced Schleicher to his friend and fellow Bavarian, Ernst Roehm, the chief-of-staff–designate of the SA.

A strange rapport developed between Schleicher, the woman chaser, and Roehm, the homosexual. What Schleicher and the Army feared more than any other possibility was a simultaneous Communist-Nazi revolt, which would have to be put down by the Reichswehr. The Army was too weak to quell a major rebellion and defend its eastern frontiers, where a Polish invasion of East Prussia and what was left of Silesia seemed to be a very real possibility. Roehm assured Schleicher that this would not happen—that Hitler really did intend to attain power by legal means—and the general believed him. Hitler's testimony in the Leipzig Trial also influenced Schleicher's thinking. As a result, on January 2, 1931—only one day after Roehm assumed command of the SA— the Army rescinded its order against employing Nazis as civilian workers. Although this gesture was of little significance in and of itself, it did indicate that the Army's attitude toward National Socialism was softening and also that the most influential member of Hindenburg's inner circle was a man who believed that it was possible to work with the Nazis. It is indeed ironic that, less than four years later, Roehm and Schleicher would die within 48 hours of each other, at the hands of Adolf Hitler's assassins.

Meanwhile, the depression continued to deepen, the unemployment lines continued to grow, and the Nazi Party continued to slowly climb the ladder to political power. In May 1931 the unemployment rate neared the 4,000,000 mark, the Creditanstalt (Austria's largest bank)

failed, and the NSDAP won more than 37 percent of the vote in the Oldenburg provincial elections. Then, on July 13, 1931, the powerful Darmstaedler und Nationalbank failed, forcing the government to close all banks temporarily. By September, Germany had 4,350,000 unemployed, and the Nazis scored another major success in the Hamburg state elections. Then, with unexpected suddenness, the wheels almost came off, and the party was shaken by a suicide, a scandal, and the near loss of its Fuehrer. These unexpected developments all centered around a woman named Geli Raubal.

9 The Suicide of Geli Raubal

When one discusses Adolf Hitler's love life, one leaves the world of fact and enters the realm of speculation. There is no documentation; Hitler did not write or talk about it; the only available sources are secondary; and many of these are suspect. We do know that his first love was a girl named Stephanie Jansten, who was a teenager in Urfahr in 1907. Young Hitler professed to Gustl Kubizek that he was in love with her, and he wrote many love poems to her but never mailed them and never approached her—he worshipped her from afar, as it were. She was seeing a lieutenant to whom she was about to become engaged; she was quite surprised many years later when she learned that she was the object of the Fuehrer's adoration.

Unrealized "calf love" of the type the future dictator experienced is not unusual in teenage boys. Hitler's love life, however, remained frustrated well into the 1920s. Even prior to the Beer Hall Putsch, when he underwent his first orientation into polite society, he never allowed himself to be paired off with one woman, even for a single night. He did, however, enjoy evenings out with groups of men, accompanied by a number of elegant women, and he liked the company of beautiful females, provided that they were not too bright. Intelligent women, generally speaking, made him nervous, although there would be occasional exceptions to this rule. Perhaps part of his sexual repression stemmed from the fact that he had only one testicle. (We know this from Soviet autopsy reports.) This physical defect should not have prevented him from functioning normally in a sexual situation, unless it created mental inhibitions, although it may have prevented him from reproducing.

Early in his career, Hitler associated a great deal with older women, the most prominent of whom were Winifred Wagner, the daughter-in-law of the musical genius, and Helene Bechstein, the wife of a famous piano manufacturer and a woman at least 20 years his senior. This has led some historians to suggest that he had a mother fixation. The real reason was probably largely monetary. Both of these women contributed heavily to his financial war chest (perhaps explaining the red Mercedes Hitler suddenly acquired in 1924) and both introduced him to wealthy businesspeople and industrialists, some of whom also contributed to the NSDAP.

There is some evidence to suggest that Hitler may have had a masochistic streak in him. In 1936, Renate Mueller, an actress whom Hitler met in 1932, allegedly told film director Adolf Ziessler that Hitler became sexually excited when he lay naked on the floor and she (also naked) kicked him repeatedly. Hitler, however, refused to see her after she took a vacation to England and spent several days with her former lover, Frank Deutsch, who was Jewish. Presumably this information was conveyed to him by the Gestapo. In any case, Renate began to take morphine and had to be confined to a sanatorium. One night she jumped out a window, an apparent suicide.[1]

After more than 50 years, it is, of course, impossible to judge how much of this story is true, if any. There are, however, strong hints that Hitler exhibited masochistic tendencies in other affairs, and sexologists report that it is not uncommon for brutal tyrants to want their women to enslave them;[2] therefore, the Renate Mueller story should not be dismissed lightly.

Apparently Hitler's first affair occurred in 1925, when he was 36 and he met 16-year-old Mitzi Reiter, who ran a boutique in Berchtesgaden with her sister, Anni. Mitzi first caught his eye while he was walking his Alsatian dog, Prinz, and she was out with her police dog. She recalled later that she would not cooperate when he first tried to kiss her; he then declared that they must not see each other again. Later, however, he seduced her, and she had visions of marriage. Hitler, however, only wanted her for a mistress, so she tried to commit suicide by hanging herself with a clothesline and was only saved because her brother-in-law happened to walk in after she had lost consciousness.[3] Hitler apparently broke off the affair after the incident, and Mitzi went on to marry a hotel owner in Seefeld. The match was not a happy one, however. In 1931 or early 1932, Hitler sent Rudolf Hess to visit her—the

Fuehrer wanted to spend a night with her. She left her husband without further ado, and she and Hitler spent a night together in Hitler's Prinz-regentenplatz apartment. "I let him do whatever he wanted with me," she recalled later.[4] Hitler promised to give her anything if she would become his mistress, but she wanted to be his wife, and this Hitler refused her. They parted company until 1934, when Hitler summoned her again; once more, however, he refused to marry her, and they never saw each other again. Mitzi divorced her husband in 1934 and married an SS officer named Kubisch in 1936. When he was killed in action in 1940, Hitler sent her 100 red roses.

Hitler's next recorded affair was with his own niece, Geli Raubal. In the summer of 1928 Hitler rented Villa Wachenfeld on the Obersalzberg for $25 a month and persuaded his half-sister, Angela Raubal,[5] to leave Vienna and keep house for him. Angela's husband (a Czech civil servant whom Hitler despised) was now dead, but she brought her two daughters with her: Angela (called "Geli") and Friedl. Geli was 17 years old, blonde, vivacious, and noted for having that kind of cheerful Viennese charm that made her exciting to men. One man she definitely did not excite was Putzi Hanfstaengl, who described her as "an empty-headed little slut" who had neither "brains nor character."[6] Hitler, however, soon fell in love with her and took her everywhere with him—even to party conferences—which caused a great deal of gossip within the NSDAP. Apparently Hitler intended to marry her, despite the fact that she was his niece. When Hitler finished the second volume of *Mein Kampf* and moved back to Munich, he took Geli with him. No longer, however, did he rent an apartment above a store on the Thierschstrasse; now he occupied a nine-room apartment covering the entire second floor of 16 Prinzregentenstrasse, in one of the more fashionable sections of Munich. One of these rooms was Geli's.

Geli Raubal's feelings about Hitler and his marriage plans are unknown; it is almost certain that they had sexual relations, but it is even more certain that Geli did not feel for Hitler what he felt for her. Putzi recalled that she "certainly never gave any impression of reciprocating Hitler's twisted tenderness."[7] In any case, Uncle Adolf was not her only lover. She was also having an affair with Emil Maurice, the SA organizer who was also Hitler's bodyguard, and there were others—apparently quite a few others. Frau Anny Winter, Hitler's housekeeper in Munich, recalled that she was "a flighty girl who tried to seduce everybody."[8] Maurice, however, was her most serious lover and "was furious one day to find her *in flagrante delicto* with a student, whom he threw out of the room . . . ," Hanfstaengl recalled; but even after that he "had no compunction about continuing to enjoy her easy favors."[9] He enjoyed them, that is, until he told Hitler that he intended to marry her. Hitler immediately threw one of his famous temper tantrums and forced them

to break off the affair. He accused Maurice of being disloyal and replaced him as chauffeur. Their relationship was never the same after
that.[10]

For her part, Geli was flattered by Hitler's attentions but was very
upset when she heard rumors that he was planning to marry Winifred
Wagner. Geli also became furious one day when she was rifling through
Hitler's pants and found a love note from Eva Braun (an assistant to
party photographer Heinrich Hoffmann), whom Hitler was taking out
on the sly. Geli became increasingly resentful of the way her jealous
uncle restricted her freedom and became more and more possessive of
her. After he forced her to break off a liaison she was having with an
Austrian artist, she decided to return to Vienna to resume her opera
studies. Hitler flatly forbade it. The next morning, September 17, 1931,
Hitler left his apartment to begin a trip to Hamburg. As he left, Geli
screamed at him from the window, causing a scene. Neighbors recalled
that she cried: "Then you won't let me go to Vienna?"

"No!" snapped Hitler.

The next morning one of the housekeepers became alarmed when she
could not open Geli's door and could not get her to answer. She telephoned Franz Schwarz and Max Amann, who summoned a locksmith.
They found Geli lying on the floor, a 6.34-caliber pistol bullet in her
heart.

All sorts of rumors and myths have sprung up about her death. One
was that Hitler personally shot her in a fit of rage. This is not true: He
was on the road with Hoffmann and Julius Schreck, his new chauffeur,
when her death took place. Their Mercedes had just left the Deutscher
Hof Hotel in Nuremberg on the morning of September 18 when Rudolf
Hess telephoned and urgently demanded to speak to Hitler. A page boy
in a taxi caught up with the Hitler party and asked him to return to the
hotel to take the call. Hitler went into a frenzy when he heard the news.
There were also rumors that Heinrich Himmler committed the murder
to eliminate an embarrassing situation for the party. This is obviously
untrue. Himmler would have never done anything like this without Hitler's approval, and, if he had been behind it, he certainly would not
have committed the murder in the Fuehrer's own apartment! In any
case both the state's attorney and the coroner made thorough investiga-
tions and both concluded that the fatal wound was self-inflicted. He
may have murdered millions of others, but Adolf Hitler did not kill Geli
Raubal.

Hitler himself was inconsolable for weeks after her death and would
not eat for days. Her room in the villa on the Obersalzberg became a
shrine and remained just as she left it. After he became ruler of Germany, Hitler had his favorite painter, Adolf Ziegler, produce several
portraits of her, and they were hung throughout the Chancellery. Flow-

ers were placed around them each year on the anniversaries of her birth and death.

Geli was buried in the Central Cemetery in Vienna. A week after her death, Hitler received a special dispensation from the Austrian government to visit her grave, where he spent an evening, weeping. Two or three days later, Hitler was en route to a Gauleiter's conference. At breakfast the following morning he refused to eat a piece of ham, stating that it was like eating a corpse. From that point on, he was a vegetarian. Except for liver dumplings, he never ate meat again.

10 Continuous Electioneering and "Cattle Trading"

Three weeks after Geli Raubal's suicide, in a meeting arranged by General von Schleicher, Adolf Hitler talked with President von Hindenburg for the first time. The would-be Fuehrer had not yet recovered from Geli's death and was visibly ill at ease in the presence of this legendary German leader who, at 6' 5", towered above the former Austrian corporal. Hitler tried to dominate the conversation and talked too much, boring Hindenburg instead of impressing him. "Make that man my chancellor?" the old Prussian snapped after the visit. "I'll make him a postmaster, and he can lick stamps with my head on them!"[1] He privately commented that he would never make Hitler chancellor. On October 13, three days after the Hindenburg-Hitler meeting, Chancellor Bruening presented the Reichstag with a new cabinet. As suggested by Schleicher, Groener became the new minister of interior (as well as of defense), and Bruening himself became the new foreign minister. He appeared to have a new lease on political life, but the Depression continued to deepen. In November the unemployment figures neared 5,000,000 and the Nazi Party triumphed in the provincial elections in Hesse, more than doubling the number of votes they received in 1930 and increasing their numbers in the provincial Diet from 1 to 27. In December, Hindenburg signed new emergency decrees that further reduced wages, prices, and interest rates while simultaneously increasing taxes. Dr. Bruening was not the man to sell this plan to the German public, who were sick of the *"Kuhhandel"* (cattle trading) and the "politics as usual" attitude of the government of the Republic. Many thought

Adolf Hitler might be the answer to their problems, and others thought that he could not be any worse; they continued to join the NSDAP in record numbers.

By January 1932 Bruening decided that it would be ill-advised for Hindenburg to run for reelection against the energetic Nazi leader, and the old marshal was ill-disposed to seeking office again in any case. Bruening, Groener, and Schleicher therefore met with Hitler and Roehm three times between January 6 and 10, in hopes of securing Reichstag approval to extend Hindenburg's present term for one or two years. During that time, Bruening said, he would be able to settle the reparations issue and press his claims for German equality in armaments. Then he promised that he would resign.

Hitler retired to the Kaiserhof, the big hotel on the Wilhelmstrasse opposite the Reichschancellery and the Presidential Palace, to consider the proposal. He was not fundamentally opposed to the idea, because, like Strasser, he was afraid that if Hindenburg did run again, he would prove to be unbeatable. On the other hand, Roehm, Goebbels, and Hugenberg (again temporarily allied with Hitler)[2] were strongly opposed, because they felt Hitler's agreement would only strengthen Bruening's hand. In the end, Hitler tried to get the best of both worlds: He wrote to Hindenburg directly, saying that he would support the president's reelection bid if he would publicly repudiate Bruening's economic decrees. This Hindenburg refused to do. As a result a presidential election was scheduled for March 13, and (predictably) the men around him convinced Hindenburg to stand after all. Hitler, however, was not sure that he wanted to run in what, in all likelihood, would be a forlorn hope. From mid-January until mid-February he toyed with the idea of supporting Ritter von Epp or Wilhelm Frick as the Nazi standard-bearer. In the end, however, he let Joseph Goebbels announce his candidacy for president of the Reich to an enthusiastic audience at the *Sportspalast* (Sports Palace) in Berlin on February 22. In allowing this announcement to be made, Hitler broke his alliance with Hugenberg and the Nationalists for the second time, because the National Party and the Stahlhelm had already announced their plans to run a candidate. Eventually they settled for Theodor Duesterberg, a colorless former lieutenant colonel and (along with Franz Seldte) the cofounder of the Stahlhelm.

Four days after Adolf Hitler's candidacy was announced, Hitler formally became a citizen of Germany when the Nazi minister of the interior of Brunswick made him a councilor of that province—a post that carried automatic citizenship with it.

Goebbels was delighted that Hitler had finally decided to run. It was his first campaign as propaganda director of the party, and he was eager to show "der Fuehrer" what he could accomplish. This was to be the first of five major political campaigns in nine months, and it was a bitter one. It was also a very strange one, for the sides seemed to be reversed. Hindenburg, the Protestant Prussian field marshal, became the symbol of the Constitution of the Weimar Republic and was supported by the Catholic Center Party, the antimilitaristic trade unions, the Social Democrats, and a host of smaller democratic parties, mostly from the moderate left. Hitler, the Austrian Catholic and former corporal, received much of his support from the Protestant north and from the conservative right. Even General von Seeckt and several members of the Royal family backed Hitler against Hindenburg. However, much of the conservative upper class (with which Hindenburg most closely identified) supported Duesterberg.

It was a vicious campaign, characterized by unbelievable energy on the part of the Nazis. Hitler himself spoke in 50 cities in the last 2 weeks alone; Goebbels made 19 major speeches in Berlin and addressed mass meetings in 9 other large cities. The NSDAP plastered the cities with tens of thousands of color posters, distributed tens of millions of pamphlets and copies of various party newspapers, and used loudspeakers on sound trucks for the first time in German political history. The most-telling charges were leveled against Duesterberg, when the Nazis revealed that his great-grandfather, Abraham Selig Duesterberg, was a Jew. A badly shaken Duesterberg swore that he had no idea that there was Jewish blood in his ancestry, but he was ruined all the same. Hindenburg himself was badly shaken when the Nazis labeled him as the candidate of "the party of the deserters" (that is, the Social Democrats). The president was upset because *he* believed the charges to be fully justified: To him, the Social Democrats *were* the party of the deserters. He never forgave Bruening for putting him in this position.

For his part, Bruening worked tirelessly for Hindenburg's reelection and even went so far as to reserve all of the time on the state-controlled radio networks for his own speakers—a move that made Hitler furious. Hindenburg himself spoke only once, in a recorded broadcast, aired on March 10. It was a brilliant speech under the circumstances: simple, straightforward, and dignified—the way the Germans expected a Prussian field marshal to speak.

On election day, Hindenburg received 18,651,497 votes to 11,339,446 for Hitler. Thaelmann, the Communist candidate, polled 4,983,341 votes (13.2 percent), as opposed to 2,557,729 for Duesterberg (6.8 percent of the total). Hindenburg, however, had gotten only 49.6 percent of the vote—just short of an absolute majority. The runoff was scheduled for April 10.

The next day, Goebbels was on the edge of despair. Hitler, however, was merely determined to try again. This time he changed his tactics. Instead of continuing to stress the misery of the people in the depths of the Depression, he tried a more positive tact, promising jobs, happiness, and prosperity if he were elected. Like most politicians, he promised things he could not possibly deliver; for example, he promised that, under his leadership, every German girl would find a husband.

This was the first "Hitler Over Germany" campaign—the first time a candidate relied heavily upon the airplane as an election tool. He flew rapidly from city to city, speaking to one mass meeting and then moving quickly to the next. The flights began on April 3, when he spoke to a quarter of a million people in four meetings in Saxony (at Dresden, Leipzig, Chemnitz, and Plaven). In the next week, he spoke in 20 different cities from East Prussia to the Ruhr, from the Baltic Sea to the Bavarian Alps. The novel campaign approach captured the imagination of many voters. As a result, Hitler received 13,418,547 votes on April 10. He had still been defeated (Hindenburg got 19,359,983, or 53 percent of the total), but he gained more than 2 million ballots, despite the fact that 1 million fewer people voted than during the first primary. Hindenburg had gained only 700,000 votes; Thaelmann lost more than 1 million, ending up with 3,706,759 votes (10.2 percent of the total). Duesterberg had dropped out after the first primary, and most of his supporters went over to Hitler or had not bothered to vote at all.

Meanwhile, state investigators in Hesse searched the home of Dr. Werner Best, a legal advisor to the Nazi Party.[3] Here they found a draft of a proclamation to be issued by the SA in the event of a Nazi election victory followed by a Communist revolt. Among other things, it called for abolition of the right to own private property and the immediate execution of anyone who opposed the Nazis. On election day the cabinet, urged on by General Groener, decided to suppress Hitler's private army as a result of the proclamation. Hindenburg did not care for the idea but was finally pursuaded to sign the decree on April 13, and it was promulgated the next day.

The Best proclamation was a major embarrassment to Hitler, who said that he knew nothing about it—and almost certainly did not. Ernst Roehm, whose SA was now 400,000 strong (and thus outnumbered the army 4 to 1) toyed with the idea of resisting, but the Fuehrer insisted that he not do so. Hitler was determined to pursue the path of legality to the end, and he had another election campaign to run.

The provincial elections of 1932 were scheduled for April 24, when 80 percent of the country went to the polls, and Hitler wanted to make another good showing. Between April 15 and 23 he spoke in 26 cities. His major target was Prussia, which had a population of 40,000,000 people: ⅔ of the population of the Reich. On election day the NSDAP garnered 36 percent of the vote (8,000,000 votes) and became the largest party in the Prussian Diet but, even with the Nationalists, were not strong enough to form a government. On the other hand, Prussian Premier Otto Braun's Social Democrat/Catholic Center coalition[4] could no longer form a government without Nazi support, either. As a result, the government of Germany's largest province was deadlocked.

After this campaign, the Nazi Party was nearly exhausted, physically and financially, and even Goebbels was ready to concede that it needed a rest from the constant strain of campaigning. Even though "it made him puke," he wrote an editorial in favor of adopting a conciliatory attitude and entering into negotiations with other parties.[5]

In fact, these negotiations were already secretly going on. The man behind them was Lieutenant General Kurt von Schleicher, the power behind the throne in Hindenburg's Presidential Palace. As he had already told Roehm and the SA, Schleicher had decided that both Groener and Bruening had been disappointments to him and therefore had to be forced out of office. The decision to ruin Groener was a particularly underhanded one, even by Schleicher's standards, because the general had always regarded him almost as an adopted son and had largely been responsible for his advancement. Groener, however, had disregarded Schleicher's advice when he banned the SA and SS; therefore, he had proven himself to be an insufficiently pliant tool and had to go.

After April 10 a malicious whispering campaign began, based upon information supplied by Schleicher. The chief of the ministerial office personally told Hindenburg that Groener had disgraced the army, because his new wife had had a child only five months after their wedding day. The president was shocked to learn that the Officers' Corps had nicknamed the baby "Nurmi," after the Olympic runner from Finland.

The trap was sprung on May 10, when Hermann Goering delivered a particularly violent attack against the defense minister in the Reichstag. Groener, who was seriously ill with diabetes at the time, rose to defend himself, only to be met by a torrent of abuse from the Nazis. He had barely sat down when Schleicher and his crony, General Kurt von Hammerstein, the commander-in-chief of the Reichsheer, informed him that he no longer had the confidence of the army. Bruening alone defended Groener, but he needed the support of Hindenburg. When this was denied to him, Wilhelm Groener submitted his resignation on May 13. The loss of this former Quartermaster-General was a major blow to the government, for he was the only senior officer of stature who had honestly supported the Weimar Republic and had worked to bridge the gap between military traditionalism and the democratic/constitutional principles of the Republic.[6]

Meanwhile, Schleicher had been plotting to further advance his own career by ousting Bruening and becoming minister of defense under a new puppet chancellor, Franz von Papen. On April 28 and May 8 Schleicher secretly met with Adolf Hitler at the estate of Walter Granzow (the new Nazi premier-designate of Mecklenburg). He offered to have the ban against the SA and SS lifted and to have new Reichstag elections; in exchange, he asked only that Hitler remain neutral to a presidential cabinet under Papen. Hitler agreed to these terms, even though it is highly unlikely that he had any intention of living up to his agreement one moment longer than it was convenient to do so.

In May 1932 Schleicher told President von Hindenburg that Papen could form a government that could secure a majority in the Reichstag. (This was an out-and-out lie. Although not without personal charm, Franz von Papen was a political nonentity who had never even been able to secure a seat in the Reichstag for himself—much less form a majority coalition in that corrupt and hostile Byzantine circus.) Schleicher, however, knew how to strike a responsive cord in the aging president, who had been trying for two years to return to a government based on the principle of majority rule. Quickly the pressure to oust Bruening mounted. Schleicher told Hindenburg that the chancellor no longer had the confidence of the army (which, coincidentally, was not a lie); the large industrialists opposed him because of his failed economic policies; and the Junkers (the aristocratic landowners in the East) demanded his dismissal because of his "Agrarian Bolshevism" (that is, because he had proposed taking over insolvent estates in the East and using them for land colonization projects). This last factor weighed especially heavily with von Hindenburg, who was himself a Junker. On Sunday, May 29, he called Dr. Bruening in and abruptly demanded his resignation. He received it the following day. Then, on June 1, 1932, he named Franz von Papen chancellor of Germany.

Meanwhile, the number of officially registered unemployed people in Germany exceeded 5.5 million out of a work force of 29,000,000. No one knows how many who had exhausted both their benefits and their hopes no longer bothered to register. The tent cities grew, as did the Nazi Party. On May 29, the day Bruening fell, the NSDAP captured more than 48 percent of the votes in the elections in Oldenburg, a province on the North Sea. Hitler's party now controlled or participated in the governments of Brunswick, Mecklenburg, Anhalt, Thuringia, and now Oldenburg.

Franz von Papen was a man of some ability, but not very much. He was born in Werl on October 29, 1879, and grew up in the Westphalian nobility. He became a lieutenant in a cavalry regiment in 1907, attended the War Academy, and became a captain on the General Staff in 1913. He served as a military attaché in Mexico and Washington, where he was known for his clumsy undercover/secret service activities. He was expelled from the United States in 1916 for planning sabotage operations (which never got off the ground). After briefly serving as a battalion commander in France, he was sent to Turkey and was in Palestine in 1918, acting as chief of staff to the Turkish 4th Army when that area fell to the Allies.

Papen resigned from the army after the war and entered politics. From 1921 to 1932 he served as a Catholic Center deputy to the Prussian *Landtag*, where he represented the agrarian interests of the party and was identified with the extreme right wing, which called for the restoration of the Hohenzollern monarchy. A man of wide social acquaintances, Papen married the daughter of a wealthy Saar industrialist, which broadened his circle of contacts and gave him access to money. Despite all of his efforts and ambitions, he never did manage to secure a seat in the Reichstag. His choice as chancellor surprised everybody. "No one but smiled or tittered or laughed," the French ambassador recalled, because Papen was "taken seriously neither by his friends nor enemies. . . . He was reputed to be superficial, blundering, untrue, ambitious, vain, crafty and an intriguer. . . ."[7]

Although most of what the French ambassador said about Papen was true, not everybody smiled or laughed about his appointment. The Catholic Center, for example, was furious. They promptly expelled him from the party and went over to the opposition. Hindenburg instructed Papen to form a government above parties, and he was able to do so almost at once, because Schleicher already had a list of cabinet members on hand. Known as the "Barons' cabinet," 7 of its 10 members were from the nobility, 1 was a member of the board of directors of I. G. Faben, and another (the minister of labor!) was a member of the board of Krupps, the munitions conglomerate. The minister of justice was Dr. Franz Guertner, Hitler's protector in Bavaria in the early 1920s. The defense minister was, of course, Kurt von Schleicher. All in all, the cabinet was considered mediocre, right-wing, a bit of a joke, and totally unrepresentative of the views of the German people. Strangely enough, however, four of its members managed to hold office far into the Third Reich. These were Dr. Guertner (who died in office in 1941); Count Lutz Schwerin von Krosigk, who was the minister of finance until 1945; Baron Constantin von Neurath, foreign minister until 1938; and Baron Paul von Eltz-Ruehenach, who served as minister of post and communications until he died at Linz in 1943.[8]

On June 4, 1932, Papen kept Schleicher's promise to Hitler when he dissolved the Reichstag and set July 31 as the date for new elections. He did not, however, lift the ban on the SA and SS until June 15, which caused suspicion and animosity among the Nazis. When he finally did lift it after considerable prodding by Hitler, the stage was set for some of the worst political violence in Germany since the days of the Freikorps. By July 20 there had been 461 riots in Prussia alone, and they had left 82 people dead and 400 seriously wounded. Thirty of the dead were Communists and 36 were Nazis.

The worst fighting occurred on July 17, when a group of Nazis under police protection marched through Altona, a working-class suburb of "Red" Hamburg. They were met by a volley of Communist bullets, which they quickly returned. By the time order had been restored, 19 people lay dead and 285 were wounded.

Papen used the Altona riot as an excuse to end the political deadlock in Prussia and to extend his own power base. On July 20 he used his emergency presidential powers and ordered General Gerd von Rundstedt to remove the Social Democratic/Center coalition (which had remained in office without a majority in the Landtag) on the grounds that it had failed to maintain law and order and had failed to deal firmly with the Reds. Otto Braun, the Prussian premier since 1920, was ousted.[9] By this act, Papen hoped to portray himself as the protector of the Republic against the Red menace, and thus steal some of Hitler's thunder. He named himself commissioner of Prussia and Franz Bracht, the mayor of Essen, as his deputy and minister of the interior—the man in charge of the Prussian police and two-thirds of the police in the Reich. In ousting the democratic government of Prussia, Papen removed another pillar from the crumbling edifice that was the Weimar Republic.

Chancellor von Papen also scored a notable foreign policy success on July 9, 1932. At last realizing the dangers a Nazi government would present to world peace, the Allies concluded the Lusanne Agreement with Germany, under which the German reparations burden was practically abolished. The German diplomats at the Disarmaments Conference in Geneva then began to negotiate for equal rights in the field of armaments and found the Allies much more pliable than they had ever been before.

Although he was justifiably proud of his diplomatic victories, Papen's actions did him no good. "The eyes of the masses were now upon home affairs," Maurice Baumont wrote, and "work and bread took the first place in their demands. . . ."[10]

During its fourth major election campaign in five months, the Nazi propaganda machine was in top form. Hitler spoke to crowds of up to 120,000 and, no longer feeling it necessary to keep his promise of neutrality toward the Papen government, blasted the Cabinet of Barons. He also concentrated his campaign attacks against the Reds, capitalizing upon the German fear of Communism, which, to a large extent, replaced hatred of the Jews in his campaign speeches. "The German Communists . . . ," John L. Snell wrote, "did much to earn a large measure of responsibility for Nazi success. Several scholars have shown that the German Communists placed a slavish loyalty to Moscow far above any national concern for Germany."[11] Finally, and most significantly, the

Depression continued to worsen. National industrial output was only half of what it had been in 1929, and there was no relief in sight. As a result, more people turned to Adolf Hitler. On July 31 his party received 13,745,000 votes and 230 out of 608 seats in the Reichstag—more than twice its previous total, making it the largest party in the German national parliament. Their nearest rivals, the Social Democrats, polled just under 8,000,000 votes and lost 10 seats in the Reichstag. The Communists finished third in the voting, capturing 89 seats; the Catholic Center Party received 73 delegates. The other moderate middle-class parties were overwhelmed. The Nationalists lost 1,500,000 votes, and the strength of the Democrats, People's Party, and Economic Party fell from a combined total of 5,582,500 votes in 1928 to 954,700 in 1932. No doubt about it—except in the predominantly Catholic regions, the middle classes had gone over to the Nazis. Table 10-1 shows the exact voting totals for the election of July 31.

Hitler, with 37.3 percent of the popular vote, now felt that he was in an extremely strong position. Since the Nazi and Communist parties controlled more than half of the seats in the Reichstag, parliamentary government without the NSDAP was impossible. Also, because the majority party normally receives the chancellorship in a parliamentary government, he was in an "all or nothing" mood when he met Schleicher at the Fuerstenburg barracks, north of Berlin, on August 5. He demanded the chancellorship for himself, and that other Nazis be placed in the Prussian premiership; the Reich and Prussian ministries of the interior;

Table 10-1
Reichstag Election of July 31, 1932 (6th Reichstag)

Party	Votes (Percentage)	Delegates
Nazi	13,765,781 (37.3%)	230
Social Democrat	7,959,712 (21.6%)	133
Center	5,782,019 (15.7%)	97
Communist	5,282,626 (14.3%)	89
Nationalist	2,177,414 (5.9%)	37
People's	436,012 (1.2%)	7
State	371,799 (1.0%)	4
Splinter Parties	1,126,991 (3.0%)	11
Total	36,902,354	608

84 percent of those eligible voted.

Source: Wilhelm Dittmann, *Das politische Deutschland vor Hitler* (Zurich and New York: Europa Verlag, 1945).

the Reich ministries of justice, air, education; and a new national ministry of popular enlightment and propaganda, which he had earmarked for Dr. Goebbels. He also demanded an Enabling Bill, which would allow him to govern without the Reichstag. General von Schleicher was duly impressed, and, when he left, the Fuehrer thought he had accomplished his objectives.

Hitler had, in fact, overplayed his hand. The election results of July 31 were impressive, but they were not decisive. They also suggested that Hitler's popularity had peaked and that it was unlikely that the Nazis would ever receive an absolute majority in a free and democratic election. In addition, all of these elections and its growing bureaucracy had strapped the funds of the NSDAP, and the violent behavior of the SA had caused many in business, finance, and industry to question whether or not the Nazis were fit to govern Germany.

Hitler became more and more nervous as the days passed and no word came from Berlin. Eventually he sent Roehm to the capital to arrange a meeting between himself, Schleicher, and Papen. The conference was set for noon on August 13.

When they met, Hitler found that Schleicher's attitude had changed since August 5. Nazi violence during and after the election had solidified opinion against them in the upper-middle and upper classes, and in the Army. All Papen and Schleicher would offer Hitler was the vice-chancellorship and the Prussian ministry of the interior. Hitler's claim to power on the traditional basis of having the largest party in the Reichstag was politely brushed aside, and he was informed that Papen would remain in office with a presidential cabinet. Hitler suddenly lost control of his temper and started to rage, shocking both Schleicher and Papen by his violence and his demand to the same power Mussolini had in 1922. What Hitler meant was that he wanted a coalition government *à la* Rome in 1922, but Schleicher and Papen thought he was referring to the dictatorship of 1923. After a prolonged and heated argument, Hitler left in a state of agitated frustration and was driven to Goebbels' flat on the Reichskanzlerplatz. He was still there at 3 P.M. when the Presidential Palace telephoned and asked him to come see Hindenburg. Hitler said he saw no point in doing so because the governmental decisions had been made, but Hindenburg insisted, and in the end Hitler relented.

It was an extremely frigid interview. Hindenburg received him standing up and coldly informed him that, under the present circumstances, he could not risk handing the government over to a new party that did not command a majority in the Reichstag—especially one that was "intolerant, noisy, and undisciplined." After referring to several clashes between the Nazis and the police and to SA excesses against the Jews, he called upon Hitler to join a coalition government as vice-chancellor. If he could achieve positive results, the octogenarian marshal pointed out, he would eliminate the fear many had of the NSDAP, and his influence would increase. Then, he implied, Hitler might advance further. Hitler, however, adamantly refused to accept these terms, so the brief interview was terminated.[12]

Throughout August and September, the Nazis maintained desultory contacts with the government, but they led nowhere. Papen was convinced that the Nazis had reached their peak and were ebbing. By keeping Hitler on the threshold of power, he felt that he could force him to crack. Meanwhile, Hitler made contact with the Catholic Center Party, which agreed to support his candidate for president of the Reichstag. When the German parliament convened on August 30, this post went to Hermann Goering. The Reichstag then adjourned for almost two weeks.

Hermann Goering had gone through quite a lot since the failure of the Beer Hall Putsch. After being critically wounded by bullets in the groin and hip on November 9, 1923, he was spirited out of Germany and into Austria in mid-November, where he was in constant pain and had to be injected with morphine twice a day. Eventually he went into exile in Italy but, when Mussolini refused to give him aid, he and his wife returned to Sweden. By now Goering was up to six injections a day and was a morphine addict. Karin Goering's family agreed to pay for his medical expenses, and he was sent to the Aspudden Hospital, where it was decided to wean him from the drug gradually. This procedure did not work, because the staff cut him back too quickly, in what amounted to a "cold turkey" treatment process. Before long, Goering was pleading for the drug.

Compassion and sympathy have never been hallmarks of the Swedish medical system. One of the nurses bluntly told him to start acting like a man instead of a sniveling coward. The former commander of the Richthofen Wing paused a moment and then threw himself at her throat. Orderlies came to her rescue before he could kill her; and that is how Hermann Goering ended up in a straitjacket in a padded cell in the Langbro Asylum for the Insane. He remained there for three months, without drugs, until his morphine addiction had been cured.

The combination of morphine, other drugs, and his bullet wounds permanently altered Hermann Goering's metabolism. No longer the slim, trim fighter pilot, he gradually ballooned out to more than 300 pounds. Then, in the fall of 1927, he was allowed to return to Germany under a general political amnesty. Adolf Hitler had no full-time job for him, so he went to work as a sales representative for the Bavarian Motor Works (BMW), which was trying to reestablish itself as a manufacturer of airplane engines. Working in Berlin, Goering made a good living and even found time to work his way back into the Fuehrer's inner circle by becoming a Nazi Party speaker. He modeled his speaking technique after Hitler's and was soon drawing large crowds. He also used his contacts in Berlin to raise money for the party. After the election of 1928 Hitler rewarded him with one of the NSDAP's 12 seats in the Reichstag. Soon he was representing several aircraft firms and was taking bribes from Erhard Milch, the half-Jewish director of Lufthansa, the German national airline, whose interests were well represented by Goering in the Reichstag. Also, Lufthansa put airplanes at Hitler's disposal free of charge after 1930.

Hermann Goering was very good at communicating the Nazi message to the upper classes and soon recruited Prince August Wilhelm ("Auwi") among others, into the party, and was largely responsible for introducing Adolf Hitler into the high society of the capital. Goering, now called "The Fat One," arranged the first meeting between Hitler and Dr. Hjalmar Schacht, the economic genius, and accompanied the Fuehrer on his ill-fated first meeting with Hindenburg on October 10, 1931. Goering was not of much help, for he, too, was distracted. His own first love, Karin, lay seriously ill in Sweden. She died a week later, before Goering could return to Scandinavia.

Goering was present when Papen offered the vice-chancellorship to Hitler, and indignantly protested that the Fuehrer would never be *vice* to anybody. Then Hitler picked him to be president of the Reichstag as a result of a Nazi-Center-Nationalist agreement in August 1932. When he convened the national assembly on September 12, 1932, the 39-year-old Goering was probably the youngest man to ever hold that chair. He was also one of the most able, although he certainly did not use his talents in the service of a noble cause.

Foreseeing trouble, Franz von Papen had already taken the precaution of having Hindenburg sign an order dissolving the Reichstag. It was typical of the man that he forgot to bring it to the opening session, however. As soon as it convened, Ernst Torgler, the Communist leader, introduced a motion of no confidence against the Papen government. Frick, the Nazi floor leader, asked for a half an hour's delay to consider the matter. The Communist resolution had created a dilemma for the Nazis, as well as for the Nationalists and Centrists. None of them wanted the Reichstag dissolved, but they did not want to give the public the impression that they supported Papen. At a hurried meeting in the palace of the Reichstag president, Hitler, Goering, Strasser, and Frick decided to vote with the Communists and defeat the government before Papen could dissolve the Reichstag.

Shortly after the second session began, Papen appeared with the traditional red portfolio, which contained the dissolution order. Goering, however, ignored him and began the vote on the motion of censure. Papen screamed until he was red in the face; still Goering pretended not to see him. Finally, Papen flung the order on the Reichstag president's desk and stormed out of the hall, followed by members of his cabinet. Goering calmly continued with the roll call, overlooking the raging chancellor, much to the amusement of the Reichstag. Finally he announced that the German parliament had voted "no confidence" in the Papen administration by a margin of 513 to 42 and that the government was overthrown. Only then did he "discover" the red portfolio. Amid general laughter he declared it worthless, as it had been issued by a government that no longer existed. Elections to choose a new Reichstag were set for Sunday, November 6.

As amusing as the fall of the Papen government was, its ramifications were not at all humorous to the Nazis, for Franz von Papen was still chancellor and would continue to be, as long as he enjoyed Hindenburg's confidence. The NSDAP position was much less secure. The Reichstag had been dissolved after only one day, the Nazis faced their fifth major election in less than a year, and the party was almost out of money. Although Hitler spoke with his usual hypnotic furor, the German people seemed less interested than before: They had had enough of the seemingly endless election campaigns. Goebbels did not help matters by acting on his own initiative and joining the Communists in supporting the Berlin transportation workers' strike. Once Goebbels took this step, Hitler could not publicly disavow Nazi backing for the strike, which was caused by Papen's policy of cutting wages. The Fuehrer acted swiftly behind the scenes to bring the strike to a quick conclusion, but the damage had been done. Big business and industry had seen the Nazis walking the picket lines beside the hated Reds, and fighting strikebreakers side by side with them. The entrepreneurs promptly cut off what funds they were conduiting to the NSDAP. As the Nazi propaganda machine sputtered due to a lack of money, Hitler himself left the campaign trail four days before the voting for personal reasons. Back in Munich his latest mistress, Eva Braun, had shot herself in the neck, severing an artery. As a result of all of these factors, the Nazis polled less than 12 million votes—2 million fewer than they had received in July. This marked the first time they had lost votes since the Depression began. Although they were still the largest party in the Reichstag, their percentage of the national vote had fallen from 37.3 to 33.1 (see Table 10-2), and their representation in the Reichstag dropped from 230 out of 608 seats to 196 out of 584.

Papen, of course, was delighted by the results. He felt that the Nazi tide had begun to ebb. Realizing that the NSDAP was near bankruptcy and that resignations from the Nazi Party were exceeding new membership applications, Papen was perfectly willing to put the country through yet another election, in order to bring Hitler to his knees. His strategy may well have worked, too, had it not been for Kurt von

Table 10-2
Reichstag Election of November 6, 1932
(7th Reichstag)

Party	Votes (Percentage)	Delegates
Nazi	11,737,010 (33.1%)	196
Social Democrat	7,247,956 (20.4%)	121
Communist	5,980,162 (16.9%)	100
Center	5,326,067 (15.0%)	90
Nationalist	3,019,099 (8.5%)	52
People's	661,796 (1.8%)	11
State	336,451 (1.0%)	2
Splinter Parties	1,102,409 (3.1%)	12
Total	35,410,950	584

80.5% of those eligible voted.

Sources: Wilhelm Dittmann, *Das politische Deutschland vor Hitler* (Zurich and New York: Europa Verlag, 1945).

Schleicher. This master intriguer had been frightened by the increase in the Communist vote (they had scored a modest gain of 11 seats in the Reichstag); he was convinced that he could control Hitler in a coalition government; and he was irritated by Papen's increasingly independent attitude. In fact, Papen acted as if he, the chancellor, was the real governing power in Germany, instead of General von Schleicher! Schleicher now conspired to depose Papen, as he had deposed (or helped to depose) Seeckt, Mueller, Blomberg, Groener, Bruening, and so many lesser lights. When Papen called his first cabinet meeting after the elections, he found that Schleicher had lined up most of the ministers against him. Sure of his strength, the general came out into the open and personally urged him to resign. Swallowing his anger, Franz von Papen agreed. He was confident that Hitler would never compromise on the issue of power, that Hitler would not be able to form a majority coalition with himself as chancellor, and that Hindenburg would never appoint him to that office unless he could secure a majority in the Reichstag. Therefore, Papen reasoned, the parliamentary deadlock would continue, and he would eventually regain the chancellorship with a stronger hand than before. He resigned on November 17.

Events unfolded exactly as Papen had foreseen—to a point. Hindenburg summoned Hitler to the palace on November 19. Arriving amid cheering crowds, he found the atmosphere much warmer than it had been on August 13. The aging president invited him to sit down, and they talked for an hour. They met again two days later. The gist of these meetings was that Hindenburg agreed to name Hitler chancellor if he could obtain a working majority in the Reichstag. Although this seemed like a fair offer on the surface, it was designed to ensure that Hitler would not be successful. Privately, Hindenburg told Meissner: "One can't put a house painter in Bismarck's chair!"[13] (Incidentally, Hitler had never been a house painter, but a rumor to that effect had spread throughout Germany, and some people still believe it.)

To secure a parliamentary majority in the new Reichstag, Hitler would have to get the support of both the Nationalists and the Catholic Center—something that Hindenburg (and Hitler) knew he could not do. Even if he were successful, he would only be the head of a shaky coalition, because Hindenburg refused to grant Hitler the same sweeping powers he had given to Papen. Thus cornered and hamstrung, Hitler broke off the talks on November 24.

Meanwhile, Schleicher continued to weave his web of intrigue. He secretly opened up negotiations with Gregor Strasser and called upon the Nazis to join a new anti-Papen coalition cabinet under Schleicher's designee for the next chancellor. Initially Schleicher's choice fell on Hjalmar Horace Greeley Schacht, but the financial "wizard" had joined the NSDAP after the July elections, and he was too smart to trust Schleicher in any event. After being turned down by Dr. Schacht, Schleicher decided to step from behind the throne and assume the mantle of power himself. He persuaded Strasser that shared power was better than no power; the Nazi chieftain agreed to put the question of joining the coalition to Hitler.

Meanwhile, the unemployment roles reached the 6,000,000 mark.

11 Hitler Achieves His Goal

The next 60 days were the most complicated in the political history of the Weimar Republic, because everybody seemed to be trying to make a deal with everyone else; everyone seemed to be trying to double-cross someone; and some people were trying to double-cross everyone. Coincidentally, the proceedings began in Weimar on December 1—not because the Republic was born there, but because Hitler was there, preparing for the Thuringian provincial elections. That evening, in a meeting of the top Nazi leadership, Gregor Strasser came out strongly in favor of joining a coalition government under Schleicher. He received some lukewarm support from Frick and Feder but was heatedly opposed by Goering and Goebbels. After listening to both sides for some time, Hitler accepted the views of his propaganda chief and "the Fat One." Then he had a long meeting with Lieutenant Colonel Eugen Ott, Schleicher's charming personal representative, who offered him the vice-chancellorship and the Prussian premier's posts for himself and the minister of the interior positions for other Nazi leaders. Their talks came to nothing; much to Strasser's disgust, Hitler still insisted upon becoming chancellor.[1]

Meanwhile, back in Berlin, Hindenburg saw Papen and Schleicher together. Papen wanted to reassume the chancellorship, dismiss the Reichstag indefinitely, and rule by presidential decree. Schleicher strongly objected on the grounds that this would cause civil war. He pointed out that the voters had already rejected Papen twice by huge majorities. Then he asserted that he, Schleicher, could form a majority coalition in

the Reichstag. The aging president, who was at last seeing Schleicher
for what he was, was shocked by his proposal. He charged Papen with
the task of forming a new government.

Schleicher, however, was not through. At a cabinet meeting at 9 P.M.
the following evening he played his trump card: the Army. As defense
minister, he stated that the Reichsheer had no confidence in Papen and
was not prepared to risk civil war against both the Nazis and the Communists for his sake. Papen got up and left without saying a word. His
government was finished.[2] Later that night, Kurt von Schleicher became
the first general to become chancellor of Germany since Count Georg
Leo von Caprivi, who succeeded Bismarck in 1890. The new chancellor
was confident that he could detach the Strasser faction from the Nazi
Party and thus woo at least 60 Reichstag delegates away from Hitler. He
also believed that he could get the support of the Social Democrats and
the middle-class parties, and perhaps even the trade unions. Ironically,
in obtaining power, Schleicher had destroyed the one prop he would
need to stay there, and that was his relationship with Hindenburg. The
old field marshal had grown quite close to Franz von Papen and saw
no reason why he should be forced out of office. He was angry and
resentful toward the new chancellor and viewed him with increasing
suspicion.

Schleicher began his quest to remain in office on December 3, when
he invited Gregor Strasser to his home and offered him the vice-chancellorship of Germany and the premiership of Prussia. This act set in motion a series of events that, four days later, ended in a clash at the Kaiserhof, where Hitler bitterly accused Strasser of trying to go behind his
back and oust him. (The fact that the NSDAP vote in the December 3
election in Thuringia was 40 percent less than it had been in July may
have had something to do with Hitler's foul mood, as did the fact that
Hitler was in his usual Christmas depression. It will be recalled that his
mother had died in the glow of a lighted Christmas tree.) In any case,
Strasser was outraged by Hitler's accusations. He had always been entirely loyal, he declared, and walked out. Back in his room at the Hotel
Excelsior, he wrote Hitler a long letter of resignation from the party. By
the time the would-be chancellor received it the following day, Strasser
had already left for a vacation in Italy with his family. On December 9
a declaration condemning Strasser in the sharpest terms was submitted
to the party leaders and the Gauleiters, meeting in the Palace of the
President of the Reichstag. Only Feder initially refused to sign. Then he
was told to sign the document or resign. He signed.

The following day Hitler broke up Strasser's political organizational
department and handed most of its functions over to Dr. Robert Ley, a

longtime enemy of Strasser. The rest of the functions were transferred to Hess, Goebbels, and Walter Darre, the party agricultural expert. Hitler, incidently, was quite wrong about Strasser. He was not planning to depose Hitler and defect to Schleicher, because he lacked the mental toughness necessary to oppose Hitler, much less betray him. The Fuehrer, however, tended to believe that even the slightest opposition to his ideas on any issue could only be attributed to malicious intent and pure blackhearted evil. He soon convinced himself that Strasser's motives were treasonable, and he never forgave him.[3]

Having failed to break up the Nazi Party, Schleicher now tried to woo the unions, the Catholic Center, and the Social Democrats. Everywhere he turned, however, he found that he was paying the price for his former intrigues. Nobody trusted him or wanted to work with him. The Center Party remembered the part he had played in overthrowing Bruening; the industrialists were repelled by his conciliatory attitude toward the unions; and the unions and Social Democrats refused to collaborate with a Prussian general—especially one as untrustworthy as Schleicher. The farmers opposed his plans to reduce protective tariffs on agricultural products, and the Junkers denounced his land reform package as "Agrarian Bolshevism." He had absolutely no success in forming the Reichstag majority that he had promised to Hindenburg.

Adolf Hitler was also at his lowest ebb, for his party was near bankruptcy. Konrad Heiden stated that Hitler himself admitted it was 12,000,000 marks in debt;[4] others put this figure at 20,000,000 or more,[5] and George W. F. Hallgarten estimated that it was 70–90 million marks.[6] Whatever the actual amount, it was clear that the Nazi Party needed help soon, or it would collapse on the very threshold of power, just as von Papen had foreseen.

Their rescue came from a most unexpected source: Franz von Papen. The former chancellor was determined to "get even" with Schleicher and ruin him politically, even if it meant propelling Hitler into the chancellorship in the process. On January 4, 1933, he and Hitler met in the home of Baron Kurt von Schroeder, a Cologne banker. The meeting was arranged by Wilhelm Keppler, one of the Nazi contact men with the business world. Also present were Hess and Himmler, but only Schroeder was present during the discussions. Papen suggested that he and Hitler form a coalition and serve together in a joint chancellorship. Hitler rightly rejected this fundamentally unworkable arrangement. He said that he alone must be chancellor, although he had no objection to retaining many of Papen's ministers, so long as they would go along with his policies of changing things, including the elimination of Jews, Communists, and Social Democrats from positions of leadership in Germany. Papen, laboring under the illusion that he could control Hitler and the Nazis, agreed to help pay off the NSDAP's debts and to restore and increase the flow of contributions from the business world, which he had cut off in November.

Hitler realized that he could do nothing further to forward the intrigue against Schleicher. Leaving this mission to his new partner, Papen, he worked on the task of removing the impression that the Nazi Party was a spent force. He concentrated all of the party's efforts, best speakers, and new money in the tiny province of Lippe, which was having an election on January 15. He and Goebbels moved in to the Schloss Vinsebeck (the castle of Baron von Oeynhausen) and campaigned day and night. Hitler spoke with great force and enthusiasm in practically every village and town in the province, which had only 90,000 voters. The results were impressive, as Table 11-1 indicates. The Nazis received almost 40 percent of the ballots, a gain of 17 percent over the previous election. The group around Hindenburg was quite impressed by this performance, for it indicated that the party's declining popularity had ended, and it was rebounding.

The Hitler snowball to power continued to roll on January 17, when even the Nationalists defected from the Schleicher regime, after he threatened to publish secret Reichstag reports that linked successive governments to the *Osthilfe*, a series of scandals involving the loaning

Table 11-1
Lippe Landtag Election of January 15, 1933

Party	Vote (Seats in Diet)
National Socialist	38,844 (9)*
Social Democrat	29,735 (7)
Communist	11,626 (2)
Nationalist	5,923 (1)
People's Party	4,352 (1)
Catholic Center	2,531 (1)
Other parties	4,510 (1)

*The Nazis received 42,280 votes in Lippe in the Reichstag elections of July 31, 1932. They fell to 33,038 on November 6, 1932.

Sources: Christian Gneuss, comp., *The Path to Dictatorship, 1918–1933*, p. 209; *Schulthess' Europaeischer Geschichtskalender* (Munich: C. H. Beck, 1933), p. 20.

of public funds to landowners in the east. Considering Hitler the lesser of two evils, Hugenberg and his party turned again to the Nazis, even though this time they were clearly the junior partner in the firm.

The anti-Schleicher intrigues reached a high point on the night of January 22, when Hitler met with Frick, Papen, State Secretary Meissner, and Colonel Oskar von Hindenburg at the home of a then relatively unknown Nazi named Joachim von Ribbentrop, a friend of Papen's who had served with him on the Turkish Front in World War I.[7] Up until this meeting Oskar had been very much opposed to Adolf Hitler and the NSDAP. Then the Fuehrer insisted that they have a private conversation in another room. When they emerged an hour later, young Hindenburg was unusually quiet. On the ride back to the Presidential Palace, however, he remarked to an astonished Meissner that they would have to take Hitler into the government. What Hitler said in this fateful meeting was never revealed, but it is almost certain that he both bribed and blackmailed Hindenburg. Oskar was not noted for his strong moral fiber, and it is almost certain that Hitler threatened to reveal his part in the *Osthilfe* scandals; also, both Oskar and his father had taken part in a tax-evasion scheme when they put the presidential estate at Neudeck in Oskar's name in order to avoid future inheritance taxes. It is also interesting to note that, 7 months after Hitler became chancellor, 5,000 acres were added to the Hindenburg estate—tax free.[8]

The following day, Schleicher went to President von Hindenburg and confessed what everybody knew: He could not form a majority coalition in the Reichstag. His position was exactly the reverse of what Papen's had been two months earlier. He asked for emergency powers to govern without the Reichstag. The old marshal, who no longer trusted him, reminded him of the fact that he had called for the ouster of Papen because he could not form a majority and told him that what he (Schleicher) had said then still held true. He told him to go and resume the task of assembling a majority coalition. When Schleicher left the Presidential Palace that evening he was through, and he knew it. "I stayed in power only 57 days," Schleicher later exclaimed during a luncheon attended by the French ambassador, "and on each and every one of them I was betrayed 57 times."[9] This may have been true, but, even so, it is difficult to feel sorry for him.

On the morning of Saturday, January 28, Schleicher asked Hindenburg's permission to dissolve the Reichstag. When Hindenburg refused, Schleicher had no choice but to submit his resignation. For a moment the old field marshal felt a wave of sympathy for his former friend and tried to console him. "I have one foot in the grave already," he said, "and I am not sure that I shall not regret this action in heaven later on."

"After this breach of trust, sir, I am not sure that you will go to heaven!" Schleicher shot back, and then he left the palace.[10] His date with death at the hands of an SS murder squad was less than 18 months away.

At noon that same day, Hindenburg charged Franz von Papen with the task of negotiating the formation of a new government. Despite his January 4th agreement to back a coalition government under Hitler, Papen had been toying with the idea of double-crossing the Nazis and becoming chancellor again, as the head of a presidential cabinet. Schleicher was aware of this and preferred to see Hitler in power, instead of his former friend, von Papen. On Sunday, January 29, he sent General of Infantry Baron Kurt von Hammerstein-Equord, whom he had made chief of Army Command in one of his earlier intrigues, and Lieutenant General Baron Erich von dem Bussche-Ippenburg, the chief of the Army Personnel Office, to warn Hindenburg against von Papen and his plans.[11] Hindenburg told them in no uncertain terms that he would not appoint "that Bohemian corporal" (Hitler) to the chancellorship; furthermore, if the generals did not obey his orders, he would dismiss them all. Hammerstein hurriedly backed down and assured the old Prussian that the generals stood behind him. Privately, however, he confessed that he feared the task of defending a Papen government against the rest of Germany. Papen, after all, would have the support of only the Nationalists, which represented only 9 percent of the population; all of the other political parties—and 91 percent of the people— opposed him.

Berlin was a city in turmoil on Sunday, January 29. There were rumors of a military *coup*, and they were well founded. General von Hammerstein had already met with Erwin Planck (Schleicher's state secretary), Colonel Kurt von Bredow (head of the ministerial office of the defense ministry), Lieutenant Colonel Ott, and Major Erich Marcks, Schleicher's press officer.[12] These men agreed that Hindenburg should be presented with an ultimatum, insisting that Hitler be named chancellor. If he rejected this overture, then Hammerstein would declare a military state of emergency and, in effect, arrest him. The ultimate decision, however, lay with Schleicher, who refused to declare an emergency. He still wanted to hold on to power and be the defense minister in a Hitler cabinet, and Hitler did not seem to be adverse to the idea.[13] Reducing the chief of the Army Command to the role of message bearer, Schleicher sent the general to see Hitler at the Bechstein's house in the Berlin suburb of Charlottenberg. Hammerstein warned Hitler of a possible attempted double-cross by Papen; in that case, Schleicher proposed that he and Hitler join forces against Papen, form a Hitler-Schleicher coalition, and rule with a united Nazi-Army front. The Fuehrer replied noncommittally, for he was still pursuing the path of legality and still hoped to form a coalition with Papen and Hugenberg. That afternoon he returned to the Kaiserhof, where he was having cake and coffee with his aides when Hermann Goering appeared and informed him that the elder Hindenburg had relented. Adolf Hitler would be sworn in as chancellor the following day.

That night the NSDAP leaders were celebrating at the Goebbels' home on the Reichkanzlerplatz when a minor Nazi rumormonger named Werner von Alvensleben arrived and told them that Schleicher and Hammerstein had put the Potsdam garrison on alert, and that they planned to kidnap Hindenburg, launch a putsch, and establish a military dictatorship.

This news threw the Nazis into hysteria. Hitler placed the Berlin SA (under Count Wolf von Helldorf) on full alert and ordered Police Major Wecke, a loyal Nazi, to have six battalions of police ready to occupy the Wilhelmstrasse, where the main government buildings were located.[14] Hindenburg had also acted to remove the possibility of a putsch, as well as to keep the army out of the hands of either Hitler or Schleicher. He appointed General of Infantry Werner von Blomberg as defense minister and ordered him to report to the Presidential Palace as soon as he arrived from Geneva, where he was representing Germany at the Disarmament Conference. Blomberg was an officer who could be counted upon to back the government against Schleicher and Hammerstein. In 1930 he had been deposed as chief of the General Staff in one of Schleicher's intrigues. He had been replaced by General Baron Kurt von Hammerstein.

Blomberg arrived at the Anhalter Bahnhof, a Berlin railroad station, at 8:30 A.M. on January 30. He was met by two officers: Oskar von Hindenburg and Major von Kuntzen—Hammerstein's adjutant. The Baron had ordered Kuntzen to intercept Blomberg and bring him to army headquarters on the Bendlerstrasse. No one knows for sure, but this is an indication that Hammerstein (who was blindly loyal to Schleicher) was indeed planning a last-minute *coup* to prevent Adolf Hitler from attaining power. (Hammerstein was a fanatical anti-Nazi. Later he actively plotted to murder Hitler when the dictator was at the height of his popularity, and long before the war broke out. The general died in Berlin of natural causes on April 25, 1943, but his son, Lieutenant Baron Ludwig von Hammerstein-Equord, played an exceedingly active role in the July 20, 1944, coup attempt, in which Hitler was wounded by a bomb blast and narrowly escaped with his life.)

That cold, snowy morning in that Berlin railroad station, Werner von Blomberg made the first of many momentous decisions. He decided to ignore Hammerstein's orders and go with the younger Hindenburg to the Presidential Palace, where he was sworn in as minister of defense.[15] This act decided the issue: The armed forces would support the new government, which was sworn in at 11:20 A.M. on Monday, January 30, 1933. The ceremony was exceedingly brief, as if President von Hindenburg wanted to get this distasteful duty over with as rapidly as possible. He even managed to avoid offering the post directly to Hitler, who was the only chancellor in the history of the Weimar Republic to be so slighted. Nevertheless, when Adolf Hitler emerged from the Presidential Palace shortly before noon, he had attained his goal: He was chancellor of Germany.

Ironically, it was Hitler's former partner and Hindenburg's former chief of staff, General Erich Ludendorff, who was the most accurate prophet that day. As soon as he heard what Hindenburg had done, he wrote him a letter. "I predict most solemnly that this man will die in incredible misery," he said. "Coming generations will curse you for naming him chancellor." [16]

Notes

CHAPTER 1

1. Erich Ludendorff was born on April 9, 1865, in Kruszewnia (near Posen) the son of an improvished landowner and captain of cavalry. He was educated in various cadet schools, graduated from the Cadet Academy at Gross Lichterfelde in 1908, and was commissioned second lieutenant in the 57th Infantry Regiment at Wessel in 1881. Later he served in the 2nd Marine Battalion at Kiel and in the 8th Grenadier Guards Regiment at Frankfurt on the Oder. He entered the War Academy in 1893 and became a member of the General Staff in 1895. Following a tour of duty as an infantry company commander at Thorn, he held General Staff positions with the 9th Infantry Division at Glogau and the V Corps at Posen. In 1904 he was assigned to the famous "Red House" of the Army General Staff at Koenigsplatz in Berlin where he was head of the deployment section, which planned the invasion of Belgium and France under the direction of Generals von Schlieffen and von Moltke the younger.

In August 1909 at the age of 44, he married divorcée Margarethe Pernet, who had three sons. Franz, an aviator, was killed in action in September 1917. Erich, also a pilot, was killed in Operation "Michael." The third son, Heinz, survived the war and took part in the Beer Hall Putsch. Meanwhile, Ludendorff was promoted to captain (1895), major (1900), and lieutenant colonel (1907). In January 1913 as a colonel, he was rather abruptly transferred to Duesseldorf as commander of the 39th Rhenish Fusilier Regiment. In 1914, when World War I broke out, he was a major general, commanding a brigade at Strasbourg, and personally led the German forces in the capture of Liège. Meanwhile, the Russians invaded East Prussia, and Ludendorff was rapidly transferred to the danger point as chief of staff of the 8th Army, under Paul von Hindenburg. After their victories in the East, Hindenburg became chief of the General Staff and Ludendorff was named Quartermaster-General on September 28, 1916. In this post he became virtual dictator of Germany and directed the Imperial war effort until his dismissal on October 26, 1918.

In 1923 Ludendorff met a Nazi widow named Dr. Mathilde von Kemnitz (1877–1966). Whereas Frau Margarethe Ludendorff disapproved of the Nazis, Kemnitz was "always properly adoring" and considered Ludendorff the greatest soldier of all time. Her belief that everything in history could be explained by a conspiracy contributed to Ludendorff's later instability. Ludendorff divorced Margarethe in 1926 and, at the age of 61, married Kemnitz (who was described as "unattractive, with her plain face and dumpy figure . . .") on September 14, 1926. See D. J. Goodspeed, *Ludendorff: Genius of World War I* (Boston: 1966).

2. Charles B. MacDonald, "World War I: The U.S. Army Overseas," Chapter 18 in Maurice Matloff, ed., *American Military History* (Washington, D.C.: 1973), p. 396.

3. James L. Stokesbury, *A Short History of World War I* (New York: 1981), pp. 297–99.

4. See John W. Wheeler-Bennett, *The Forgotten Peace* (London: 1938).

5. Samuel William Halperin, *Germany Tried Democracy* (New York: 1946; reprint ed., New York: 1965), p. 39.

6. C. R. M. F. Cruttwell, *A History of the Great War, 1914–1918*, 2nd ed. (London: 1982), p. 487.

7. Wilhelm Souchon was born in Leipzig on June 2, 1864. He joined the navy as a cadet in 1881 and received his commission as an ensign in 1884. After a long and distinguished career, which included a tour as captain of the ship of the line *Wetten*, he became a rear admiral in 1911. From 1913 to September 1917 he was commander of the Mediterranean Division of the Imperial Navy. Souchon was promoted to vice-admiral in 1915 and to admiral in 1918. He received the *Pour le Merite* in 1916. After the war he served for four months as state secretary for the Reich Naval Office. He retired in March 1919 and died in Bremen on January 13, 1946. For a full chronological listing of his appointments, see Hans H. Hildebrand and Ernest Henriot, *Deutschlands Admirale, 1849–1945* (Osnabrueck: 1990), Volume 3, pp. 347–48.

Ritter Franz von Hipper was born in Weilheim, Bavaria, on September 13, 1863. Like Souchon, he joined the navy as a cadet in 1881 and was commissioned ensign in 1884. He spent most of the 1890s in the torpedo boat branch, commanding several torpedo boats, a torpedo boat squadron, a reserve torpedo boat division, torpedo boat divisions, and torpedo boat flotillas. He commanded the light cruiser *Leipzig* (1906) and the heavy cruisers *Friedrich Carl* (1906–1908) and *Gneisenau* (1908). He commanded the Imperial Navy's reconnaissance ships from the outbreak of World War I until August 12, 1918, when he was promoted to admiral and became Fleet Chief. Hipper had become a rear admiral in 1912 and a vice admiral in 1915. He held the Pour le Merite and the Max Joseph Order (1916). Admiral von Hipper retired in December 1918 and died in Hamburg on March 25, 1932. See Hildebrand and Henriot, *Deutschlands Admirale*, Volume 2, pp. 106–8.

For the best account of the German naval mutinies of 1917 and 1918, see

Daniel Horn, *The German Naval Mutinies of World War I* (New Brunswick, N.J.: 1969).

8. Charles B. Flood, *Hitler: The Path of Power* (Boston: 1989), p. 47.
9. Cruttwell, p. 595.

CHAPTER 2

1. Robert G. L. Waite, *Vanguard of Nazism: The Free Corps Movement in Postwar Germany, 1918–1923* (Cambridge, Mass.: 1952), p. 6.; Erich Otto Volkmann, *Revolution ueber Deutschland* (Oldenburg: 1930), p. 68.
2. Sefton Delmer, *Weimar Germany: Democracy on Trial* (London: 1972), p. 21.
3. Waite, *Vanguard*, pp. 17–20.
4. Ibid., pp. 29–30.
5. Theodore Abel, *Why Hitler Came into Power* (New York: 1938), p. 24.
6. Delmer, p. 35.
7. Ibid., p. 36.
8. The rank of *Oberfuehrer* has no exact English equivalent. It lies between colonel and brigadier general in the U.S. Army and between colonel *(Oberst)* and major general *(Generalmajor)* in the German Army of the Nazi era. *Oberfuehrer* will remain untranslated, as will Reichsfuehrer-SS, Reichsmarschall, and a few other words that have either no exact English translation or have a uniquely German meaning. Appendix I gives the translations of American, British, and German ranks and also shows the tables of equivalent ranks.
9. Richard Hanser, *Putsch!* (New York: 1971), p. 148.
10. It is notable that women were allowed to vote in this election. They were not allowed to vote in Great Britain, France, or the United States at this time. See Charles B. Flood, *Hitler: The Path to Power* (Boston: 1989), p. 47.
11. Otto Friedrich, *Before the Deluge: A Portrait of Berlin in the 1920's* (London: 1972), p. 49.
12. A. J. P. Taylor, "History Unfolds, 1918–1933," in John L. Snell, ed., *The Nazi Revolution: Germany's Guilt or Germany's Fate?* (Boston: 1959); also see A. J. P. Taylor, *The Course of German History: A Survey of the Development of Germany since 1815* (New York: 1946), pp. 189–92 and 203–14.
13. Waite, *Vanguard*, p. 68.
14. Hanser, p. 159.
15. Ibid., p. 167.
16. Waite, *Vanguard*, p. 86.
17. Ibid., p. 86, citing von Oertzen, *Die deutsche Freikorps,* p. 331.
18. Waite, *Vanguard*, pp. 285–96.

CHAPTER 3

1. Erich Eyck, *A History of the Weimar Republic* (Cambridge, Mass.: 1962), Volume I, pp. 92–95.
2. Samuel William Halperin, *Germany Tried Democracy* (New York: 1946; reprint ed., New York: 1965), p. 140.

3. Sefton Delmer, *Weimar Germany: Democracy on Trial* (London: 1972; reprint ed., New York: 1972), p. 82.

4. Ibid., p. 83.

5. Count von Brockdorff-Rantzau was later named ambassador to the Soviet Union and served until his death in 1928.

6. Halperin, pp. 152–53.

7. Theodore F. Abel, *Why Hitler Came Into Power* (New York: 1938), p. 24.

8. "World War I," Columbia Broadcasting System Documentary, 1965.

9. Eliot B. Wheaton, *Prelude to Calamity: The Nazi Revolution, 1933–1935* (Garden City, New York: 1968), p. 7.

10. Herbert M. Mason, Jr., *The Rise of the Luftwaffe: Forging the Secret German Air Weapon, 1918–1940* (New York: 1973), p. 36.

CHAPTER 4

1. Werner Maser, *Hitler: Legend, Myth and Reality,* Peter and Betty Ross, trans. (New York: 1973), p. 19. Germany at that time was dominated by two religious groups: Northern Germany formed a great Evangelical Lutheran bloc; Bavaria, Rhenish Prussia, and Westphalia were Catholic. Hesse, the Palatinate, Baden, Wuerttemberg, and Silesia were mixed.

2. William L. Shirer, *The Rise and Fall of the Third Reich* (New York: 1960), p. 10.

3. August Kubizek, *The Young Hitler I Knew,* E. V. Anderson, trans. (Boston: 1955; reprint ed., Westport, Conn.: 1976), p. 30. William Patrick Hitler, Alois, Jr.'s son from his first marriage, was living in New York under an assumed name in the 1970s. Heinz Hitler, a son by his second wife, became an officer in the German Army and was killed in action on the Eastern Front.

4. Adolf Hitler, *Mein Kampf* (Munich: 1925; reprint ed., Ralph Manheim, trans. Boston: 1943, 1971), p. 6.

5. Another son, Edmund, was born on March 24, 1894, and another daughter, Paula, was born on January 21, 1896. Edmund died of measles on February 2, 1900.

6. Kubizek, p. 49.

7. Shirer, *Rise and Fall,* p. 12, citing *Hitler's Secret Conversations, 1941–44,* August 29, 1942.

8. Ibid., Sept. 7, 1942.

9. Adolf Hitler, *Mein Kampf* (Munich: 1925; reprint ed., Alvin Johnson et al., trans. New York: Reynal and Hitchcock, 1940), p. 19.

10. Kubizek, p. 52.

11. Maser, *Hitler: Legend, Myth, and Reality,* p. 32.

12. Robert Payne, *The Life and Death of Adolf Hitler* (New York: 1973), p. 39.

13. Maser, *Hitler: Legend, Myth, and Reality,* pp. 35–36.

14. Hitler, *Mein Kampf,* Manheim trans., p. 18.

15. Kubizek, p. 12.

16. Maser, *Hitler: Legend, Myth, and Reality,* pp. 39–40.

17. Kubizek, p. 124.

18. John Toland, *Adolf Hitler* (New York: 1976; reprint ed., New York: 1977), p. 38.

19. Ibid., pp. 19–20.

20. Ibid., p. 37, citing Colliers (1941).

21. Hitler, *Mein Kampf*, Manheim trans., p. 21.

22. Eliot B. Wheaton, *Prelude to Calamity: The Nazi Revolution, 1933–1935* (Garden City, New York: 1968), p. 37.

23. Werner Maser, *Hitler's Mein Kampf: An Analysis*, R. H. Barry, trans. (London: 1970), p. 87.

24. Kubizek, p. 157

25. Maser, *Hitler's Mein Kampf*, pp. 90–91.

26. Charles B. Flood, *Hitler: The Path to Power*, citing Hitler, *Mein Kampf* (Boston: 1989), p. 35.

27. Maser, *Hitler's Mein Kampf*, p. 67.

28. Maser, *Hitler: Legend, Myth, and Reality*, pp. 87–88.

29. Flood, p. 24, citing Toland Container 48; Konrad Heiden, *Der Fuehrer: Hitler's Rise to Power*, Ralph Manheim, trans. (Boston: 1944), p. 83.

30. Engelhardt eventually recovered from his wounds and retired as a major general.

31. Richard Hanser, *Putsch!* (New York: 1971) pp. 89–90.

32. Toland, p. 82.

33. Ibid., p. 89.

34. Hitler, *Mein Kampf*, Johnson translation, p. 191.

35. Ibid., p. 192.

36. Ibid., pp. 193–194.

37. Ibid., p. 202.

38. Ibid., pp. 204–5.

39. Ibid., p. 206.

CHAPTER 5

1. Hitler, *Mein Kampf*, Manheim trans., p. 219.

2. Anton Drexler, *Mein Politisches Erwachen* (Munich: 1920).

3. Hitler, *Mein Kampf*, Manheim trans., pp. 180–81.

4. Charles B. Flood, *Hitler: The Path to Power* (Boston: 1989), p. 76.

5. Ibid., p. 97.

6. General von Oven, a famous Freikorps commander, was named to succeed Baron von Luettwitz.

7. General Baron Walter von Luettwitz, who was born in 1859, retired after the failure of the Kapp putsch and died in 1942. Mortally ill, Wolfgang Kapp returned to Germany shortly before his death on June 12, 1922.

8. Baron von Watter's command included Wilhelm Friedrich Loewenfeld's 3rd Naval Infantry Brigade, the notorious Freikorps Rossbach, Freikorps Luetzow, von Aulock, von Epp, Oberland and von Oven, as well as other Freikorps and various *Zeitfreiwillige* (emergency volunteer) formations. For a full account of the conquest of the Ruhr, see Robert G. L. Waite, *Vanguard of Nazism: The Free*

Corps Movement in Postwar Germany, 1918–1923 (Cambridge, Mass.: 1952), pp. 177–82. Watter was the commander of Wehrkreis VI.

9. Waite, *Vanguard*, p. 182.

10. Samuel W. Halperin, *Germany Tried Democracy* (Hamden, Conn.: 1963), p. 206.

11. Konstantin Fehrenbach (1852–1926), who had been president of the Reichstag in 1918, retired.

12. Scheidemann, who was born in 1865, died in 1939.

13. Richard Hanser, *Putsch!* (New York: 1971), p. 259.

14. Count von Lerchenfeld held no further major offices and died in 1944.

15. William L. Shirer, *The Collapse of the Third Republic* (New York: 1969; reprint ed., New York: 1971), p. 127.

16. Flood, pp. 392–93; Hanser, pp. 288–89.

17. Hanser, pp. 288–89.

18. Eliot B. Wheaton, *Prelude to Calamity: The Nazi Revolution, 1933–1935* (Garden City, New York: 1968), p. 67.

19. Ibid., p. 294.

20. Anton Drexler, who was born in Munich on June 13, 1884, described by Rosenberg as a man with a "simple, direct heart," was a toolmaker foreman in one of the machine shops of the German railroads. He was elected to the Bavarian Landtag in 1924 on a non-Nazi list. Alfred Rosenberg, *Memoirs of Alfred Rosenberg*, Eric Posselt, trans., Serge Lang and Ernst von Schenck, commentaries (Chicago and New York: 1949), p. 45.

21. Drexler died, a forgotten man, on February 24, 1942. Robert Wistrich, *Who's Who in Nazi Germany* (New York: 1982), pp. 57–58.

22. Ernst Hanfstaengel, *Unheard Witness* (Philadelphia and New York: 1957), pp. 34–37.

23. Randall L. Bytwerk, *Julius Streicher* (Briarcliff Manor, New York: 1983), pp. 67–68.

24. Ibid., p. 68, citing Martin H. Bertram, ed., *Luther's Works* (Philadelphia: 1971), Volume 47, p. 275.

25. James D. Forman, *Nazism* (New York: 1978; reprint ed., New York: 1980), p. 8.

26. Bytwerk, p. 66. See Shakespeare, "The Merchant of Venice."

27. Edmond Vermeil, "Pre-1914 Roots" in John L. Snell, ed., *The Nazi Revolution: Germany's Guilt or Germany's Fate? Problems in European History* series, Ralph W. Greenlaw, editorial director (Boston: 1959), p. 16. Also see Edmond Vermeil, *Germany in the Twentieth Century* (New York: 1956), pp. 14–20, 31.

28. Bytwerk, p. 65, citing Heinrich von Treitschke, *Ein Wort ueber unser Judenthum* (Berlin: 1880), p. 4.

29. Forman, p. 14.

30. Ibid.

31. Ibid., p. 25.

32. Leonard Mosley, *The Reich Marshal: A Biography of Herman Goering* (New York: 1974; reprint ed., New York: 1975), pp. 22–23.

33. Loerzer, who was born on January 22, 1891, later became a colonel general in the Luftwaffe and chief of the personnel and air armaments office. He retired on December 20, 1944, and died on August 22, 1960. Rudolf Absolon, comp.

Rangeliste der Generale der deutschen Luftwaffe Nach dem Stand vom 20. April 1945 (Friedberg: 1984), p. 18.

34. Robert Manvell and Heinrich Fraenkel, *Goering* (New York: 1962), p. 27.

35. Ibid., p. 37.

36. Some of Karin Goering's original letters, together with English translations, are located in the archives of the Military History Institute, U.S. Army War College, Carlisle Barracks, Pennsylvania.

37. Flood, p. 137.

38. Rudolf Hess was named Deputy Fuehrer in April 1933 and Minister without Portfolio in December 1933. He was chief of the NSDAP until May 10, 1941, when—apparently in a mentally deranged state of mind—he stole a Messerschmitt and flew to England in an attempt to negotiate a peace between Britain and the Third Reich. Imprisoned for the rest of the war, he was tried as a major war criminal at Nuremberg and sentenced to life imprisonment. He died under mysterious circumstances at Spandau prison in August 1989—an apparent suicide.

39. Hanfstaengl, p. 30.

40. Hanfstaengl was appointed Foreign Press Chief of the NSDAP in 1931 but fled the Third Reich in March 1937, because he believed Hitler was trying to have him killed. He served as an adviser to President Roosevelt during World War II and died in Munich on November 6, 1975.

41. For the best biography of Streicher, see Bytwerk's *Streicher.* Streicher was ousted as Gauleiter of Franconia in late 1939 for corruption and a number of excesses, including rape and horsewhipping prisoners—although his major offense seems to have been the fact that he charged that Goering was impotent and that his daughter had been conceived by artifical insemination or other means. Even so, Hitler allowed him to continue to publish *Der Sturmer* until the end of the war. He was hanged at Nuremberg on October 16, 1946.

42. Dietrich Eckart, the son of a Bavarian lawyer, was born in Neumarkt, Upper Palatinate, on March 23, 1868. He was an eccentric intellectual, a journalist, and an extreme anti-Semite. A "man of the world," he liked wine, women, and pleasures of the flesh. Eckart had a great deal of influence on Hitler, and many of the views expressed in *Mein Kampf* came from him. Eckart had a heart condition, aggravated by alcoholism and a morphine addiction. He died on December 23, 1923, and is buried in Berchtesgaden. Hitler wrote an emotional tribute to him in *Mein Kampf.*

Rosenberg became chief of the NSDAP's Foreign Affairs Department in 1933 and was Minister of Occupied Territories in the East in July 1941. He was hanged at Nuremberg on October 16, 1946.

43. Hans Frank became Reich Minister of Justice in 1934 and Governor-General of Occupied Poland on October 12, 1939. Responsible for the deaths of tens of thousands of Jews and Poles, Frank was executed at Nuremberg on October 16, 1946.

44. Wilhelm Frick, Reich Minister of the Interior in the first Hitler cabinet, was partially responsible for the Nuremberg Laws and other anti-Jewish measures. He was executed at Nuremberg on October 16, 1946.

45. Heinrich Himmler committed suicide at the end of the war. Sepp Dietrich died in 1966.

CHAPTER 6

1. Cuno died in 1933.
2. Charles B. Flood, *Hitler: The Path to Power* (Boston: 1989), p. 401.
3. Johannes Steinhoff, Peter Pechel, and Dennis Showalter, *Voices from the Third Reich* (Washington, D.C.: Regnery Gateway, 1989), p. xxvi. Also see Ernst Hanfstaengl, *Unheard Witness* (Philadelphia and New York, 1957), p. 101.
4. Hanfstaengl, p. 102.
5. Richard Hanser, *Putsch!* (New York: 1971), p. 321.
6. Ibid., pp. 102–4.
7. Hanser, *Putsch!*, p. 321.
8. Hanfstaengl, pp. 104–5.
9. Oskar Cantzler later became a lieutenant general in World War II and distinguished himself as an engineer. At various times he was chief engineer officer of the 9th Army (1939), 2nd Army (1939–1940), 11th Army (1940–1941), Army Group Center (1941), Army Group South (1942), OB West (1943–1944), and Army Group G (1944). He was named Inspector General of Engineers and Railroad Engineers with the Home Army in September 1944. He became commander of the defensive works in the middle Baltic Sea region in January 1945. He was living in Feldkirch in 1957. Wolf Keilig, *Die Generale des Heeres* (Friedberg: Podzun-Pallas-Verlag, 1983), p. 58.
10. Flood, p. 520.
11. Ulrich Graf, who was born in Bachhagel on July 6, 1878, was a miller and butcher by vocation. He was later elected to the Munich City Council in 1925 and became a Nazi Reichstag delegate in 1936. During World War II, he held the rank of SS major general *(SS-Brigadefuehrer)*.
12. Hanser, p. 367.
13. Flood, p. 578; John Toland, *Adolf Hitler* (New York: 1976; reprint ed., New York: 1977), p. 258.
14. Shirer, *The Rise and Fall of the Third Reich* (New York 1960), p. 75.
15. Ibid., pp. 75–76.
16. Lossow was succeeded as commander of Wehrkreis VII on February 18, 1924, by General Baron Friedrich Kress von Kressenstein (1870–1948), an officer loyal to Seeckt and Berlin. Kress commanded the Bavarian military district until 1928. General von Lossow died in 1938.

Ritter Gustav von Kahr was President of the Bavarian Supreme Court from 1924 to 1927 and then retired from politics. He was nevertheless murdered by the Nazis during the Blood Purge (the "Night of the Long Knives") on June 30, 1934.
17. Flood, p. 580; Konrad Heiden, *Der Fuehrer: Hitler's Rise to Power*, Ralph Manheim, trans. (Boston: 1944), pp. 204–5.
18. Hanser, p. 370.
19. Flood, p. 585, citing *Hitler Trial*, v. 3, pp. 393–94.
20. Hanser, p. 371.

CHAPTER 7

1. General von Seeckt was the architect of what eventually became Hitler's army. He was dismissed as chief of the Army Command on October 8, 1926, for

allowing former Crown Prince Wilhelm to attend a military training exercise in uniform. He was elected to the Reichstag in 1930, reached an agreement with the Nazis, and eventually became a Hitler supporter. He was senior military adviser to Chiang Kai-shek from May 1934 to March 1935. Hans von Seeckt died in Berlin on December 29, 1936.

2. Held remained in office until 1933, when he was overthrown by General Ritter Franz von Epp.

3. The first volume was published by Franz Eher II of Munich on July 18, 1925, and there were 10,000 copies in the first edition. The second volume (also published by Eher) was released on December 11, 1926. Like the first volume, the style was that of Hitler's oratory.

4. Julius Barmat was eventually sentenced to 11 years imprisonment after a public trial that lasted more than a year. Dr. Anton Hoefle, the Centrist minister of the post, was also forced to resign as a result of the scandal and died in prison in April 1925 under very mysterious circumstances. Ernst Heilmann, the Social Democratic leader in the Prussian Landtag, was also implicated in the scandal, as was Richter, the commissioner of the Berlin police. He was fired by the provincial minister of the interior—a fellow Social Democrat.

Gustav Bauer, who was born in 1870, died in 1944.

5. Otto Friedrich, *Before the Deluge: A Portrait of Berlin in the 1920's* (London: 1972), p. 171.

6. Dr. Walter Simon, who was born in 1861, retired from the supreme court in 1929 and died in 1937.

7. After Hitler took power, Ernst Thaelmann (who was born in Hamburg on April 16, 1886) was tracked down and arrested at his hiding place in the Charlottenberg section of Berlin on March 3, 1933. After 11 years in solitary confinement at various locations, he was taken to Buchenwald in August 1944. He was shot on August 28.

8. Robert Ley became head of the Reich Labor Front (RAD) in 1933 and became known as the "Reich Drunkmaster." Unstable and an incompetent administrator, his influence declined considerably during the war, although he continued to hold high office until the end. He was captured by American soldiers near Berchtesgaden at the end of the war and committed suicide in his cell at Nuremberg on October 24, 1945.

Bernhard Rust became Reich Minister of Education in 1934. Following the collapse of the Third Reich, he committed suicide in May 1945. Koch went into hiding after the war and was not arrested until 1950. Sentenced to death by a Polish court in 1959, he was not executed because of a Polish law prohibiting the execution of bedridden persons. At last report (1971), the 85-year-old Koch was in prison at Bartchero, Poland.

9. Otto Strasser, *Hitler and I*, Gwenda and Eric Mosbacher, trans. (Boston: Houghton Mifflin Co., 1940; reprint ed., New York: AMS Press, 1982), pp. 86–87.

10. Ibid., p. 86.

11. Roger Manvell and Heinrich Fraenkel, *Adolf Hitler: The Man and the Myth* (New York: Pinnacle Books, Inc., 1973), pp. 73–74.

12. Helmut Heiber, *Goebbels*, John K. Dickinson, trans. (New York: Hawthorn, 1972; reprint ed., New York: De Capo Press, Inc., 1972), p. 40.

13. Strasser, pp. 89–90.

14. Heiber, p. 5.

15. Ibid.

16. Helmut Heiber, ed., *The Early Goebbels Diaries, 1925–1926*, Oliver Watson, trans. (New York: Frederick A. Praeger Publishers, 1962), p. 78, dated April 13, 1926.

17. Heiber, *Goebbels*, p. 42.

18. Dietrich Orlow, *The History of the Nazi Party*, Volume I, *1919–1933* (Pittsburgh: University of Pittsburgh Press, 1969), p. 129.

19. Richard F. Hamilton, *Who Voted for Hitler?* (Princeton, N.J.: Princeton UP, 1982), p. 476.

20. Ibid., p. 147.

21. These were seven additional Gaus for Austria, Danzig, the Saar, and the Sudentenland.

22. Orlow, Volume I, pp. 138–41.

23. Fritz Reinhardt became State Secretary to the Reich Minister of Finance when the Nazis came to power. He served four years in prison after the war and died in 1969.

24. Goebbels remained Minister of Propaganda and Gauleiter of Berlin throughout the Nazi era. A major figure in the Third Reich, Hitler named him Chancellor of Germany in his political testament. The Fuehrer committed suicide on April 30, 1945. That night, Goebbels and his wife poisoned their six children. The following day, May 1, Joseph and Magna Goebbels committed suicide in the Fuehrer Bunker in Berlin.

25. See Orlow, Volume I, pp. 180–82, 197–200.

Gottfried Feder had lost considerable influence by the time Hitler assumed power and, in 1933, was given the minor post of Undersecretary in the Ministry of Economics. Schacht dismissed him from this post in December 1934; he died in obscurity in Murnau, Upper Bavaria, on January 24, 1941. Richard-Walter Darre became Reich Minister of Agriculture in June 1933 but was dismissed in May 1942 because of his failure to organize the German food supply efficiently. He was sentenced to five years' imprisonment at Nuremberg for deliberately starving civilians. Released in 1950, Darre retired to Bad Harzburg and died in a Munich clinic on September 8, 1953.

26. Hjalmar Schacht became Minister of Economics in 1934 but was dismissed in 1937 because he opposed Hitler's aggressive military buildup. Later a member of the anti-Nazi resistance, he was arrested by the Gestapo on July 29, 1944 (nine days after Colonel Count Claus von Stauffenberg narrowly failed to assassinate the Fuehrer). He was liberated from Flossenburg concentration camp by American troops in April 1945. Tried at Nuremberg as a major war criminal, he was acquitted, despite the protests of the Soviet judge. He was sentenced to eight years' hard labor by a Stuttgart Denazification court in 1946 or 1947, but his conviction was overturned on appeal in 1948. He then started a highly successful career as a banker and financial adviser to developing countries and sired a second family. "The Old Wizard" died in Munich on June 3, 1970.

27. The Young Plan was named for Owen D. Young, an American banker who worked out the reparations formula.

28. Flood, p. 197.

CHAPTER 8

1. Alan J. Bullock, *Hitler: A Study in Tyranny* (New York: Harper and Row, 1964), p. 143, citing C. S. R. Harris, *Germany's Foreign Indebtness* (Oxford, 1935), c. I.

2. Otto Friedrich, *Before the Deluge: A Portrait of Berlin in the 1920's* (London: 1972), pp. 300–1.

3. Ibid., p. 302.

4. Hermann Mueller died of liver failure in the spring of the following year, 1931.

5. Mueller had been plagued by ill health throughout his second chancellorship.

6. Bruening was born in Muenster, Westphalia, on November 26, 1885, the son of an industrialist. After obtaining his doctorate from the University of Bonn in 1915, he volunteered for the army and was sent to the front. He distinguished himself in battle and was commanding a machine gun company at the end of the war. Conservative and sincerely Catholic, he was elected to the Reichstag in 1924 as a deputy from Breslau.

7. H. W. Koch, "1933: The Legality of Hitler's Assumption of Power," in H. W. Koch, ed., *Aspects of the Third Reich* (New York: St. Martin's Press, 1985), p. 39.

8. William L. Shirer, *The Rise and Fall of the Third Reich,* (New York: 1960), pp. 119–20.

9. John Toland, *Adolf Hitler* (New York: 1976; reprint ed., New York: 1977), p. 309.

10. A. J. P. Taylor, "History Unfolds, 1918–1933," in John L. Shell, ed., *The Nazi Revolution: Germany's Guilt or Germany's Fate?* (Boston: 1959), p. 21; A. J. P. Taylor, *The Course of German History: A Survey of the Development of Germany since 1815* (New York: Coward-McCann, Inc., 1946), pp. 189–92 and 203–14.

11. Koch, "1933," p. 55.

12. Henry Ashby Turner, Jr., "Big Business and the Rise of Hitler," *American Historical Review,* Volume LXXV (October, 1969), p. 59.

13. Ibid., p. 59.

14. Koch, "1933," p. 55.

15. Turner, p. 66.

16. Friedrich, p. 315.

17. Theodore F. Abel, *The Nazi Movement* (New York: 1965), p. 100.

18. Helmut Heiber, *Goebbels,* John K. Dickinson, trans. (New York: 1972; reprint ed., New York: 1972), pp. 53–54.

19. Abel, *The Nazi Movement,* p. 104.

20. Hoehler's accomplices were executed by the Nazis in 1934. Diels was killed in a hunting accident in 1957.

21. Otto Strasser was born in Windsheim, Middle Franconia, on September 10, 1897, and joined the NSDAP in 1925.

22. Bullock, p. 165.

23. Shirer, p. 140.

24. Roehm, the son of an old Bavarian family of civil servants, had been born in Munich on November 28, 1887.

25. Dietrich Orlow, *The History of the Nazi Party*, Volume I (Pittsburgh: 1969), p. 215.

26. Ibid., pp. 218–19.

27. Franz Xaver Schwarz was born in Guenzberg on November 27, 1875, and graduated from the Gymnasium there. After a tour of military service, he became a municipal clerk in Munich. He joined the Nazi Party in 1922 and replaced Max Amann as *Reichsschatzmeister* (national treasurer) of the NSDAP in 1925. He held this post until the end of World War II.

Philip Bouhler was born in Munich on September 2, 1899, the son of a retired colonel. He served as business manager of the NSDAP (1925–1934) and police president of Munich (1934). He was later chief of the Chancellery and in charge of the euthanasia institutions. He committed suicide with his wife at Goering's headquarters (Zell-am-See) in early May 1945, shortly before the Americans arrived.

28. John W. Wheeler-Bennett, *The Nemesis of Power: The German Army in Politics, 1918–1945* (New York: St. Martin's Press, 1964; reprint ed., New York: The Viking Press, 1967), p. 183.

CHAPTER 9

1. Glenn S. Infield, *Hitler's Secret Life* (Briarcliff Manor, N.Y.: Stein and Day, 1979; reprint ed., Briarcliff Manor, N.Y.: Day Books, 1981), pp. 79–81. For a biography of Renate Mueller, see Cinzia Romani, *Tainted Goddesses: Female Film Stars of the Third Reich* (New York: 1992).

2. William L. Shirer, *The Rise and Fall of the Third Reich* (New York: 1960), p. 132.

3. John Toland, *Adolf Hitler* (New York: 1976; reprint ed., New York: 1977), pp. 288 and 313.

4. Robert G. L. Waite, *The Psychopathic God: Adolf Hitler* (New York: Basic Books, Inc., 1977; reprint ed., New York: New American Library, 1977), pp. 271–72.

5. Angela Hitler Raubal married her first husband in 1903. She married again after Geli's death, this time to a Dresden architect. Hitler disapproved and did not attend the wedding. Angela died in 1949.

6. Ernst Hanfstaengl, *Unheard Witness* (Philadelphia and New York: 1957), p. 169.

7. Ibid.

8. John Toland, *Adolf Hitler* (New York: 1976; reprint ed., New York: 1977), p. 334.

9. Hanfstaengl, p. 169.

10. Emil Maurice later became a watchmaker, married, and had two children. Rumors of his Jewish origins are totally unfounded. Nerin E. Gun, *Eva Braun: Hitler's Mistress* (New York: Meredith Press, 1968), p. 11.

CHAPTER 10

1. Leonard Mosley, *The Reich Marshal: A Biography of Herman Goering* (New York: 1974; reprint ed., New York: 1975), p. 167.

2. This alliance, called the Harzburg Front, had been made in mid-October 1931.

3. Dr. Werner Best, the son of a postmaster, was born at Darmstadt on July 10, 1903. He took his doctorate of law at the University of Heidelberg in 1927 and accepted a position with the justice ministry of the province of Hesse in 1930.

4. Except for two brief interruptions in 1921 and 1925, Braun had been minister-president of Prussia since 1920. The coalition had governed since 1925.

5. Dietrich Orlow, *The History of the Nazi Party,* Volume I (Pittsburgh: 1969), p. 255. Goebbels *Diary,* 25 Apr 1932.

6. Wilhelm Groener was born in Ludwigsburg, Wuerttemberg, on November 22, 1867, the son of a paymaster of a Wuerttemberger regiment. He became an officer, graduated from the War Academy, and, as a lieutenant colonel, was named chief of the Railway Section of the General Staff in 1912. In August 1914 he directed the German mobilization, which went very well. A trusted adviser to both von Moltke and Falkenhayn, he was appointed a member of the Food Control Office in May 1916 and was named chief of the War Office (under the Army High Command) in autumn 1916. He succeeded Ludendorff as First Quartermaster-General in 1918. A republican by reason rather than by conviction, he served as Minister of Railway Reconstruction (1920–1923), Minister of Transportation (1923–1928), and Defense Minister (January 1928–April 1932). He died in Bornstedt, Potsdam, on May 3, 1939.

7. Andre Francois-Poncet, *The Fateful Years: Memoirs of a French Ambassador in Berlin, 1931–1938,* Jacques Le Clerge, trans. (New York: Harcourt, Brace, 1949), p. 23.

8. Dr. Franz Guertner died in office in Berlin on January 29, 1941.

9. Otto Braun went into exile in Switzerland on March 2, 1933, and was joined by his wife four days later. He never returned to Germany and died in 1955. Braun was born in 1872.

10. Maurice Baumont, "The Role of Foreign Policy in the Success of the National Socialist Party," in John L. Snell, ed., *The Nazi Revolution: Germany's Guilt or Germany's Fate?* (Boston: 1959), p. 14.

11. See John L. Snell, *The Nazi Revolution: Germany's Guilt or Germany's Fate? Problems in European History* series, Ralph W. Greenlaw, editorial director (Boston: 1959).

12. Alan J. Bullock, *Hitler: A Study in Tyranny* (New York: 1964), pp. 221–22.

13. John Toland, *Adolf Hitler* (New York: 1976; reprint ed., New York: 1977), p. 376.

CHAPTER 11

1. Eugen Ott was sent to Japan on April 17, 1933, and was attached to the Imperial Japanese Army. He was named military attaché to Tokyo on April 1, 1934, and ambassador to Japan on April 1, 1938.

2. Franz von Papen became Hitler's envoy to Austria in 1934 (following the assassination of Chancellor Dollfuss by Austrian Nazis) and was named ambassador to Vienna in 1936. Following the Anschluss, he served as ambassador to Turkey (1939–1944). Acquitted at Nuremberg in 1946, he was sentenced to eight

years' imprisonment by a German denazification court in 1947. He was released on appeal in January 1949 and died in Obersasbach on May 2, 1969, at the age of 89.

3. Gregor Strasser was murdered on July 1, 1934, during the Blood Purge (the "Night of the Long Knives"). His brother Otto, who had already fled the country, did not return to Germany until the 1950s. Otto died in Munich in 1974.

4. Konrad Heiden, *A History of National Socialism* (New York: 1935, abridged edition).

5. Alan J. Bullock, *Hitler: A Study in Tyranny* (New York: 1964), p. 242.

6. George W. F. Hallgarten, "German Industrialists Paid Hitler," in John L. Snell (ed.), *The Nazi Revolution* (Boston: 1959), p. 42.

7. Ribbentrop later became German ambassador to London (1936–1938) and foreign minister (1938–1945). He was executed at Nuremberg on October 16, 1946.

8. For cooperating with Hitler, Oskar von Beneckendorf und von Hindenburg was promoted to major general (on the retired list) on September 30, 1934. During World War II he commanded Special Purposes Divisions 422 and 401 (1939–1941) and was commander of *Kampfgruppen* (battle groups) in East Prussia from 1941 until December 1944. He was still living in Medingen in 1955 (Wolf Keilig, *Die Generale des Heeres* [Friedburg: 1983], p. 27). President Paul von Hindenburg died at Neudeck on August 2, 1934, after which Hitler abolished his office and assumed its functions.

9. Andre Francois-Poncet, *The Fateful Years: Memoirs of a French Ambassador in Berlin, 1931–1938,* Jacques Le Clerge, trans. (New York: 1949), p. 43.

10. John W. Wheeler-Bennett, *The Nemesis of Power: The German Army in Politics, 1918–1945* (New York: 1967), p. 54. Schleicher was murdered on June 30, 1934, during the Night of the Long Knives. His wife of 18 months was shot and killed by the Gestapo at the same time.

11. Baron von Hammerstein-Equord was commissioned second lieutenant in the 3rd Grenadier Regiment of Foot in 1898 and became Chief of the General Staff on October 1, 1929. He was named Chief of the Army Command on October 1, 1930, and was discharged (with the honorary rank of colonel general) on February 1, 1934.

Baron Erich von dem Bussche-Ippenburg retired as a general of artillery on September 30, 1933, and was named honorary commander of the 6th Artillery Regiment. He was living near Fulda in 1955.

12. Erich Marcks was born in Berlin in 1891. He joined the army as an officer-candidate in the 76th Field Artillery Regiment in 1910. During World War II he served as chief of staff of the VIII Corps in Poland (1939) and chief of staff of the 18th Army in the invasions of the Netherlands, Belgium, and France (1940). He was in charge of the initial planning of Operation "Barbarossa" (the invasion of Russia) in 1940. On the fifth day of the invasion, Marcks (now commander of the 101st Light Division) was seriously wounded and lost a leg. He returned to active duty in March 1942 as commander of the 337th Infantry Division in France. Later he commanded the LXVI, LXXXVII, and LXXXIV Corps, all in occupied France. Despite his anti-Nazi views Marcks was promoted to general of artillery in late 1942. On June 6, 1944, his corps was struck by the D-Day

invasion. He was killed by an Allied fighter-bomber 13 days later (Keilig, p. 217).

13. H. W. Koch, "1933: The Legality of Hitler's Assumption of Power," in H. W. Koch, ed., *Aspects of the Third Reich* (New York: 1985), p. 54.

14. Count von Helldorf later turned against the Nazis and was executed for his part in the conspiracy of July 20, 1944.

15. Werner von Blomberg was promoted to field marshal in 1936 but was forced to retire at the end of January 1938, when it was discovered that his new wife was a former prostitute. Never reemployed, he retired to Bad Wiessee, Bavaria, where he was arrested by the Americans in 1945. He died of cancer in detention at Nuremberg on March 14, 1946.

16. Donald G. Brownlow, *Panzer Baron: The Military Exploits of General Hasso von Manteuffel* (North Quincy, Mass.: The Christopher Publishing House, 1975), p. 49.

Bibliography

Abel, Theodore F. *The Nazi Movement*. New York, 1965. Revision of the 1938 edition.

————. *Why Hitler Came Into Power*. New York, 1938.

Absolon, Rudolf, comp. *Rangeliste der Generale der deutschen Luftwaffe Nach dem Stand vom 20. April 1945*. Friedberg, 1984.

Adam, Uwe Dietrich. *Judenpolitik im Dritten Reich*. Duesseldorf, 1972.

Baumont, Maurice. "The Role of Foreign Policy in the Success of the National Socialist Party," in John L. Snell, ed. *The Nazi Revolution: Germany's Guilt or Germany's Fate?* Boston, 1959.

Baynes, Norman H., ed. *The Speeches of Adolf Hitler*. London, 1942. 2 Volumes.

Berghahn, V. R. *Der Stahlhelm, Bund der Frontsoldaten*. Duesseldorf, 1966.

Bertram, Martin H., ed. *Luther's Works*. Philadelphia, 1971. +47 volumes.

Bessel, Richard. *Political Violence and the Rise of Nazism: The Storm Troopers in Eastern Germany, 1925–1934*. New Haven, Conn., 1984.

Brownlow, Donald G. *Panzer Baron: The Military Exploits of General Hasso von Manteuffel*. North Quincy, Mass., 1975.

Bullock, Alan J. *Hitler: A Study in Tyranny*. New York, 1964.

Bytwerk, Randall L. *Julius Streicher*. Briarcliff Manor, N.Y., 1983.

Childers, Thomas. *The Nazi Voter: The Social Foundations of Fascism in Germany, 1919–1939*. Chapel Hill, 1983.

Columbia Broadcasting System. "World War I." Documentary produced in 1965.

Craig, Gordon A. *The Politics of the Prussian Army*. New York, 1956.

Cruttwell, C. R. M. F. *A History of the Great War, 1914–1918*. 2nd edition. London, 1982.

Delmer, Sefton. *Weimar Germany: Democracy on Trial*. London, 1972. Reprint ed., New York, 1972.

Dittmann, Wilhelm. *Das politische Deutschland vor Hitler.* Zurich and New York, 1945.

Dorpalen, Andreas. *Hindenburg and the Weimar Republic.* Princeton, N.J., 1964.

Drexler, Anton. *Mein Politisches Erwachen.* Munich, 1920.

Eschenberg, Theodor, et al. *Path to Dictatorship, 1918–1933: Ten Essays.* New York, 1967.

Eyck, Erich. *A History of the Weimar Republic.* Harlan P. Hanson and Robert G. L. White, trans. Cambridge, Mass., 1962. 2 volumes.

Flood, Charles B. *Hitler: The Path to Power.* Boston, 1989.

Forman, James D. *Nazism.* New York, 1978. Reprint ed., New York, 1980.

Francois-Poncet, Andre. *The Fateful Years: Memoirs of a French Ambassador in Berlin, 1931–1938.* Jacques LeClerge, trans. New York, 1949.

Friedrich, Otto. *Before the Deluge: A Portrait of Berlin in the 1920's.* London, 1972.

Goering, Karin. "Papers." Military History Institute, U.S. Army War College, Carlisle Barracks, Pa.

Goodspeed, D. J. *Ludendorff: Genius of World War I.* Boston, 1966.

Gordon, Harold J. *The Reichswehr and the German Republic, 1919–1926.* New York, 1972.

Gun, Nerin E. *Eva Braun: Hitler's Mistress.* New York, 1968.

Hallgarten, George W. F. "German Industrialists Paid Hitler." John L. Snell, ed. *The Nazi Revolution.* Boston, 1959.

Halperin, Samuel William. Germany Tried Democracy. New York: 1946; reprint ed., New York: 1965.

Hamilton, Richard F. *Who Voted for Hitler?* Princeton, N.J., 1982.

Hanfstaengl, Ernst. *Unheard Witness.* Philadelphia and New York, 1957.

Hanser, Richard. *Putsch!* New York, 1971.

Harris, C. S. R. *Germany's Foreign Indebtedness.* Oxford, 1935.

Heiber, Helmut, ed. *The Early Goebbels Diaries, 1925–1926.* Oliver Watson, trans. New York, 1962.

———. *Goebbels.* John K. Dickinson, trans. New York, 1972. Reprint ed., New York, 1972.

Heiden, Konrad. *Der Fuehrer: Hitler's Rise to Power.* Ralph Manheim, trans. Boston, 1944.

———. *A History of National Socialism.* New York, 1935.

Hildebrand, Hans H., and Ernest Henriot. *Deutschlands Admirale, 1849–1945.* Osnabrueck, 1990. 3 volumes.

Hitler, Adolf. *Mein Kampf.* Munich, 1925. Reprint ed., Ralph Manheim, trans. Boston, 1943 and 1971.

———. *Mein Kampf.* Munich, 1925. Reprint ed., Alvin Johnson et al., trans. New York, 1940.

———. *My New Order.* Raoul de Roussy de Sales, ed. and trans. New York, 1941.

Holborn, Hajo, ed. *Republic to Reich: The Making of the Nazi Revolution.* New York, 1972.

Horn, Daniel. *The German Naval Mutinies of World War I.* New Brunswick, N.J., 1969.

Infield, Glenn S. *Hitler's Secret Life.* Briarcliff Manor, N.Y., 1979. Reprint ed., New York, 1981.

Jetzinger, Franz. *Hitlers Jugend.* Vienna, 1956.

Jonge, Alex de. *The Weimar Chronicle.* New York and London, 1978.

Keilig, Wolf. *Die Generale des Heeres.* Friedberg, 1983.

Koch, H. W., ed. *Aspects of the Third Reich.* New York, 1985.

———. "1933: The Legality of Hitler's Assumption of Power," in H. W. Koch, ed. *Aspects of the Third Reich.* New York, 1985, pp. 39–61.

Kubizek, August. *The Young Hitler I Knew.* E. V. Anderson, trans. Boston, 1955. Reprint ed., Westport, Conn., 1976.

MacDonald, Charles B. "World War I: The U.S. Army Overseas," in Maurice Matloff, ed. *American Military History.* Washington, D.C., 1973.

Machiavelli, Niccolo. *The Prince.* Thomas G. Bergin, ed. and trans. New York, 1947.

Manvell, Roger, and Heinrich Fraenkel. *Adolf Hitler: The Man and the Myth.* New York, 1973.

———. *Goering.* New York, 1962.

———. *The Hundred Days to Hitler.* London, 1974.

Maser, Werner. *Adolf Hitler: Das Ende der Fuehrer-Legende.* Duesseldorf, 1980.

———. *Hitler.* Peter and Betty Ross, trans. New York, 1971.

———. *Hitler: Legend, Myth and Reality.* New York, 1973.

———. *Hitler's Mein Kampf: An Analysis.* R. H. Barry, trans. London, 1970.

Mason, Herbert M., Jr. *The Rise of the Luftwaffe: Forging the Secret German Air Weapon, 1918–1940.* New York, 1973.

Matloff, Maurice, ed. *American Military History.* Washington, D.C., 1973.

Merkl, Peter. *Political Violence under the Swastika.* Princeton, N.J., 1975.

Mosley, Leonard. *The Reich Marshal: A Biography of Herman Goering.* New York, 1974; reprint ed., New York, 1975.

Nicholls, Anthony J. *Weimar and the Rise of Hitler.* New York, 1968.

Orlow, Dietrich. *The History of the Nazi Party.* Pittsburgh, 1969. 2 volumes.

———. *Weimar Prussia, 1925–1933: The Illusion of Strength.* Pittsburgh, 1991.

Papen, Franz von. *Memoirs.* Brian Connell, trans. London, 1952.

Payne, Robert. *The Life and Death of Adolf Hitler.* New York, 1973.

Peterson, Edward N. *Hjalmar Schacht: For and against Hitler. A Political-Economic Study of Germany, 1923–1945.* Boston, 1954.

Pridham, Geoffrey. *Hitler's Rise to Power: The Nazi Movement in Bavaria, 1923–1933.* London, 1973.

Romani, Cinzia. *Tainted Goddesses: Female Film Stars of the Third Reich.* Robert Connolly, trans. New York, 1992.

Rosenberg, Alfred. *Der Mythos des 20. Jahrhunderts.* Munich, 1931.

———. *Memoirs of Alfred Rosenberg.* Eric Posselt, trans. Serge Lang and Ernst von Schenck, commentaries. Chicago and New York, 1949.

Shirer, William L. *The Collapse of the Third Republic.* New York, 1969. Reprint ed., New York, 1969. Reprint ed., New York, 1971.

———. *The Rise and Fall of the Third Reich.* New York, 1960.

Snell, John L., ed. *The Nazi Revolution: Germany's Guilt or Germany's Fate? Problems in European History* series, Ralph W. Greenlaw, editorial director. Boston, 1959.

Snyder, Louis L. *Encyclopedia of the Third Reich.* New York, 1976.

———. *Hitler's Elite.* New York, 1989.

Steinhoff, Johannes, Peter Pechel, and Dennis Showalter. *Voices from the Third Reich*. Washington, D.C., 1989.

Stokesbury, James L. *A Short History of World War I*. New York, 1981.

Strasser, Otto. *Hitler and I*. Gwenda and Eric Mosbacher, trans. Boston, 1940. Reprint ed., New York, 1982.

Taylor, A. J. P. *The Course of German History: A Survey of the Development of Germany since 1815*. New York, 1946.

———. "History Unfolds, 1918–1933," in John L. Snell, ed. *The Nazi Revolution: Germany's Guilt or Germany's Fate?* Boston, 1959.

Toland, John. *Adolf Hitler*. New York, 1976. Reprint ed., New York, 1977.

Turner, Henry Ashby, Jr. "Big Business and the Rise of Hitler." *American Historical Review*. Volume LXXV (October, 1969).

Vermeil, Edmond. *Germany in the Twentieth Century*. New York, 1956.

———. "Pre-1914 Roots," in John L. Snell, ed. *The Nazi Revolution*. Boston, 1959.

Volkmann, Erich Otto. *Revolution ueber Deutschland*. Oldenburg, 1930.

Waite, Robert G. L. *The Psychopathic God: Adolf Hitler*. New York, 1977. Reprint ed., New York, 1977.

———. *Vanguard of Nazism: The Free Corps Movement in Postwar Germany, 1918–1923*. Cambridge, Mass., 1952.

Wheaton, Eliot B. *Prelude to Calamity: The Nazi Revolution, 1933–1935*. Garden City, N.Y., 1968.

Wheeler-Bennett, John W. *The Forgotten Peace*. London, 1938.

———. *The Nemesis of Power: The German Army in Politics, 1918–1945*. New York, 1967.

Wistrich, Robert. *Who's Who in Nazi Germany*. New York, 1982.

Index

About the Author

SAMUEL W. MITCHAM, JR. is an internationally recognized authority on Nazi Germany and the Second World War and is the author of more than a dozen books on the subject, including *Rommel's Desert War, Hitler's Legions, Hitler's Commanders,* and *Men of the Luftwaffe.* He teaches at Northeast Louisiana University.